BONE AND DREAM

I am reality.
You are reality.
But the sun
is the only seed.

Who are you? What am I
but a body on loan
that casts a shadow?

— Gonzalo Rojas,
"The Sun Is the Only Seed"

BONE AND DREAM

➤

Into the World's Driest Desert

LAKE SAGARIS

Alfred A. Knopf Canada

PUBLISHED BY ALFRED A. KNOPF CANADA

Copyright © 2000 by Lake Sagaris

An earlier version of chapter 1, "Trails Through Time,"
won first prize in the Periodical Writers Association of Canada
National Writing Contest (1996). An earlier version of chapter 7,
"The Earth's Refusals," was published in *Descant*. Some of the
information on desertification in Chile (chapter 10) is from
an article I wrote, originally published in *EcoAméricas*.

Canadian Cataloguing in Publication Data

Sagaris, Lake
Bone and dream : into the world's driest desert

ISBN 0-676-97223-3

1. Atacama Desert (Chile) — Description and travel.
2. Atacama Desert (Chile) — History.
3. La Tirana, 16th cent.
4. Sagaris, Lake — Journeys — Chile — Atacama Desert.
I. Title

F3131.S23 2000   983'.1   C00-930369-3

Map: CS Richardson

First Edition

Printed and bound in the United States of America

10 9 8 7 6 5 4 3 2 1

For Joan Simalchik and
Robin Breon, unexpected muses

For Camilo,
the shadow travelling beside me,
eyes drinking in the desert

For Jaime and Daniel

And for Patricio,
twenty years later, still

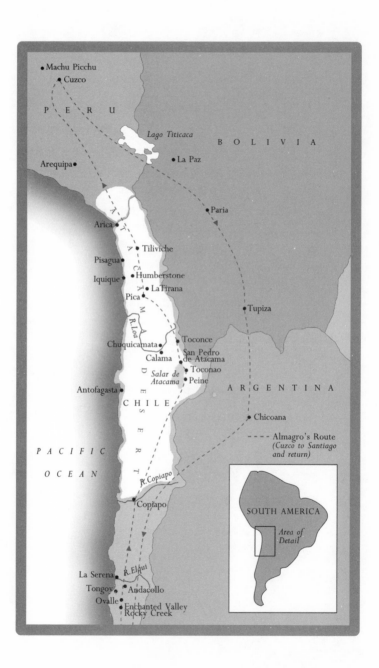

• Machu Picchu
• Cuzco

P   E   R   U

Lago Titicaca

B   O   L   I   V   I   A

Arequipa•

• La Paz

• Paria

Arica•

A
T
A
C
A
M
A

• Tiliviche

Pisagua•

• Humberstone

Iquique•

• La Tirana

Pica•

• Tupiza

R. Loa

Chuquicamata•

• Toconce

Calama•

San Pedro
de Atacama

• Toconao

*Salar de
Atacama*

• Peine

Antofagasta•

A   R   G   E   N   T   I   N   A

C H I L E

D
E
S
E
R
T

• Chicoana

- - - Almagro's Route
(Cuzco to Santiago
and return)

R. Copiapó

Copiapó•

SOUTH AMERICA

*Area of
Detail*

PACIFIC

OCEAN

La Serena•

R. Elqui

Tongoy• • Andacollo

Ovalle•

• Enchanted Valley

Rocky Creek

CONTENTS

INTRODUCTION

➤

Norte Grande

I N THE SILENCE of the desert, voices ring out, echo
hollowly, keen, wail, burst into unexpected peals of
laughter. On my journeys and in my dreams I wander
amongst the gardens of stones and gravel, the delicately
carved and fitted rocks, fallen walls, salt crystals, mountains
of salt, and the voices come to me clear as spring water, preserved by the Atacama, the Norte Grande, the Great North.

In my homeland, we move in reference to a True
North, *strong and free*. So too do these voices that speak
Quechua, Aymara, that once spoke Kunza, that drift like fragrance through my senses. What is the Great North? Where
is it to be found? In the icy desert of the North Pole or in
the dry clear air of the Atacama, where you can see forever?

North has somehow become confused with freedom,
strength, a place, a space, where like compass needles we can
move to our own rhythms, seeking something essential
where the eyes see nothing.

Samuel Johnson said that a traveller must take knowledge along if he or she hopes to bring knowledge back from a journey. Perhaps that was what most frustrated me on my early visits to the Atacama Desert. I could feel that everywhere I looked I saw something extraordinary, but I did not know how to read what I was looking at. Chilean guidebooks, pamphlets, the flashy flyers of city councils anxious to flaunt their wares were no help. My questions, fed by a little knowledge, became fascination, then obsession. Hence this retracing of the desert's trails and voices over time, as much as over the scarred surface of the earth.

I cannot stay put, cannot write a whole book in one place. So this book is a quilt, pieced together during journeys, like those illusions we call maps, with their neat little countries, each one divided by a clear line, marked by a specific colour. My book is my map of memory, but also a search for those who left the desert scarred with their trails, and roads seared by their voices.

Like our collective subconscious, the desert holds the past, shoots strange disparate images into our conscious mind. The desert is also a kind of living book and I have pored over it endlessly. But time reads over my shoulder, is faster than I, flips each page before I finish, slams another volume shut on my eager fingers. Like other people who left their footprints in the Norte Grande, I write because to write is to tell beyond the boundaries of our own time and place, to reflect, but above all to hope. As the flood of "progress" thrusts us over the cliff into the abyss of yet another century, I can't help groping blindly, unfashionably backward, believing that we must find a meeting place, must perhaps build one where none exists, between who we are and those whom we have refused to let be.

To travel the Atacama is to retrace the paths of memory in search of a better future, to discover a new variation on the great romantic tragedy that is perhaps the founding myth of the Americas. We think we know the world we live in, but we have forgotten more than we have learned. Others have travelled here before and their views make the lost objects from violated graves shine again, as they did when they were the private treasure of specific beings whose voices linger in the desert winds, below the great dome of the Atacama's only temple, the sky that reflects the earth. In between stands humanity, the horizon between the possible and what will never be again.

The Norte Grande is also a journey through death, but death made palpable, intimate, in some way less terrifying. In our extremely specialized world we put all the religion into churches, all the science into museums. There is a kind of reverence in a good museum, but it is muffled, strangled even, by the need to look scientific. In an increasingly secular society that has tired of gods, as we have tired of big bosses pushing us around, we still need the freedom for reverence and wonder, to let death back in to walk hand in hand with life—and we can bear to see it do that, can even hang on its elbow, show it around.

One day I will be dead (ah, yes, in your forties you start to face this fact) and if it means becoming a part of the colours of the salt fields, a molecule of flawless air, part of the algae that make the flamingo pink, I think I can live with that, can feel about death as if there will be something of a homecoming to it, something of celebration, and rest from the fearful part of living.

It is odd how as our society has become dependent on specialization, we as people are more obsessed with individualism. Yet it's clear that specialization requires complex cooperation and an ever more collective approach to knowledge. Individualism, of course, makes death so much more terrible. Death becomes the end of the world, the universe, instead of a mere shift in the cosmic energies, one person falling out of line, another moving in, a whole new shape created, a new act really, eventually a whole new circus.

So the desert is the arena between performances, the circus just ended and the one about to begin, waiting for the voices to play across it.

1

TRAILS
OVER TIME

➤

The Atacama Desert

D
ESERTS. Shifting hills of sand inhabit some essential
corner of the human brain, turning a few square inches
of spongy cells into a changing landscape where our
nomadic thoughts trudge endlessly, heads bowed against
the driven sand, toward the next oasis or mirage. We seldom know which. The journey is all.

Nevertheless, not even two of my favourite books, *The
Songlines* by Bruce Chatwin and *The English Patient* by
Michael Ondaatje, both of which explore deserts of earth
and soul, could convince me that I had any interest in
these waterless spots. After all, my name is Lake and while
I have travelled long and hard, it is the landscape informed
and defined by water that draws me outside myself, connecting me to something larger.

I had lived for fifteen years in Santiago, Chile, but not
even my regular journeys to the country's southern fjords,
inner seas, turquoise lakes and watchful volcanic peaks had

quelled my thirst for water in all its incarnations. A quick trip to the northern desert for the inauguration of a copper mine left me cold. Never had my eyes seen so much, my spirit remained so mute. And yet. In December 1995, armed with a couple of assignments, I once again entered the Atacama. Flying toward Calama, a flat, gritty town 1,566 kilometres north of Santiago, I was struck by how the land looks river-carved: enormous ravines rumbling down from the Andes toward the ocean, cliffs and clefts slashed by flash-floods thousands of years old, the surface rippling like sand in shallow water.

As our plane banked and glided earthward I studied the roads scarring the surface below me. Later, as Patricio, my companion, and I climbed into our rented car and shot toward a furred and empty heart of light, astonishment shivered along my nerves. We roared across a landscape of horizontal lines of violet and pink, pearly grey and steely blue, shifting, stretching, thinning under a relentless cobalt sky. We screeched to a halt by a roadside shrine, an *animita*, erected where some previous traveller had died. A tamarugo tree, the desert's weeping willow, trembled in the breeze, two feet tall. The attached sign pleaded, not for loose change like those hanging round the necks of beggars in downtown Santiago, but for water.

As we wound through the last crystal peaks and down into the valley toward San Pedro de Atacama, the mountains of salt looked like works of art, charged with dramatic meaning. Lost voices keened along the hollows of my bones.

The landscape's very stillness seemed to shiver. This desert was breaking every rule of the imagination. The rocks proclaimed, *Your expectations make the landscape lie.* I had expected sand, but this was a land of stone and salt. I took the tufts of silver-plated grass for sheep huddled together. The tawny curves of lions' backs were golden moss; a prickly porcupine, some shrub; a jagged flock of birds, mere stones.

How many thousands of years, how many generations have measured these mountains with their feet, leaving their secrets buried under sand or marked by a lone figure standing out against the distance, transformed, as I approach, into a cairn?

The Atacama rises gently out of the Pacific Ocean, the world's largest body of water, but it is the driest desert on our planet. It stretches 970 kilometres north to south, starting from Arica at the Chile-Peru border and ending in Copiapo, about a third of the way down the long ladder that is Chile. There's nothing virgin or untouched about the Atacama. Rather, everyone and everything that has perished on its rocky plain or among its mountains of salt has left a mark.

For thousands of years, the bodies of those who ventured here shrivelled into the desert's surface of rock and bone, but their voices blended with the air. The desert is so silent that if you stand still, those voices come back to you, telling their stories: the Incas, expanding their empire southward through the mauve solitudes of rocks; the Aymaras, the Chinchorros, the Atacamenians and the Diaguitas, building the oases that made life possible; the conquistadors, dying in droves as they stumbled blindly over the scars left by others; the British businessmen, goading Chile into the War of 1879, by which Chile, and its English "patrons," seized control of the north's vast mineral wealth.

Before the Europeans reached this continent, the Atacama was sparsely populated, but heavily travelled by caravans linking the fishing and hunting peoples of the Pacific coast to the empires and isolated village oases of the high Andes nestling along what are today the border areas of Peru, Bolivia, Argentina and Chile. The main ethnic groups included the Diaguitas, known for their pottery of round bellies and precise geometrical designs in red, white and black; the fishing peoples known as the Changos, who lived not on the arid coast but in their canoes of inflated seal bladders, floating on the rolling surface of the sea; the Atacamenians, of the oases; and the Aymaras, the former lords of the high Andes.

When, with the arrival of the Spanish, the map of the Incas' Andean empire shattered into individual settlements that were in turn gathered together again to form Spain's colonized kingdoms of Peru and Bolivia, the Atacama too was divided up. Peru grabbed the northernmost reaches, Chile the southernmost and Bolivia held on to a stretch that reached to the Pacific Ocean.

In the nineteenth century, the War of the Pacific (1879–1883) pitted Chile against Bolivia and Peru. The upshot was a Chilean victory, thanks in part to support from the British, and a heritage of bitter distrust and contempt that underlies Chile's relations with Peru and Bolivia to this day. However, the war did bring the Atacama, with all its mineral wealth, into the sphere of Chileans eager to build if not an empire at least a country, stretching from Arica at the Peruvian border and the northern edge of the Atacama, all the way down to Punta Arenas and Tierra del Fuego in the south. Once the war was over, the British nitrate mines fuelled prosperous towns—mere ghosts today—and a union movement that changed Chilean history.

Since the late eighties, American and now Canadian mining companies have been tearing out the desert's very entrails in their search for the high-grade copper, silver and gold that make the figures on their balance sheets shine. To do so, they often find themselves battling the surviving native people for the desert's lifeblood, water.

These are the bare facts, but they don't explain the way this seemingly empty tract of land has filled itself over the years with the sighs and shouts of past adventurers, how their whispering still moves the sun-shot air.

For five years, the Atacama desert has haunted me, a ghostly presence composed of majestic silence and brutal conflict, the shadows of men and women struggling to wrest a green shoot from its rocky surface or stumbling through palaces of ice to the golden mansions they hoped to build, their hearing assaulted by the strangled screams of massacres, the distant chime of hammer on stone, alarm bells, the warning buzz before the *tronadura*, the massive daily explosion that blasts free new ore to be trucked to the surface of its open-pit mines.

But there are also the shouts and laughter of giggling children as they slap and spray each other, crowding around the tap in the central square of San Pedro de Atacama. Another illusion shatters in the bright sunlight. Oases, at least here in the Atacama, are not found but built. Over thousands of years the channels were dug and lined with stones, then painstakingly cleaned and feasted over every year, to keep the water racing into the fertile ground. They mine these waters, loaded with salt and arsenic, like rock until they find enough to green the rushes and feed the hungry flocks of llama, donkeys, sheep. The water's poisonous, but still life survives.

The descendants of those who built the oasis still live there quietly, among the green fields sliced into neat rectangles by rows of poplars and high adobe walls.

San Pedro de Atacama's Central Square has become a key to the mental map that pins me to the earth. At one edge stands the Padre Le Paige Museum, squat and white, its generator humming incongruously day and night, as if it were the motor that keeps the world spinning on its axis. The museum's contents offer a rather ironic tribute to human history as told by the surrounding earth. It makes everything look so easy, so accessible, even this desert seeded with thousands of mummies, preparing its bizarre crop. Some are the result of sophisticated effort, but most are natural, prepared by mourners, then dried and preserved by the land itself.

There were times on later visits when I would experience the museum as a relentless, godless kind of crypt, with its polished glass cases, the neatly printed labels, the locked doors behind which lurk headless bodies and lonely skulls, chipped rocks and weapons, the raw chaos of human detritus that gets shaped into its tidy presentations.

But that first time, I found marvels inside, sounds and sights that clung to my senses long after I returned to Santiago's pressured roar: golden objects that lie dented, scarred and crumpled as if someone had crushed them in his fist, tossed them away in rage. Among the earrings and beads, the golden headbands and ornaments, nine tiny vertebrae, a thousand years old, spelled out the brief life of a child.

In the central hall, a round chamber from which emanate the galleries that contain the museum's displays, lurked the shadows of lives trapped behind glass. In one large case, a woman's figure hunched over the ragged bundle of her newborn child. So lifelike was her pose that I could imagine the child growing up, running and shouting to friends, the mother grinding pestle against rock as she transformed nuts into flour, ears sharpened to her child's footfall or cry.

Such are the illusions of the museum curator's craft: this image of them, which rekindled movement in my mind's eye, was only the dried essence of a moment captured by the desert, in which death froze mother and child, ushering them forever out of life, at the moment of birth. Her dark braids, which made her feel so alive to me, had been neatly combed fifteen hundred years before, when someone wrapped her in a fine wool shawl and sang or said a last farewell.

That presence, those lives behind our lives, that sense of life surviving, penetrating death, the echoes of voices like radio waves filling the air, the sense, always that sense that this was a pregnant emptiness, shivering toward labour, bent on telling *something*, if someone would just tune in. It would call me back, over and over in the years to come, invisible threads tangled around my mind, tugging, gently, unforgiving. What or whom was I searching for? Why?

She could be a woman, I thought, travelling from the heights of the altiplano to the lowlands of the coast, travelling from north to south, from triumph through failure to hope and death, and something after. From certainty to doubt. From presence to memory. From physical reality to myth. How would I know her, find her, and what could we possibly say to each other? The whole shape of her mind, her life, would be crafted by spirits and gods

I might find interesting, but would not feel. At best a pagan atheist, in the Atacama I would be travelling through a landscape of faiths, every landmark a site for ritual prayers, offerings of spirits to spirits, candles lit to attract or deflect beings I could grasp like Joseph Campbell's myths, but could not experience as living forces.

I am a city creature, although I love the land. I love my tree-lined street, the bitter fight to hold a place for people against the neo-conservative logic that has tried to drive us from our homes. For almost as long as I've been obsessed by the Atacama, I've been fighting a highway project that would cut through our neighbourhood and our lives, severing the north bank of the Mapocho River—the historical heart of Santiago—from the rest of the city, forcing artists and writers, market vendors, professionals and retired workers out of our habitat, turning us into refugees in our own city. I'm addicted to Internet and virtual worlds, the computer's synthetic mind and speed, the high-pitched tone of the fax machine at all hours of the night. Who would this woman be and why should I try to find her?

But in the end, there's not much point in arguing with an obsession. We don't choose them. They're born in us and drive us until we die. Like an addict eager for reform, I've tried to kick the writing habit many times. But here I am, terrified and fierce, setting out on another book, another journey, trying to create what I must find, because for some reason I can only sense, I can't live without it.

During that first visit to the anonymous woman's glass cage in the museum, there was a coda that I did not see: the parchment-like skin covered only her forehead and one cheek; on the other side of her face, white bones gleamed.

People here believe that the soul does not go to another land, Alonso Barros, a young lawyer working with the Atacamenian communities told me. *When one of these bodies is disturbed from their trip back to the Pachamama [earth], then the spirit emerges and starts to haunt those who have disturbed it.*

When I played back my tapes from that first journey, what I noticed most were the sounds of water I had recorded, how it punctuated the wind, the voices, the tape's quiet hiss, shifted the meaning of everything I'd heard. The sound of a splash spilled out the memory of a fat, brown-skinned boy wearing a green T-shirt as he dove into the rock pool in the Atacamenian village of Peine. Past him, past the frame of giant ferns and primal shrubs around the pool, the horizon was an endless line of smoky rock and dust.

Then came the hissing geysers of Tatio, boiling up out of the earth, bringing the damp heat that swirled around me as I tried to wrap my shivers in those warm shrouds of steam, tried to absorb the heat, at 5:00 a.m., 4,500 metres above sea level. On the way back down to San Pedro de Atacama, more bubbling, splashes and laughter even, to mark my discovery of Puritama, an Eden-like oasis complete with hot spring, dammed to produce shallow pools for chilly bathers.

Water is the source of life, said Barros. *Indigenous people have known that for a long time. It's part of their culture and their cosmovision. They worship water.*

But today, even as I sit down to write this, another well's gone dry in the heart of the Atacama salt fields. The water is vanishing—sucked up by the dry, hot skies, pumped out by lithium miners, gulped down by copper mines or piped away by water utilities trying to quench the bottomless thirst of coastal cities, their endless suburbs garnished with swimming pools.

We forget that deserts are results, not only of the massive geological changes the earth's crust has undergone, but also of the processes humankind can thoughtlessly unleash. Deforestation. Blasting. Building. Global warming. Every year, the desert's frontier creeps 500 metres farther south into Chile's fertile central valley.

Crucial moments of our history, as homo sapiens and peoples of the Americas, remain mummified, encrusted among its rocks and salt. Much of our future must lie there too, if we only knew how to read it. The desert lies wordlessly at our feet, speaks only through the peculiar objects it preserves, waiting for someone to pick them up, turn them over, listen with their fingertips.

Silence was its first gift to me, after fifteen years in noisy Santiago, where buses operate at 70 decibels and discotheques boom all night. After that silence, which cleansed the ears, I heard—water tinkling in a rusty culvert, children teasing each other, my footsteps crunching through the salty crust, memories of trudging to school in Canada among the frozen leaves.

And the desert has gone on, teaching me to experience anew, colour, space, texture: the guanacos—graceful Atacamenian camels—prancing together against a backdrop of brown velvet, or the green tongues of a plant, clinging to sand, fragile and stubborn as starlight.

Most of the landscapes I had known until then *like a mirror, turn you inward* as the poet, Gwendolyn MacEwen, wrote. But the desert turns you outward, stretches you beyond your skin.

On the last day of that first visit, we hurtled toward the Salar de Atacama, which is a shallow, briny lake shrinking amidst an enormous salt field. The rims of coastal mountains to our west deepened to blue, while in the east the peaks of Argentina smouldered, flared orange, dimmed to mauve. Farther south loomed mountains of dust and steel. We stopped the car and stood alone on the vast plain of salt and brine, surrounded by a land composed of lines and shades of grey. The sharp scent of iodine rasped our nostrils. The faint cries of long-legged birds pecking at microscopic lives underlined not our solitude, but the solitary majesty of this place, graced by brilliant cerulean blues, the sharp pinks and greens of chemicals aflame, the gentle wash of yellow light soaking the skies, the hills, our eyes. When I gazed upward, the pink arrows with black-tipped wings that flung themselves across the sky were Andean flamingos.

Life and death live back to back, are halves of one whole. In the city, both crowd so close we cease to see them. Death seems unnatural. It usually takes us by surprise. Here, life stunned, delighted. And begged. In that salty heart of the world's driest desert, the flamingos lay their single annual egg in water, safe from rodents, birds of prey. But if the water evaporates, so does their fledgling future, and their kind.

Death is a shadow that always follows the body, an old English proverb says. In that bare and open plain, where the sun falls bright and even on every nook and rock, the line between earth and flesh has grown transparent. There is much to learn. Time and the land may look endless, but life is absolute and brief.

I did not know it then, but I had just taken the first step on this journey. And so had she.

2

HEADS
WITHOUT
HANDS

The Incan Empire

We order that in all the towns of this reign the main chiefs, the Indians large and small, eat together in the public square, so that all the poor, orphans and widows, sick, old, blind and one-eyed people, pilgrims and wanderers, may join them without shame, and without feeling they eat from charity, but rather, because that is our custom.

— A common regulation of the Incan authorities of Cuzco

Tiwanaku (Bolivia) 1535

SHE STOOD IN THE MIDST of what in the dim pre-dawn light appeared to be a vast plain, where the line between earth and heaven was barely distinguishable. Embroidered with wisps of fog, the occasional arrow of a bird's flight vanished from sight before she'd really seen it, the sharp whistle of its need for company extinguished before she was even sure she'd heard it. She drew the robes of fine llama wool tighter around her to shut out the cold wind that blew off the sacred lake, somewhere to the north. It was nearby. She could tell by the smell of water and her memory of the last days of their journey from Cuzco, a journey whose rhythm was marked by the clank of the Spaniards' armour and the chains around the necks of her fellows.

As Huillac Ñusta, daughter of the great Incan pope Huillac Uma, she did not travel in chains. Nor was she expected to join the thousands of Incan subjects who struggled up the rugged staircase of the Andes carrying live chickens, sacks of corn, Spanish armour and sometimes even the Spanish themselves. A young girl—a child, really—helped her carry her belongings, helped her to dress her hair and don her clothing in the morning. A young girl who helped maintain the illusion that she somehow had more in common with Diego de Almagro, the conquistador, than with the Indian slaves that were already beginning to die from his treatment of them.

She and her father and Paullu were travelling as a kind of safe-conduct pass for Diego de Almagro, the Spaniard who was a friend of the Inca Manco Capac, Paullu's brother. Francisco Pizarro had tried to resolve the struggle between two of his brothers and Almagro over Cuzco by granting the latter the right to conquer the Incas' southern domains. Manco, who had waged his own bitter struggle of attrition with the Pizarros, had even spent a night hidden under Almagro's bed, while a mob looted his house. Near Titicaca the cacique of Copacabana, Challco

Yupanqui, would join and accompany them to Chile, showing them the roads and making the Indians along the way obey them. The mainly Aymara peoples of Lake Titicaca still held more sway over the Atacama than the Incas themselves.

She was troubled and she had slept badly, rising early to climb a low hill to try to catch a glimpse of where they were headed. For Ñusta, as an Inca, the future lay behind her because it was unknown, she could not see it. Before her spread the known world, her own past.

She knelt on the ground, feeling the rough tufts of the brown grass of the altiplano bite into her knees, scoring it with hieroglyphs that would fade, as she continued the long march southward. To still her thoughts she closed her eyes, letting her mind sink into a greater darkness than that around her, letting the stories of this place that were part of the foundation of her own universe blaze against the dark walls of her fear. She could sense the musicians' breath echoing hollowly, plaintively through the quenas and the ocarinas, the deep sighs of the pan flute, which accompanied every important ritual in her temple and her life.

For a moment her mind slipped back to her narrow room in the Acllawasi, the Incan nunnery at Pachacamac where she had become one of the Chosen Ones, studying to become a high priestess and perhaps eventually the wife of a noble or even a concubine of the Inca himself. Her room was always a refuge, cool and dark even at the hottest hour of the day. In her memory she drew that familiar space around her, like the woollen folds of her tunic. In that humble stone cell, in the enormous hive that formed Acllawasi, her life had learned to pulse with the

rhythms of their faith, punctuated by the tales she had
memorized, their Bible learned by heart, preserved by the
Chosen Ones.

. . . They say that in the olden days, when the earth was com-
pletely covered by night, in the eastern province of Collasuyo, a
lord named Kon Tiksi Viracocha emerged from the lake and went
to a place nearby where the town of Tiwanaku stands today; he
went there with his own and they say that then he made the sun
and the day and started the sun along the path it now travels. And
then, they say, he made the stars and the moon. But he grew
angry with the people in that place and made everything dark
again, and later he turned them to stone . . .

But just as he had emerged and at that same time, they say,
he made the sun and day, moon and stars; and in that place of
Tiwanaku he moulded stone into the people he would later pro-
duce, and at first he governed and was lord of many pregnant
women and women with children in their cradles, according to their
ways; all made of stone that he set apart; and then he made an-
other province there in Tiwanaku, forming them from stones just
as I've said, and when he had finished he sent them all off, keep-
ing only two with him, telling them as he watched the others
leave, "These will be called the so-and-so's and they will emerge
from that fountain, in that province, and they will populate it and
grow; and these will emerge from that cave, and they'll be called
such-and-such and they will populate that place; and just as
I have painted and carved these stones, so they will emerge from
fountains and rivers, caves and hills, in the province I have named
to you; and you must go forth along this path"—he pointed to the
sun—"dividing them up and telling them what they must do."

. . . His back to the sun he sent off one of the last of his stone
people to Condesuyo, on his left, and he sent the other off to

Andesuyo, on his right. Then, his back still to the sun, Viracocha himself began to walk straight to Cuzco, between the two provinces, along the royal road that crosses the sierra toward Cajamarca. He himself went walking and calling people out as I described.

Now the heartland of this past and their most cherished religious traditions lay at her feet. She and her father had retraced Viracocha's steps, accompanied by these aliens who wanted to continue southwards, crossing the Andes and moving down and through the crystal mountains and salt plains of the Atacama Desert, driven by their hunger for gold and silver.

But with this journey they were no longer creating or even celebrating the known world of the Incas, with its tightly structured society based on a foundation of hard work, stringent honesty, worship, sacrifice. Viracocha's supremacy had been challenged and shifted slightly downward in the hierarchy of their gods. Now Inti, the sun god of the Incas, their highest ruler and king, ruled supreme. But perhaps even his reign now faced a tragic challenge?

She was troubled with doubts as she had never been before. It was as if the murmur of the feet of the 570 Spanish cavalry and foot soldiers and the 12,000 Indians flowing up the endless terraces of the Andes to Tiwanaku were beginning to unravel Viracocha's tightly spun thread of life. Her legs had grown numb, in the chill morning. She stirred and rose to her feet, stumbling slightly.

The low "hill" where Huillac Ñusta stood was really the tip of Akepana, a seven-terrace pyramid, part of the greatest city-state the Andes had known, a civilization known as Tiwanaku that had flourished and died between A.D. 600 and A.D. 1100 near the shores of Lake Titicaca (a name meaning "sacred stone") 3,400 metres above sea level. In the ensuing years, the surviving feudal lordships of the Aymaras had used the great ruins as a kind of quarry, taking the finely carved and fitted stone blocks—some weighing as much as 140 tons—to use in their buildings. Later the Spanish would even use them for the foundations of a Christian church. But the Aymara lords weren't the only ones to take their future from these ruins. Psychologically, economically, morally, the Incan empire itself was firmly built on the foundations of Tiwanaku, one of the world's longest-lived and most sophisticated civilizations.

A thousand years earlier, villagers on this site had experimented with farming and irrigation techniques and created a simple irrigation system that generated enough of a surplus to allow for the development of a new class of artisans and priests. These specialized in the prayers and rituals, the music and the engineering techniques, that later gave birth to the rich, colourful city of Tiwanaku.

Their culture was enriched by the endless caravans of llamas and their drivers, who carried dried fish and other products from the Pacific Ocean upward into the heartland of the Andes, trading for the highly prized textiles, potatoes, quinua and other highland crops, then continued in a diagonal line northwest toward Cuzco and then from there down again to the Pacific Ocean.

As she wandered the ruins of Tiwanaku, Ñusta paused to meditate on the history carved into the hard Andean rock above the massive stone gateways into its main temples. Her fingers traced the grooves of a carving that was vaguely familiar, the four figures of the Sacrificer floating from left to centre, where they met four similar figures floating toward them from the right. Their heads were elaborate masks, crowned with ritual diadems. In one hand, each figure held the same raised sceptre, while from the other dangled an axe and a human head. These masked faces had no eyes, but bared huge teeth, a leaf-like hallucinogen clamped between them, as they floated with their terrible message within the stone.

Born in the Pukara empire that preceded Tiwanaku and perhaps even before that, the shaman known as the Sacrificer wielded the power of death over the known universe, including the people who worked the land, creating the surplus crops that maintained the lords and engineers, the architects and magicians, the artisans and messengers, and finally the soldiers who would turn Tiwanaku from a village into an empire.

By the time Ñusta stood worrying over the view from Akepana, four hundred years after the empire crumbled, the essential rites and messages of Tiwanaku had vanished, leaving only the footprints of their thoughts in the finely painted ceramics, the intricately carved stone panels and the monumental stone buildings that have been compared to the palace of Teotihuacán in Central America. Not even the Incas, their finest students, could surpass their mastery of stone.

As the differences between those who produced the food and those who planned and controlled the irrigation systems and the religious festivities that accompanied them began to grow more significant, the relationship between the Sacrificer and the other ritual figures as portrayed by the stone carvings and painted figures also began to undergo a transformation. From their original positions, floating equally in the same space, all of the same size, face to face, the figures with the sceptre began to transform themselves and one in particular began to swell and mutate. As time passed and the patient fingers of the artisans grew more skilled, more sure of the metaphor they were teaching the hard Andean rock, one figure began to climb higher and higher in the hierarchy of their carvings, standing on pillar-like legs, staring out of a dread-inspiring mask, with an axe, a sceptre, a human head gripped firmly in his thick, strong fingers.

Tiwanaku's Puerta del Sol, "Gate of the Sun," is now badly cracked, but still stands. It remained a proud whole, attached to the adjoining walls of one of the temples, when Diego de Almagro's party stopped there overnight. Wandering among those stone walls, Ñusta studied the huge figure, firmly planted on a pedestal that lifted him high above his writhing attendants, some with the heads of birds. He firmly clutches two magnificent sceptres and clearly rules over tens of smaller figures, arranged in neat rows of three by his side and under his feet.

Whom did they sacrifice? How often? How did they decide? In her time and theirs, ritual death was not simply a punishment to be meted out to society's worst transgressors; it was the maximum sacrifice, a kind of reward, although not perhaps one that many would seriously aspire to. Tiwanaku's Sacrificer, a fearsome man with a mass of dreadlocks and the blood and gore of his office staining his clothes and hands, was called forth from his temple to practise his grisly trade on some of the best and purest offerings that society could provide.

The sacrifices were a genuine part of religious practices throughout the vast territory that Tiwanaku came to rule. The Sacrificer's dreaded visage was already a part of the Pukara culture that thrived on the northwestern shores of Lake Titicaca during the first centuries A.D., well before Tiwanaku. The Incas themselves continued the tradition during their rule, carrying the shaman and his bloody rituals with them as they conquered the other peoples who formed part of their empire, which lasted barely a hundred years. He was an intricate part of the terrible world that the highest rulers and shamans explored in drug-enhanced trances. His pitiless visage was often his victims' last view of this world, as they began their journey to the next. His image formed the handle of the beautifully carved tablets used to inhale hallucinogens throughout the Andean region, as far south as San Pedro de Atacama in what is now northern Chile. One variation of his menacing countenance can still be seen in the museum there, one foot slightly forward as if he's walking firmly forward, one hand clutching a human head. Under an arched topknot his eyes stare blankly outward, a flat, chilling turquoise. Only the Sacrificer ever returned from those astral journeys through death.

And he travelled the physical landscape too, moving southward with his sceptre and his axe and another loyal companion, a musical instrument, known as the *antara*, which was an integral part of his rites. Sometimes, in the ceramic or stone friezes that betray his presence, the Sacrificer has put his axe, sceptre or even the head down for a moment. In its place he holds an antara.

The antara is still played today, an integral part of the dances of the *chino* dancing groups in the small towns near the coast of Chile's central valley. It is a two- or four-column wind instrument, which produces an eerie tuneless wail unlike any other sound on earth. For most of the journey southward, the antara and the Sacrificer were inseparable companions.

In the desert oasis of San Pedro de Atacama, gravedig-gers have discovered the instruments in some of the older tombs, still keeping company with the remains of bodies without heads. Heads without hands and bodies.

For the star of the sacrifice, being the primary figure in a major religious celebration may have blunted the edge and fear of death. Hallucinogens could have helped to magnify awareness, helping to turn the experience of sac-rifice into a profound exploration of the doorway from life to death. Poised on that threshold, prepared by ritual and faith to cross it humbly, perhaps there was even a momen-tary flash of some deeper knowledge, unlike anything we can know today.

But it can't have been easy for parents to offer up a child to be made drunk with *chicha*, fermented apple juice, and then watch impassively as they were chanted and prayed over and finally slaughtered, along with llamas and other ritual animals. For young women in the prime of their lives, like Ñusta herself, chosen for her beauty and strength to receive the best education her society could give her, there must have been moments of doubt, moments of profound regret at the prospect of submitting to the Sacrificer's axe.

No matter how brief, a violent cry of horror and resis-tance must have ached to burst from the throats of those chosen for the sacrifice, an incentive for them or those who loved them to shake off the cold paralysis of fear, the passive acceptance of ancient custom.

Fear of the consequences of rebellion would have played an important role in silencing any instinct to protest. At least for the Incan society that followed, sacrifices were often chosen from among the children and daughters of royalty, a fierce but effective method of social control. But there was another reason that conspired to maintain and strengthen a custom that reinforced the growing class differences among these originally egalitarian societies and made sacrifice not only acceptable but somehow desirable and right.

It got results. Results beyond anyone's wildest dreams.

The culture and the ruling class, whose power both shielded and was strengthened by the Sacrificer's arts, was wildly successful. Without the aid of modern technology, Tiwanaku's rulers accomplished feats that would be envied by any modern-day city, unmatchable perhaps, because of the perfection with which they moved stone and animals, crops and human beings to give shape on this earth to their dream, to call forth life from the granite reaches of their empire.

City planners traced orderly streets and had neat rows of adobe homes built for the over one hundred thousand people who came to live in Tiwanaku, while engineers designed precisely angled aqueducts to carry water to and from the city and to drain the pyramid of Akepana. Architects carefully planned the monumental temples of Kalasasaya and Puma Punku, while weavers designed and wove the colourful four-pointed hats. These colours and designs, reinforced by the blouses, woven tunics and robes commonly worn, also marked the social status and place of origin of all those who visited the centre of worship and commerce, the extraordinary Andean Mecca that Tiwanaku became.

Tiwanaku's hydraulic engineers studied the irrigation techniques of the raised fields of the surrounding villages, magnified and improved them, coaxing the stingy rivers and the great sacred lake to give of their waters at the right times and in the right proportions for successful crops, remodelling thousands of hectares of the barren, marshy altiplano into the lushly successful farmland, capable of providing enough potatoes and other crops to feed the city in just four months of the year. Their system was considerably more complex than the usual irrigation ditches that still carry vital water to thirsty roots.

Farmers dug ditches about three metres wide, lining them with stones to help prevent leakage. In between the channels they piled layers of medium-sized stones, followed by finer and finer stones and finally a layer of topsoil, often fertilized with guano brought from the coast. These raised beds—*camellones*—were about six metres wide. Not only did they ensure that water was always available for their crops, the water also absorbed the sun's heat during the day, returning it to the air around the beds at night, blanketing them in a gentle mist that protected them from the frosts common on the altiplano.

In four months, the camellones could produce enough food for the population, and still allowed for enough surplus to support the empire's army, the administrative and religious elite, and the lords whose descent directly from the gods enshrined their right to rule from one generation to the next. During the rest of the year, this freed farmers to work as builders and artisans or to prepare new land for planting.

When the shamans ordered thousands of farmers to build the raised fields and stone-lined aqueducts that carried the water between them, when they called forth rain, and announced it was time to plant, the farmers sowed their seed and the fields flourished. Untouched by the harsh frosts, they produced millions of kilos of potatoes and other crops, creating an ecology where fish swam freely and ducks could nest, providing plenty of eggs and meat for hungry settlers. Massive storehouses and careful planning meant hunger disappeared, and it remained unheard-of throughout the Inca empire that followed, returning in all its horror with the ruthless exploitation of the Spanish, an indomitable scourge to this day.

At its height, Tiwanaku was the capital city of an empire whose influence reached from Lake Titicaca in what is today Bolivia, all the way to the Pacific Ocean in both Peru and modern-day Chile. It included hundreds of small farming communities as well as the sister cities of Ojje, Wankani, Lukurmata and Pajchiri, which functioned as regional administrative centres. Agricultural colonies at lower altitudes provided the cities with corn, sweet potatoes, beans, squash, peppers and other products, along with the guano, organic fertilizer, used on Andean fields, edible seaweed, dried fish and other marine products carried from the Pacific coasts by the endless caravans that criss-crossed the desert and the mountains. Between the city and its colonies the people of Tiwanaku created a civilization that used every ecological niche from the Pacific to the high Andes, without apparently damaging the land or destroying its ability to survive.

But no one is clear about why, after over a thousand years of growth, expansion and prosperity, the divine king of Tiwanaku faltered and Aymara lords in the outlying areas began to take over the land and resources, the essential accoutrements of power. Some speculate that there could have come a period of extraordinary flooding, which destroyed the camellones. Others, going on evidence gleaned from a glacier near Lake Titicaca, believe that a period of prolonged drought finally shattered the king's and the shamans' control over the water, and with that, the land and its people.

Whichever it was, Tiwanaku reflected a continuity of religious, agricultural and social principles that lasted for thousands of years and seem to have inspired the major civilizations of the Americas. Its stone architecture, sculpture, ceramics, weaving and even its extraordinary agricultural methods were born from the Pukara culture that preceded it and co-existed for some time in an adjacent region to the northwest of Lake Titicaca. In turn, painfully, but with all the power and sheer muscle that go into a human birth, Tiwanaku, like Pukara before it, gave life, instruction and inspiration to the Incan empire that followed it, some three hundred years later.

Tawantinsuyu (Ecuador, Peru, Bolivia, Chile)
1100–1532

Tawantinsuyu—the land of the four corners—was the name by which the Incas knew their empire. For its time, there was nothing to compare with Tawantinsuyu anywhere else in the world. It became one of the largest states in existence, covering an area eight times the size of Spain, with twenty million inhabitants. It stretched from what is now Quito, Ecuador, in the north, to the River Maule in southern Chile, covering a huge stretch of the Pacific coast and reaching from there up into the Andes and beyond, to the edge of the Amazon rainforests. Its network of highways, through terrain so difficult that it remains virtually impenetrable today, provided the backbone for an efficient administration that included a messenger service, sophisticated systems of aqueducts for irrigation and other purposes, and major temples and mansions characterized by extraordinary architecture and a quality of execution that is among the finest the world has ever seen. Ñusta had no reason to believe her civilization, like that of Tiwanaku, would soon become enshrined by its own ruins.

Pedro Cieza de León, who arrived in Peru some fifteen years after the Conquest and was one of its more faithful chroniclers, describes watching an old man of Tawantin-suyu gaze down upon Cuzco and *let out an enormous howl, which dissolved into tears of sadness as he contemplated the present and remembered the past, watching that city which for so many years had its own lords from among its own people, lords who knew how to attract [its citizens with attitudes of] service and friendship unknown to the Spanish.*

It was a land still populated by the living idols known as *huacas*: these could be caves, rivers, stones or other landmarks representing local gods who gave life to each of the peoples called forth by Viracocha as he walked from Tiwanaku to Cuzco. Each man, woman and child belonged to the natural landscape, their huaca being a religious and moral symbol as well as a doorway through which the people of the present could communicate with their ancestors, and the three layers of reality that composed the Incan universe—heaven, earth and underworld—could be reached. The Incan capital city of Cuzco was built in the shape of the sacred cat, a puma. Every road and building in the empire, every object, expressed essential concepts of the Incan cosmovision. And it was a cosmovision, informed as much by detailed observations of the night sky and a profound knowledge of astronomy as it was by their knowledge of the physical world, supplemented by their imagination.

The Southern Cross, a permanent point of reference in the southern hemisphere's night sky, indicated the beginning of agricultural cycles and their related festivals. It inspired the geometric designs of the ceramics, the stone and metal work, and the intricate tapestries created by pre-Columbian weavers, some of which have survived. It also provided the central organizing structure of the Incas' faith and cities. Theirs was a three-dimensional Sacred Cross. On the horizontal level or axis it divided the world, and consequently Tawantinsuyu and each of its major cities, into the four cardinal divisions, north, south, east and west.

On the vertical level, a Bolivian scholar, Roberto Restrepo, explains, it divided the world between *jananpacha*, heaven, *kaypacha*, the middle or natural world inhabited by people and animals, and *ukupacha*, the underworld, the *aquatic and earthly uterus, where celestial coitus takes place and where fertility originates*. Its main symbol, as elsewhere among the original peoples of the Americas, is the serpent, which *surges from the depths, lives, matures, reproduces and grows old*. At times that serpent could curl and rise from the underworld, surging skyward where it became a lightning bolt that reached the heavens. The symbol for the three levels of the world is the combination of the serpent, the feline and the richly feathered bird symbols so common in artefacts from Teotihuacán in Central America southward.

The faith of Tawantinsuyu recalled the ancient *sacred time*, which began when Manco Capac and Mama Ojllu emerged with other brothers and sisters from their respective huacas to build the first Incan settlements, as instructed by Viracocha who created them by the shores of Lake Titicaca. Their rule and that of their descendants lasted some two thousand years.

Then, with the emergence in the fourteenth century of a new leader, Inka Ruka, the Incan centre of beliefs shifted from the eastern edge of the empire around Titicaca to Cuzco, the centre of the universe. With this shift, Viracocha's importance also slipped slightly, giving way to a new supreme being, the Inti, or Sun.

But even with change came continuity. A straight, diagonal line stretches between the main Incan towns, from Potosi in the southwestern corner of what is now Bolivia, through Tiwanaku and the sacred Sun Island of Titicaca (the centre of the universe), and beyond through Pukara (Tiwanaku's predecessor), to Cuzco (the new centre of the Incan universe), cutting neatly across the three-dimensional Sacred Cross of the four-cornered land. The local gods, or the huacas, remained important but lesser religious entities, revered by each clan and village.

Inca was the name of both the people and the figure who ruled and exemplified them. *Inca, Inka* or *Inkka* referred to the king, who was believed to be the son of the Sun here on earth, both human and divine, but it also described him as the essential human archetype or model, the die from which the human race was cast. Along with the other Incan nobles, the Huillac Uma, Ñusta's father, was the highest religious authority. Under the Huillac Uma, the priests known as *amautas* and the priestesses, called the *mamaconas*, all lined up around the Inca and his sister-queen-wife, the Coya, the combined central point defining the order of the universe, the essential moment where communication between the multiple levels of their reality was possible.

Each *suyo*, that is, each of the four corners of the empire, had its own governing, religious and working class, which in turn was divided into administrative units organized by the ten thousand, the thousand, the hundred, and the local, family or *ayllu* (village) level. The complex accounts of the empire's twenty million citizens—their working hours paid to the empire as taxes; the products of their labours, stored for trade, maintenance of non-producing sectors or simply to cover times of want; the births and deaths, were all recorded in the *quipu*. This was the Incas' solution to writing without paper, an intricate series of knotted and coloured strings. In the hands of its well-educated keeper, each quipu was capable of recording everything from the detailed statistics of the latest population census and recent harvests, to the lines of love poems and prayers, perhaps even plays or the movements of the dances that so many of the songs seem to cry for.

Strict records required even stricter morals in the keeping of the public accounts. Even the Spanish chroniclers took their hats off to the Incas' incredibly successful administration of their vast empire, an achievement that the Spanish and their descendants in America have never equalled. Their organizing ability permitted not only the engineering marvels—inns, bridges and roads that could carry a traveller over the rugged terrain of the Andes and into the Amazon jungles, as well as over the driest expanse of desert in the world—but also created specialized storage towers using water channels at their base and currents of air in their heights to dry, chill or otherwise preserve huge quantities of food, enough to feed their nation and, as with Tiwanaku, still maintain a surplus for trade.

Those conquered by the Incas and integrated into their empire were required to pay taxes in the form of work. One-third of their land remained for the local people, one-third of the land's produce went into the storage and refrigeration towers of Tawantinsuyu, and another third was reserved for the gods. Incan law banned wars of expansion among the different member peoples, the death penalty and human sacrifices (except as provided for within its own laws), the accumulation of goods at the expense of the common good and practices that went against its basic values.

The smallest community unit was the ayllu, the village, an institution that continues to structure thousands of indigenous communities in northern Chile, Bolivia and Peru to this day. The members of an ayllu stemmed from a common mythical origin as represented by their local landmark/god, their huaca.

Collective work for the benefit of the community predated the empire and remained a common bond in every Andean community. Throughout the empire, the Inca or his representative invited regional leaders to meetings, plied them with gifts and then requested their co-operation in collective projects. The principle of reciprocity, which required that one return gifts and goodwill in kind, was the foundation that underpinned the political, social and economic system and prescribed the precise rituals employed when the Inca "requested" assistance for some task.

Celebrations, festivals and ceremonies occurred throughout the year, marking periods of intense labour in order to fulfil the quotas required by the empire and those set aside for the gods. There was drastic punishment for soldiers or bureaucrats who took advantage of their position or otherwise abused the authority bestowed upon them by the Inca. In the event of disaster in some point of the empire, food and supplies from elsewhere would be shipped in, and the common wealth also provided for widows, orphans, the physically and mentally handicapped, artists and artisans, teachers, and so on.

The Inca himself was subject to the harsh scrutiny of his own subjects and particularly the nobles who surrounded him. Although by divine right each Inca chose the son who would succeed him as Inca (not necessarily the oldest, but the one perceived to be most qualified), he himself could be and on occasion was removed by the royals, priests and priestesses who surrounded him.

The army was powerful and effective, but as with Tiwanaku before it, integration into the empire could often be achieved by negotiation, rather than devastating warfare and conquest. Local communities kept their beliefs and their languages, and their most important huacas were moved to Cuzco, where they could still be worshipped, but where they were also kept as a kind of hostage. In fact, one of the more interesting characteristics of both Tiwanaku (and perhaps Pukara before it) and Tawantinsuyu was their ability to integrate other peoples' beliefs into their own. It was an empire based not on obliteration, but on unity in difference. They surely expected the Spanish to continue this practice.

The Spanish reached Tawantinsuyu under Francisco Pizarro toward the end of 1532. After a harsh and disconcerting march up into heavily defended mountains that are hard to penetrate to this day, Pizarro and his force of some 150 conquistadors found Atahualpa, the new king, resting in Cajamarca, fresh from victory in a vicious civil war with his brother Huáscar. (In fact he was enjoying a hot bath, complete with hot and cold running water, and the company of his several wives.) The civil war had flared between the two brothers after the sudden death of their father, Huayna Capac, and his most probable heir, apparently from a European epidemic that travelled overland and caught him near Quito. He had no time to choose another successor.

After sending one of his nobles to briefly reconnoitre the Spanish forces, Atahualpa chose to allow them to climb into the Inca heartland in the Andes in Cajamarca, offering no resistance, apparently because he did not take them very seriously. In what was to become the first of a series of incomprehensible meetings between two profoundly different cultures, he had sent gifts—some chickens ready to roast and two *keros*, carefully moulded clay vases—to Pizarro. The Spanish interpreted these not as the gift and sign of good intentions (requiring a reply in kind, as dictated by the rule of reciprocity) that the Inca Atahualpa intended, but rather as a threat that they would end up skinned like the chickens if they attempted to penetrate the Incas' defensive towers, as symbolized by the vases. Nevertheless, they sent the Incan noble back to Atahualpa with similar gifts, a fine Holland shirt and two Venetian goblets, a reply that must have confused communication even further.

Following their initial meeting with Atahualpa, Pizarro and his men decided that their best strategy was to set an ambush and take him hostage, a tactic Cortés had used successfully in Mexico. They prepared the ambush carefully, relying on their horses, armour and artillery to give them the military superiority that their numbers, a small rock of 150 awash in a sea of thousands, did not.

Atahualpa spent a long day breaking a fast and celebrating his victories in the recent civil war. Then he slowly made his way across the plain toward Cajamarca, where Pizarro had organized the ambush in the central plaza. Horsemen hid in the long, low buildings that lined the square, awaiting a sign to charge. Atahualpa entered the town with *five or six thousand men, unarmed except that they carried small battle-axes, slings and pouches of stones under their tunics.** Vicente de Valverde, a Dominican friar, went forward to receive him.

But Atahualpa had arrived with his own agenda. At the beginning of each Inca's rule, he would set out to travel his empire with his court. During these journeys, the store-houses set aside for the Inca's use provided for him and his retinue, without imposing on the local population. In contrast, the Spanish troops had simply helped themselves to whatever wealth they'd found along the way, including a raid on a nunnery of *acllas*, similar to the acllawasi where Ñusta had been brought up. After parading with his troops across the plain, their chests flashing with gold and silver di-adems to mark their rank and valour, Atahualpa and some five thousand of his men arrived in full regalia. He sat, as the graven images of Tiwanaku had done before him and as Roman Catholic saints would do in the centuries to follow, on an elaborate litter, decorated with silver and gold, and lined with an intricate design of brilliant feathers. Eighty lords, dressed in rich blue livery, carried him on their shoulders. While Valverde tried to entice him away from his men by inviting him into a building where Pizarro was waiting for him to dine, Atahualpa refused, demanding that the Spanish return everything they had stolen or used.

Valverde replied by explaining his role as a priest, which culminated in his handing Atahualpa a Bible. Atahualpa struck his hand away when Valverde tried to show him how to open the book. He eventually did open it and after study-

---

* Hernando Pizarro (Hemming)

ing the writing, threw it angrily to the ground. Valverde used the incident as an excuse to call on the Christians to come out and attack *these enemy dogs who reject the things of God.*

The Spanish assault began with a burst of cannonfire, followed by the troops on horseback charging from their hiding places into the square, slashing away at the noblemen holding the litter until many lost their limbs and then their lives. Pizarro himself deflected the knife blow of a Spanish soldier who tried to stab Atahualpa, capturing him and taking him into his lodgings. The slaughter continued outside, with the Inca's desperate men, terrified at the artillery and the horses, milling around in the square, then plunging en masse against a wall, which they successfully toppled, and pouring out onto the plain. The horsemen charged through the wall and followed them, slashing and chopping and stabbing until some six thousand men lay dead.

Seeing the Spaniards' greed for gold, Atahualpa made another tragic mistake. He promised them a roomful of gold in exchange for his freedom, and proceeded to order his subjects to hammer and pry the gold slabs and other decorations from the empire's major temples in Cuzco and bring them to Cajamarca. The process took several months, but he finally filled the room. Its treasures were melted down and much of the Incas' finest craftwork was lost, one fifth of it paid to the Spanish crown in taxes, the rest going to enrich their conquerors.

Still jumpy from the tensions of the civil war, Atahualpa was more worried about his brother Huáscar. Although Huáscar was already his prisoner, Atahualpa fretted that he might somehow escape, organize his troops and take advantage of Atahualpa's being the prisoner of the Spanish to make another leap into the supreme position of Inca.

Atahualpa finally reached a decision. Huáscar was killed by the men who held him prisoner in a town not far from Atahualpa's own cell. Although Atahualpa told the Spanish that his death had nothing to do with him, his absolute authority over his universe makes that impossible.

With competition from Huáscar no longer troubling him, Atahualpa finally paid some serious attention to the Spanish. As the months in captivity wore on, he must have realized that they were unlikely to fulfil their side of the bargain and release him. From captivity he attempted to organize his own rescue and the defeat of the Spanish under a loyal Incan general, Rumiñavi. But a regional chief revealed these plans to Pizarro. After several lengthy debates, Pizarro yielded to Almagro's insistence that Atahualpa should be put to death for plotting treason. Reluctantly, he sentenced the Inca to death.

Before he died, however, Atahualpa pleaded for Pizarro to take care of his sons. When Valverde told him to stop worrying about his sons and think of his immortal soul, Atahualpa "converted" to Christianity, then continued to plead for Pizarro to take charge of his sons. Pizarro finally agreed. Atahualpa was promptly garrotted with a piece of rope. His death plunged the empire into violent mourning. Many of his wives rushed to the chamber where he was being watched over in preparation for burial, complaining bitterly that it was too small and insisting that they must be killed and buried with him. They also believed that without proper funeral rites he would return. Several spent the night searching for him.

For Tawantinsuyu, the arrival of a small force of Spaniards bent on conquest and riches at any cost must have been the equivalent of the arrival of invading armies from outer space for us today. They had no idea what to expect. The language, cultural context and ancient traditions that had always ruled Andean society, even through times of change, abruptly assumed new meanings. Meanings that were meaningless for the people subjected to them.

The Spaniards' success—against mighty armies that had conquered the better part of a continent before pummelling each other in a bitter civil war—was more than an important military victory. Just as the Sacrificer's "success" at improving crops and creating better living conditions helped to consolidate his position in Tiwanaku's early society, the Spaniards' success, backed by a powerful god unknown to the Incas, must have dealt a significant blow to their religious convictions. Time to add a new god to the pantheon, many must have thought, at least at first. Atahualpa's own conversion (and those that followed), along with his imprisonment and summary execution, suggests they were at least willing to try it on for size.

Their own experience as invaders and forgers of a new empire was firmly built on the foundations and traditions of their own Andean past, and it could not prepare them for the Europeans, whose ambition had been fed by centuries of hunger and suffering exacerbated by the Inquisition, then at its height. The policies of the Spanish often crossed the fine line between extreme exploitation and genocide. Because of the Incas' own tolerance and that of the empires that had preceded and inspired their own, no one could foresee the crusade launched by the Catholic Church to destroy every vestige of their beliefs, including the very huacas from which each local people had sprung to life on hearing Viracocha's call.

Instead, and particularly in the early years, they seem to have expected a conquest similar to those they themselves had imposed on their enemies, which would add a new and higher god to the existing pantheon and bring some changes, but would essentially respect the principles of fairness and sound administration which they had applied during their short reign.

There were other, powerful reasons that must have encouraged the leadership of Tawantinsuyu in their hope that merger rather than genocide could result from the newcomers' arrival. The cross itself, the maximum icon of the new god, was remarkably similar to their own, although its context was substantially different. And there were astounding similarities between the Christian calendar of celebrations and those of the Inca.

Among the ceremonies that Huillac Ñusta had learned and nourished throughout her life, most coincided with important events in the Christian calendar, which is remarkable given how closely religious ceremonies are related to the changing seasons. The northern hemisphere's summer months are winter in the south. Cold in the north means heat in the south. The cold, dark days of the southern winter are the negative reflection of the bright sunshine of the north's brief summers.

And yet at the height of the northern winter, their summer, between January and March, the Inca dedicated their ceremonies to penitence, offerings, invocations and sacrifices, especially in the name of rain. These overlapped the Christians' forty days of Lent. As the Christian calendar celebrates Easter and rebirth at the end of April, festivities and celebrations marked each new harvest of Tawantinsuyu's crops, along with their safe storage in the silos placed in every administrative district. By June—midwinter—the Incas practised dancing, singing and other rites to prepare the hard earth, using sacrifices and ritual drinking. In July, they prepared to sow, and by August there were more parties and singing to accompany their collective work in the fields.

In November, full spring, the Incas, like the Roman Catholics, visited their dead, carrying out rites of memory and sombre rejoicing. Part of the ceremonies included processions during which the mummified remains of former Incan rulers were paraded through the streets on fine litters to the jubilant dancing and singing of their subjects. Later, their descendants would dance and sing before Christian saints brought out to see the light of day once a year, for their own festivals.

Amazingly, in December, as Christianity celebrates its most important holiday, the birth of God and Mary's Son, the Incas held their great festivals in honour of the Sun, their highest god. These included sacrifices, ritual requests and penitence, dancing and singing in Cuzco and all the Inca centres.

Inti Raymi became Corpus Christi, while the worship of lesser deities, as symbolized by animals, would later meld into the story of Saint Francis. To the Inca, Santiago Apostle (Saint James the Apostle), patron saint of the holy wars against the Moors, must have looked like a desirable ally. People formed an intuitive connection that joined the Inca to his sister-bride, the Coya, and from the Coya it was a small step to the Virgin, who in turn easily became the Pachamama, Mother Earth.

The conquistadors themselves must have helped this process along. They were hardly deep theologians. Most, in fact, were the sons of minor nobility in crisis, soldiers of fortune, poor men, artisans and peasants with a hunger for wealth and power that could perhaps only be fully understood within the context of medieval European society, a world of social difference that few of the Incas would ever come to know. Bold, desperate men, many with sharp minds untouched by education, they came imbued with the popular culture of medieval Spain, a culture in which *fiction and reality know no clear limit between them*, as Lautaro Núñez, the author of many books about the desert, once put it.

Every living culture is constantly re-examining its own soul, Núñez also wrote. For Huillac Ñusta, travelling forward through and beyond her own past, this thread would continue to wind its way through her life story, long after she herself had died.

Ñusta may have felt comforted as she wandered among the massive stone blocks of Tiwanaku's fortress. She had come home to the very heart of her own civilization. Even the ornaments used to enlarge the ears of the Incas' ruling aristocracy had their origin in Tiwanaku. But the massive walls of the magnificent temples lay cracked and neglected around her. Many of the imposing statues that once ruled the central courts of their halls and ceremonial centres lay unceremoniously on the ground, half buried under the debris of four centuries of decay. The Spaniards were already busy tearing the gold ornaments and brass clamps from walls and thrones.

As she wandered uneasily back toward the Spanish encampment, Ñusta passed several of the temples that, together with the pyramid, formed the heart of Tiwanaku's sacred city. Just east of the massive stone staircase that led up into the main hall of the Kalasasaya temple, she found a staircase leading down into another roofless chamber, about two metres below ground level. She hesitated, then made the brief descent into this smaller, more intimate subterranean temple. Perfectly carved and fitted, the rock pillars and finely worked bricks that composed its walls were of all shades of grey and white and almost black, or rosy, pink and orange as the dawn light that fuzzed the landscape around her. She moved closer. In that light, some of these rocks protruded, casting dark shadows toward the pale earth. With her fingers she could trace human eyes and noses, the elaborate headdresses of peoples she'd never met, a wild variety of features she had perhaps heard of but never seen.

She gave a small gasp and stepped suddenly back, her fingers frozen in mid-air as if she'd found them slick with blood. These beautifully wrought walls were covered with the heads of people of many races, perhaps every race the Tiwanaku had conquered or colonized, every lord they'd ever negotiated with or sent gifts to. Heads divorced from the flesh they had once governed, people fixed in time like a coin that can only flip from essence to opposite. Their past alone lies forever before them. At first she thought they were real skulls, but then her fingers and her eyes growing accustomed to the dim light communicated stone. Perhaps these heads were surrogates for the fleshly thing they represented, and had brought an end to Tiwanaku's reliance on the Sacrificer, replacing his power over life and death. She would never know.

The underground temple was both familiar and sinister. She felt both comforted and disturbed, her mind turning back to the present. Twelve of the Incas' finest *willcas*, captains and priests, were travelling with Diego de Almagro, disguised among the Incan hosts. There were still many cords to be woven and knotted into the quipus that would tell the tale of this pilgrimage. Before the Spaniards could call her to continue the long walk into the desert, she took a deep breath and felt her lungs fill with the thin, cold air, the sharp blade of its energy cutting away her misgivings.

Then, like her sisters, her mother, her grandmothers and their mothers for centuries before, she lifted her arms to the gods, and prayed to Viracocha:

God, origin of the universe, creator of all,
gold that burns alone in the heart's night.

May the joy in your eyes come with the dawn,
may the warmth of your breath come with the wind.

May your generous hand always reach out
and your infinite will be all that flowers.

3

S T A R S

O F   S A L T

➤

Calama and
San Pedro de Atacama

Atacama Desert, July 1998

I T RAINED ON MY FIRST NIGHT in Calama. I couldn't
believe it. For three years I'd plotted and planned
and squeezed rare drops of financing from our over-
extended family budget to buy the time to research, travel
and write this book about the world's *driest* desert. And
then, thousands of kilometres and pesos later, Calama greeted
me with a heavy, leaden sky, slapped my face with a damp
breeze. All night I listened to drops of water smacking the
pavement, smacking the ceiling of my room in a cheap
hotel. I couldn't believe it.

The rain wasn't as unusual as I thought. I had already
discovered Isaiah Bowman, an American geographer who
wrote his way across the Norte Grande almost a hundred
years before. Now, he stirs at my elbow and notes that the

British consul in Iquique, north of Calama, had advised some English friends not to bring umbrellas, *for in the fourteen years that he had then known the coast no rain had fallen. Yet on the night on which they disembarked from the steamer it was raining hard.*

On my first night in Calama, it wasn't the rumbling or hissing of a steamer, but rather the roar of the plane that still buzzed in my brain, the sense that as we left Santiago behind I was embarking on my own flight into another kind of desert, the myth turned real, the point of origin for so many metaphors about city or soul. I was searching for Ñusta, whom folklore has turned into the "Beautiful Tyrant of the Tamarugo Grove," Chile's own Belle Dame Sans Merci, the Incan noblewoman who stumbled and struggled across the high Andean passes with the Spaniard Diego de Almagro. I was searching, almost against my will, for the woman and high priestess who, according to the legend, had briefly ruled the republic of her own hopes, but was then defeated, and today still serves—as the desert's most revered Christian saint.

As the plane dropped lower to land in Antofagasta, clouds hung heavy over the gleaming glass and metal boxes that composed the city, promising rain. I gazed out at what looked like the world's largest construction site. The earth was bare as bone, raw as newly killed meat. Everything looked far too small for us to land on. The pilot, however, seemed to have some of the conquistadors' fierce need to grab the devil by the balls and shake him down. He banked sharply into his landing like an aerial hot-rodder, arcing way out over the ocean above the thick layers of cloud, then plunging through them. They muffled the expanse, made the plane seem small and cramped as it dived into a

point so small we could have disappeared. We fell into the
dot, dropped steadily until a quick trick of light and dust
and vapour caught the plane, pinned us to the sky over the
ocean, then pulled the pin and pushed us back to earth, the
roar of backward jets firing to bring us to a stop.

An hour later, on the approach to Calama, we did it
again. As we swerved and dived toward the earth, the
whole desert unfolded below us for a moment, a crumpled
map spread out on a table. Back to our left, on the Pacific
Coast, Antofagasta had shrunk to the size of a spider, hunched
in its brooding web, pipelines like threads sucking the bright
juices of mines into the port, then shipping them out to a
world hungry for cables, tubes and levers.

Off to my right, to the east, toward the Andes, sat
another oasis, the one that had pulled me up and back and
away from Santiago. San Pedro de Atacama, the Atacama's
capital city for thousands of years, still stood guard over its
many buried secrets.

The plane paused for barely an instant before it sank
into the heart of the map, which rose up around us and
disappeared.

At the terminal, I collected my bags and eagerly grabbed
a taxi into Calama, where I checked in at a cheap hotel,
then rushed off to the Calama Regional Museum. This was
a one-storey adobe structure that formed the right arm of a
patio shaped like a rectangular table. At the head sat a colonial church, regal and lovely and looking, as they all did, as
if the mountains themselves had shaped it out of the mud.
From the outside, the museum looked lovely too, its adobe
walls smooth as a silk gown.

For my book *Medusa's Children*, I had toured single-
room museums in small towns in Newfoundland. With

few resources but the flotsam of troubled lives and, usually, the single-minded passion of some collector, they still managed to be depositories for surprise, sudden delights. Here in Calama, a trace of someone's passion for the past remained in the carefully hand-printed cards that tried to capture a thousand years of history in a net of fading letters. The archaeological evidence was laid out behind them, trapped and asphyxiated behind glass. A cruel indifference, thick as the dust, now shrouded the collection of arrowheads and skins, tattered woven bags and ponchos. The sight of the mummies struck me like a blow.

Alive they slept, wore woollen turbans, shook rattles. When they died, their families had carefully dressed them, wrapped them in layers of finely woven cloth, folded their faces in soft scarves, braided their hair, then planted them like seeds among the rocks, trusting in nature itself to preserve the dried essence of their loved ones.

Now their remains lay, the abandoned rag dolls of long-dead children, nibbled at by moths, spattered with dust and draped in webs.

Christians view the body as a fragile cage from which the soul eventually escapes. For the Buddhist, bodies are stepping stones that lead us upstream. But I believe we are our bodies, live and die in that brief instant of being awake to life. I think of the old theory that an infinite number of monkeys with an infinite number of typewriters would eventually type Shakespeare's works, random patterns of letters that strike the human mind with the precision and force of literary arrows. Our life is like that, utterly unlikely and yet inevitable, typed into existence by chance, a haphazard pattern of molecules that briefly knows and tries to understand itself before its components are scattered again. We are a shadow dancing in the parchment windows of the world. The blinds flick open and we vanish.

For the first people to die in the Atacama, the body became a gateway between where we come from and where we are going, a threshold to be crossed in the long journey taken by both the inanimate and living, rock and tree, by all things defined by their shadows, fleeting motes in the desert's blind eye. For us their bodies have become clues to what we don't know, an exhibit that we examine with every instrument at hand.

Whatever it is that we believe we are, we like to deny the Other, the one who is gone, the one who was different, the one who isn't going where we want to go. *We* are human, our cemeteries are shrines, protected by rites, safe from our wrongs. *They* are History, to be dug up, pried open, placed on display. At the best of times we lay them out on bright cloths in museums with the high ceilings, strong lights, hushed whispers and polished rituals of a church. At our worst, we tear them from their resting place and pile them on shelves, covering them with a mantle of forgetfulness that is worse than contempt.

Two days after arriving in Calama I set out by bus to San Pedro. For two hours we drive through seemingly endless miles of garbage, shiny windows of shattered glass interrupted by plastic buckets like tacky fountains, green and red plastic bags stuffed and overflowing with pop bottles and disposable diapers, the two most ubiquitous relics modern society has chosen to deposit in the desert's storehouses, the time capsules we're preserving for the future. The thick sweet fumes of these burning offerings to desert gods

follow us for miles, mugging our nostrils long after the
garbage is out of sight. To the north, our left, perched on a
ravaged hill, Chuquicamata, once the world's largest open-
pit copper mine and certainly its oldest, smokes like Mount
Olympus.

To ride in a bus across this landscape is to become part
of an absurd, impertinent, vertical creature on wheels,
which dares to challenge the perfect flat horizon. It's like
being inside a television camera, with the film unfolding
around me. I've become obsessed with maps, and now
I travel across a landscape as flat and apparently simple as
a map, criss-crossed with old roads and ancient borders,
seeing from so close and passing so quickly that I can
make out only the shadows of the lost territories they once
portrayed.

This is not the kind of place you'd run *to*, I think. You'd
have to be running *away* from something to end up here:
poverty, limits, fear and filth. What brilliant pictures must
they have projected across the blank screen of the Norte
Grande, dreaming of freedom and wealth, of making their
own decisions, running the republic of their own lives.
Whatever the period they lived in, when they ventured
onto this new surface they left behind them an environment largely shaped and controlled by men, cobbled or
asphalt streets, candle or gas or electric lights, walls enclos-
ing warmth, windows that let in light and sight, but keep
out wind and sound. They turned their backs on all that
and ventured out onto this flat surface like a child's game-
board. Perhaps they thought the space meant freedom.
Perhaps for some it did. But most found themselves forced
into an island existence, the oasis as prison surrounded by
hundreds of square kilometres of rock without a blade of

grass or bird, a land where only the wind lives and roams freely, killing and keeping its own counsel, tossing sand into curious eyes.

A sign in the Calama museum announced that the Pacific Ocean at one time—it didn't specify when—reached all the way through the oasis where the town is now located, 150 kilometres inland, and beyond. Some of the tourist information materials mention the same idea. But the Atacama was born almost 200 million years earlier, during the Jurassic period, when two of the earth's tectonic plates, the Nazca and the South American, crashed headlong into each other, squeezing and thrusting the molten rock from the earth's core upward until they formed the Andes mountain range, which frames the long oval bowl that is today the Atacama desert.

Sixty-five million years ago those mountains exploded again, spewing out gases and liquid rock that flowed down into the parched dust and salt of the plain. Like mad farmers they flung their seed in the air, sowing the desert with gold, silver, nitrates, copper, and the other minerals that turned it into a treasure chest, although not the kind the Spaniards expected to find in 1535.

This is the ocean bottom without the ocean, with no weeds or microscopic creatures, a landscape that has been ravaged by wind, raked by glaciers, heated and poured and moulded in the explosive crucibles of Andean volcanoes. Air masses passing over the cold currents that flow northward from Antarctica lose their moisture over the ocean, well before they reach the Pacific coastline of Latin America. Thick morning fogs, the *camanchaca*, torment the shoreline with the promise of rain, even storms, but it actually rains only once every six or seven years on the coast and may never rain in some parts of the desert's rocky interior. The fog itself rises from the Humboldt current, then drifts inland, where it doesn't survive the morning sun. Bowman takes my elbow, eager to show me around. *It is indeed a strange experience to be in the midst of desert country, so far removed from the sea that there is neither sight nor sound of it, and yet awake in the morning to find the air filled with a clammy, cold fog.*

Fog itself reflects the seasons perhaps more than any other kind of weather. *When the fog belt hangs high over the hills it is the season of dryness. When the fog belt thickens and extends from sea level to the summit of the hills rain may fall. The fog bank is thickest from June to September (winter) and in that period the sun may be hidden for weeks at a time . . .*

Day-to-day weather, Bowman reminds me, is the result of *local causes—a mountain, a regional wind . . . , a fog bank or the absence of it, a cloud belt.* A whole world unfurled, laid out on the ocean bottom, exposed to the dry air. A fertile world that could do more with a few drops of water than others could do with an ocean.

Darwin too was fascinated by this desert. He was eager to describe what a single rain shower meant: *Farmers, who plant corn near the seacoast where the atmosphere is more humid, taking advantage of this shower, would break up the ground; after a second they would put seed in; and if a third shower should fall, they would reap a good harvest in the spring. It was interesting to watch the effect of this trifling amount of moisture. Twelve hours afterwards the ground appeared as dry as ever; yet after an interval of ten days, all the hills were faintly tinged with green patches; the grass being sparingly scattered in hair-like fibres a full inch in length. Before this shower every part of the surface was bare as on a high road.*

When I first visited the Atacama, for the inauguration of the Escondida copper mine, Chuquicamata's great competitor and one of the world's richest producers, I saw what Darwin called the desert's *negative possessions*, the lack of trees, rivers, normal vegetation, animals. Accustomed to seeing forests and fields, flocks of sheep, birds and the other normal signs of life, I tended to "see" what I expected to see, and had to constantly stop and correct my own visual and mental perceptions.

When I travelled it in 1995 and now again in 1998, what most surprised me was the amazing range and variety of the landscape. Once I managed to let go of my expectations, I began to see the surreal "gardens" planted with small rocks, standing on edge as if each one had been carefully placed there by some loving farmer, millennia ago. Today, as I gaze out the bus window, I can see the crops of rocks at different stages of growth—small pebbles, barely visible as we roll by at a hundred kilometres an hour; fist-sized rocks, already starting to sprout and grow; massive boulders, mature and ripening, almost ready for harvest.

And the harvesters have come: generations of Atacamenian miners, followed by the Inca, then the Chileans in the early 1800s, followed by the Brits eager for the rare nitrates that would have washed out of any other kind of soil. Finally, in the twenties and thirties, the Americans arrived, and in the 1990s the Canadians came too, hungry to chew up the copper, the silver, the gold, spit them onto world markets. Mining is terribly unpopular, an ugly, monstrous complex of machines, smelly chemicals, war-like blasts. But a tenuous magic clings to the mines of the Atacama, the mystery of substances transformed, a rock slimming to wire, the molten gold of a lady's ring.

I'm looking forward to seeing the surprises of San Pedro de Atacama once again. I want to turn them over in my hands, decipher their secrets, play back the reels of voices that have echoed here against this enormous sounding board, this essentially empty place that has resounded with human history like a huge drum.

Between forays into the desert and along the narrow valleys of the oasis, as I wheel my bike through a landscape where only the plumed grasses speak in low, dry whispers, I will learn that the people who built and cared for San Pedro de Atacama and buried their dead under its shifting red dust, or in earlier times inside their own homes, still live and thrive there. San Pedro is above all what it has always been, an Atacamenian town, crowded with visitors, crushed by their chatter and their ignorance, half buried in the sand. The Atacamenians are all-present and as elusive as the water itself. They shape the town, direct its quiet bubbling flow through channels, bring forth green or wander off and evaporate, leaving another unnoticed scar on the desert's weathered face.

I turn my back on the sweet whisper of water running through the stone-lined irrigation canals and ride my rented bike along the red-dirt road out of San Pedro de Atacama. The bike has a small mechanical problem—at least, I hope it's small. With every few strokes of my legs, the gears slip, the pedals lose track of their sockets and I practically fall onto the crossbar. Of course, old-time feminist that I am, it didn't occur to me to insist on a woman's bike. Nor, as a cash-strapped writer, to pay a little more to rent a truly functioning means of transport.

Today San Pedro de Atacama, one of the oldest settlements in South America, remains a large oasis and a small
town, a grape-like cluster of *ayllus*, family villages where
the Atacamenians alternately sweat over red furrows or
doze in windowless rooms. After the conquest, it was controlled first by Lima, Peru; then later by Buenos Aires; and
from 1767 on it was part of the mineral-rich madness of
Bolivia's Potosi. During the nitrate era, it was a necessary
stopping place for mule and cattle-trains driven across the
mountains from Argentina.

On the crest of a hill overlooking the old town I pause,
leaning on the handlebars. There is the hill of Quitor
where the old fort stands, the ravine stretching northward
past Catarpe and on toward Bolivia. Bowman speaks in my
ear, telling me he always saw San Pedro as *the centre of a certain amount of revolutionary ferment and the refuge of those who
sought to escape from persecution . . . men come and go for political
reasons in such situations in a manner to which we are not at all
accustomed in this country . . . A politician in difficulty in Peru or
Bolivia may flee to San Pedro de Atacama, as those in political
difficulty in Chile may flee to Salta . . .*

I like the idea of San Pedro de Atacama as a refuge, a
meeting-place where difference is not questioned and a
disastrous past can be forgotten. Gerónimo de Bibar, the
old Spanish chronicler who travelled the Andean highroads
shortly after Ñusta did, must have paused, seated on his
horse on a hill similar to this one, and remembered the
words of a contemporary who reflected that *to understand the
grandeur of [the Atacama], one must bring to mind the two royal
roads of the Inca: one that goes along the coast through the entire
populated and unpopulated length of it, and is up to forty feet wide,*

*walled in on both sides . . . especially two leagues before entering
every valley and then leaving it, cobblestoned in many parts and
with well-treed shadows, and formerly most with fruit, a flavour
that now has been lost and dried out by the death and lack of the
natural people. . .*[*] Bibar observed that the people who lived
along this highway were handsome indeed. In the men's
hands were arrows and slingshots, more to bring down small
animals and prey than to wage war, although there were
periods of conflict between the land's human inhabitants.
Silver puma copper masks, tin candlesticks, lead and ala-
baster, the salt that formed the crystal mountains on the way
into San Pedro de Atacama. The women had long black
hair, wore knee-length skirts and long-sleeved blouses. In
their hands, mud became fine ceramics and the tangled wool
of llamas became delicately woven textiles, echoing the
colours of the oasis, the grief of the desert that embraced it.

The wheel of change whirls on an axis of permanence.
Perhaps it is the women with their weaving who hold the
essential patterns in place, even when the materials have
changed over time. Perhaps it is the men with their songs
and stories, a poem I find engraved on a stone in a neatly
fenced plaza hidden amidst the irrigation channels and the
reeds, behind the fort, the Pukara of Quitor.

I wheel out into the gorge past the old fort, to look for
Ñusta. Everything has changed, but I can still see the
stones that must have shifted under her feet, wearing away
the leather of her shoes, if indeed at this point in her journey she still had shoes at all. My eyes strain to trace the
lines of walls that may be two or twenty or two thousand
years old. The flock of sheep that grazes at the foot of the

---

[*] Cristóbal de Molina, a Spanish chronicler of the Conquest.

old Incan inn at Catarpe would have been llamas then, but still they continue their circular crunching among the tall grasses fed by the salty waters of the Vilama River.

Surely this spirit of rebelliousness, the fact of living on the highway, the permanent temptation of moving (*I'm going to leave this place, and make it mine*) goes way back, turning Bowman, me, Bibar and countless others into a chain connecting our time to that moment when Huillac Ñusta finally set foot on the gritty surface of the Atacama, her long journey over the Andes finally ending in the marketplace of San Pedro, the clouds of dust that announce the arrival of mules, the departure of mules, the generation of wealth by movement, the journey become a way of life.

Today the authorities demand that shepherds and other trans-Andean travellers pay more attention to official borders. During the military regime (1973–1990), the entire area was sown with land mines and they continue to blow off the legs of unsuspecting tourists who step off the main paths, or the trucks of construction companies bent on building international pipelines to deadline. Chile's elected authorities have made little effort to clean up the mines, which have drifted under the desert's surface as they would in the sea. But the town is still a crossroads, crowded with exotic visitors, some of them rebellious, if not revolutionary. They babble in many tongues, as they unwisely race to visit the Inca fort at Quitor, the buried village of Tulor, the Incan Inn at Catarpe and the museum, or drive out into the desert in fleets of vans to photograph the sunset colours of the salar, the salt fields, which coat the hollow belly of this earth, once you move away from the green wounds of the oases.

Past the massive stone fort on a steep hill that was the site of great battles between the Atacamenians and the

Incas, then the Incan–Atacamenians and the Spanish conquerors, I ride along the bottom of a broad gorge that leads
me through the cluster of fields and lonely houses that
composes Quitor, and on along what was once one of the
desert's main highways.

If the mild-mannered young woman who loaned me
the bike had asked me to be careful and not get it wet, I
would have laughed. But in fact, once past Quitor and the
fort, my main problem becomes fording shallow but
opaque puddles that stink and slouch across the road under
the hot sun. I've never ridden a mountain bike before, so
at first I stop at every watershed, walk judiciously along it,
examining every wheel track in the dust, trying to map out
the best route through it.

A true coward at heart, I usually opt for dismounting
and stepping gingerly across whatever stones happen to
thrust their blunt heads out of the muck, dragging my glo-
rious mechanical steed along behind me. It finally occurs to
me that there must be a reason why this is called a *mountain*
bike, and that I should be racing through puddles and over
and around stones and other obstacles, with nary a care in
the world. I eventually try it, at a place where a particularly
wide stretch of water has formed a two- or three-metre-
wide pool across the road, blocking my way. But no sooner
do I rev up my pedalling to dash wildly through than the
gears slip and I find my feet rotating uselessly, the bike grinding to a stop and my most precious female parts jammed
against the crossbar holding this contraption together.

The Chilean expression (please don't use this—I am not
offering you a phrase book and this is definitely not acceptable in polite company) *sacarse la chucha* (to tear out one's
female sex organ) has never echoed in my mind so literally

as it does now, along every one of the more difficult stretches of the road ahead and a few of the easy ones too.

But it doesn't matter, or shouldn't, I think, as I trundle my bike along this stately old Incan highway. The road winds along the gorge, part of the network that once joined Peru, Bolivia and the rest of Chile, pulling them all reluctantly into the empire, weaving the local people, reluctant or rebellious, fierce or docile, back into the fabric that had existed for thousands of years, criss-crossed by caravans and signposted by geoglyphs and rock paintings.

I try to imagine stumbling over these rocks, crawling up and sliding down the granite staircases of the Andes, the sun fierce as the shiny teeth in a toothpaste commercial. I try to imagine Huillac Ñusta being dragged along by Diego de Almagro's expedition, relieved after the gruelling hardships of the journey over the Andes.

I try to imagine that I'm waiting for her, for all of them, to appear at the end of these seemingly endless valleys, which the wheels of my bike refuse to consume, in spite of the endless nudging of my legs. First I would see a glint, sunlight caught and reflected off a steel lance or breastplate. Then, perhaps, a rumbling would vibrate in my ears, the distant echo of their leather-shod feet knocking the stones together as a hundred Spanish soldiers and thousands of captive Indians ground their way down the valley toward me, like a distant glacier, slow, threatening, then suddenly upon me.

But it is too soon, only July. Their journey across the mountains was in August, as they tried to avoid the worst of the winter. As I pedal I try to figure out where Huillac Ñusta's father and Paullu would have made their escape. Perhaps here, perhaps farther south in the town known as Peine.

I wonder if they really arrived through this valley or perhaps traced its winding path when they were finally headed homeward, a few paltry treasures barely weighing them down, not enough to justify the pain and the price paid in the currency of human lives. And when her father and Paullu escaped, why didn't she go with them? I can see how she might have caught Diego de Almagro's wandering eye. Maybe he kept her close to him, where he could always see her, and take her whenever the fancy took him. Did her father and his king take advantage of Almagro's obvious fascination with her and slip away when he was otherwise occupied?

The bike makes the thought of entering the desert's vast emptiness, the arrogance of attempting to cross it, or at least a piece of it, bearable. I cannot imagine measuring this enormous, waterless, lifeless, mineral existence with my feet alone, as she did. My journey north has little in common with Ñusta's long southward trek into Chile from Peru. And yet.

Yamana-n-gamata: *He who was the least likely to die, dying, and the one expected to die, recovering. To escape, survive, when the rest die or are killed.* The phrase has haunted me for years. It is from Thomas Bridges' Yamana-English dictionary, recording the language of one of the peoples who roamed Tierra del Fuego in Chile's far south until the advent of the Europeans and *civilization* wiped them out.

Bridges' words pass through my mind again as I clumsily navigate roads and trails on my faulty bicycle at the other end of Chile, a place as dry as Tierra del Fuego was damp and shrouded in fogs, as caked in heat and dust as Tierra del Fuego was a bright knife sharpened by Antarctica's icy winds.

If my bike were a dull pencil trying to trace narrow roads on a faded map I couldn't be having a harder time finding the old archaeological sites. *Just ride on past Quitor until you see a church and the ruins of Catarpe are just to the right there*, the soft-spoken young woman told me when I rented the bike. *Just follow the highway out of town, turn left and carry on until you see a sports field*, she said when I asked about the mysterious shapes of Tulor, half rescued from the desert's sucking sands.

The road I'm following takes me straight out into the desert of Atacama, the gentle greens and murmuring waters of the town giving way abruptly and totally to the road to the Valley of the Moon, a bare gravel trail snaking across a bare, gravel world, where borders dissolve and the road meanders off into space and distance, distracted by the huge sky above me. The horizon looks close and finite, easy to touch. As I hit the desert, the solitude hits me, the vastness of it, and the absurdity of trying to cross it on foot or bicycle.

If there is one use for the car it is in the desert. My years of fighting the highway project have made me hypercritical of cars—their noise, the way they cut us off from landscapes even as we fly through enormous lengths of them, the way houses are knocked down and trees uprooted, all for the almighty car. We worship it like a god, let it crack like a whip through city streets, imposing its will on all those in its way. But the metal carapace shields you as you travel, hides you from everything but where you came from and your destination, shoots you toward a future as intangible as the horizon.

Where everything else creeps, or croaks, or flickers through water, to speak in clear language, to have mastered flight and the ocean's liquid depths, to walk, to touch, to take—these abilities are important. But to scuttle across the face of immobility itself, to crave a few cold drops of water, to need the sustenance of leaf or flesh, is to be completely superfluous, absurd, a flea on a marble statue's flank. Here, the sun is a blind white pupil, life a nuisance.

I turn back. I can't help it. The woman spoke as if the road were clearly marked, but all I can find is a trail to the Valley of the Moon and the highway to Calama. All roads seem to lead away from where I want to go and in the drunken spinning of that empty place the stakes feel too high to make an experiment worthwhile. I could be a drop of blood in that vast field of stones, red and wet, dried and gone in the blink of time's eye.

Back within the green reaches of San Pedro and its high adobe walls, I keep trying to find another route, pushing my uncooperative steed along gravel roads choked with sand. I ask for directions, and a young woman carrying a toddler in her arms and pulling a small girl along beside her points me forward, and passes me as my bike fails to advance, becomes a burden to be dragged along, holding me back. Hours pass. I'm anxious because I have appointments to keep at awkward hours, crucial interviews that will eventually fall through, but I don't know that now. Those raucous birds that the Chileans call *treiles* screech along beside me, warning me off, pushing me away, turning me round, just as I seem on the verge of finding whatever it was I was after.

At the agricultural high school, I turn right and take a narrow lane, a trench of dust between the adobe walls, passing modest homes. I stop to accommodate a shepherd with his flock of sheep. The sun has dropped behind him in the sky, turning him into a giant shadow, tall and black against its gold-white globe. The sheep have become god-like creatures that travel in clouds of dust. I ask him for Tulor and he gestures up the road behind him, nodding, yes, I'm on the right path. Encouraged, I even try to mount my bike. It lasts for a few rounds of the pedals, but then I go back to my feet.

I feel safe, secure here between the high walls along the road, amidst the algarrobo and pepper trees. Vegetation is sparse but green, the sand sucks at my wheels and heels but I manage to move along. I pass the woman and children, the shepherd and his sheep. Sparrows start and fly off at my passing. I am moving through a landscape painted with life. I may be an odd-looking foreigner in my mauve cap, my blue jeans, sweater and a pack, but there is a kinship here. Something moves all of us, besides the wind. Something from within.

The trees become more sparse, the houses fewer and farther apart. I round a bend and the last sparrow flees up-river to my right. The light of the dropping sun is harsh as steel. A globe of fire burns in the river's heart, making the land that spreads beyond look as hard and dark as cast iron streaked with brittle tin.

The road dips a moment into the creek before rising on the other side, where it winds, dry and flat as a cast-off snakeskin, back into the desert.

Everywhere the roads are neatly labelled, have names as if they led somewhere. I follow them endlessly on my rented bike, but this is all a mirage. Where does the road end and the desert begin? There's nothing but desert, really, the whole world flattened and pulsing with a mineral life we creatures mesmerized by biology cannot understand.

The absence of water defines everything. Where no living creature exists, we're forced to examine the life of stones, passive, sun-warmed, harder than ice, scattered and sparkling amidst the sand. Scratched and scarred by ghosts whose voices still blow through them, whispering of water's cold caress, the inexplicable lights that flash and brand the desert's dark flanks at night. This could be "life" after death, the mineral cells with no sense of movement, no intelligence, their flat receptiveness to all the elements, their unimaginable interactions that nonetheless make life happen, or make it better.

The buried village of Tulor exists. I've seen pictures of the mud walls, straight as narrow highways for miniature feet or curving like the spines of a herd of large, gentle creatures, long extinct. They lie filled with dust up to what was once roof level. Humble and half hidden, the rooms I know will curve when I find them, shaped like the wedding cups that the Bolivians carve of wood, a honeycomb of interconnected chambers, so each guest drinks from a separate yet integrated vessel.

About thirty years ago Father Gustavo Le Paige, a Jesuit priest from Belgium, wandered across this stretch of desert, gazing at his feet. (He walked like a monk doing penance, his eyes fixed on the ground, while I tend to stride and stare into the crystal wheel of the sky, seeking the same answers to different questions.) It was he who discovered Tulor.

Le Paige turned on the desert the same fierce gaze as the sun itself. An impassioned amateur archaeologist, he spent forty years digging amongst its artefacts, questioning the native Atacamenians for clues, venturing into mysterious caves, collecting arrowheads and fragments of bones, and recording everything in notebooks whose sprawling hand began to sketch human faces across the destiny of place. He discovered and explored hundreds of grave sites; stored skulls and mummies, skeletons and individual bones on his sterile shelves. Today, most remain in the back rooms of the museum in San Pedro de Atacama that bears his name. Some are on display, some crumpled into desert dust, teaching those that followed Le Paige not to open the funeral urns.

To walk through the museum is to visit a zoo where death is neatly ordered and gazes out at you from glass cages. But I love this zoo. Just as I unfashionably love Santiago's zoo, which perches up on the hill above my house. I love even the smell of dung, the bitter reek of skunk and fox and wildcat that drifts through my windows when the wind is inclined in our direction. There is in humanity's endless seeking after knowledge, its stubborn insistence on destroying life in its efforts to discover what it is, something pathetic that endears humanity to me, even though the individual actions repel me. I can wander for days through the fields and cages of the Toronto zoo, taking my children with me as an excuse, to experience the thrill of meeting the eye of a white rhinoceros, something you can't do watching television. So I wander through the museum, learning about the way people used to live by studying their approach to death. Archaeologists and anthropologists are the professionals at this, of course. I find the anthropologist Birgit Jacobs's typed manuscript of her thesis on a shelf in the library of the Pre-Columbian Museum in Santiago. Her work and that of the scholars she cites shine a light on the fragments I see in the museum, teach me I'm seeing with my eyes only, those lenses of deceit turned outward to bring us the illusion of the world without its substance. Without scent—the sharp tang of pine, the blue rush of water, the leafless dry smell of snow—we don't connect to where we are. Without the other senses, it's just a show.

Yet this is what remains. We use the bricks of death to reconstruct the roads and edifices of past life, to reinvent "their" horizons. We dig, drill through shell and clay, beading together customs and beliefs, attempting to re-create the coloured threads that once sewed earth, heaven and the underworld together. We fill in the spaces and perhaps learn more from the gaps and how we fill them than from the objects themselves.

The quipu, the abacus, the calculator. Numbers and stars, or how they viewed the stars, measured by how they buried their old bones. Above all, we listen most closely to the bones. If we touch them, their angles and joints press back, refuse to yield or change under our questions. We turn them into numbers and measurements. How much energy it took to discard or bury them. How many treasures they chose to send with the dead on their journey, not from this world to another, but from their world to ours. Like time capsules, the dead travel from then to now.

A human body, Jacobs tells me (the old paper whispers in my fingers while I read, as I imagine her voice would), can be abandoned, eaten, burnt, mummified or buried. Religion struggles to build a bridge out of our fear of death, where we can stand and gaze past life's end, to get us across the abyss that suddenly yawns open, its hot breath singeing our hair, when someone we love disappears. We need their bodies, the shell, the symbol of their selves, to convince us that what was is no longer. We need to cry or sing, move our fingers through their hair, inhale the wrong smells rising off their skin, take a step backward and away.

In the Atacama, over the centuries, people wrapped their dead and buried them, alone or in groups, in underground chambers or in burial mounds. These could be in their homes or in the fields or in cemeteries. Sometimes they marked them with a post, a circle of large rocks, a pile of stones. Some tombs contained layers of bodies, neatly ordered underground. In many, the dead sat as they'd rested in life, cross-legged in silent circles, heads bowed, right foot over left, arms hugged to the chest. Often dead babies were wrapped together sitting on their mothers' laps or bound to their breasts. Sometimes dead couples' remains were wrapped together. Occasionally, adults alone or children alone were buried in clay containers. The conditions of the desert meant that most of those buried here became mummies.

They were wrapped in cloth both fine and coarse, some of it mended, indicating that these weren't woven specially. These in turn were tied in place using the wide woven bands that served as belts and string and cords during daily life. Sometimes the heads received a special wrapping—occasionally, part of the apparatus used to deform the skull, as was the style here. In other cases, Le Paige thought, these indicated a cult to the head. Some of the mummies simply wore hats, to keep off the sun or the cold, an indication, perhaps, of the season in which they were buried.

The bundles that accompanied them could contain knitting needles from cactus spines, llamas carved of bone, seeds of corn or the Andean grain, quinua, more rarely *tabletas de rapé* and other instruments used to inhale hallucinogens. These may have been the possessions of the dead, placed in the grave to help them in the new life ahead, or simply offerings to encourage them to intervene on their living relatives' behalf, before the gods they would soon join.

Of the bodies that Le Paige dug up and Jacobs examined, one of four wore a necklace of pearl, or beads of liparite, malachite, turquoise and copper, an indication that there was a small, privileged class. A handful wore ceremonial wigs and feathers, a clear sign of their special status, which was carried over into death.

They believed, as the people of the Andes do today, that we travel not in a straight line from life to death, but rather in a circle, where *the past is always alive and part of the present and the future exists now and always did.** The dead are extremely mobile and the living are but a fragile layer over the past, which lies close beneath our feet and can break through and influence the present. *Individual human existence, which begins and ends, is not important, but rather collective existence, in which from each human generation and its disappearance comes the next,* says Jacobs herself. In the planting season, people *bury* seed, so crops will grow. Mourners *plant* the dead, who then travel inside the mountain to its summit, from which the next generation will be born.

For three years the dead are venerated in a series of rites and remembrances, including the festival of the dead, which takes place during the planting season. Just as the seed dies to bring forth life, so the sacrificial victim must receive a ritual burial to ensure that new life will flow from the old, especially among the herds of sheep or llamas.

While the people of the Atacama were nomads moving across the surface of the earth, fertility was their most highly

---

* Gow and Condory, cited by Jacobs.

prized value, its rites played out by the wind, the sun, the moon and the rainbow, embodied in a god personified by lightning. As they settled into agricultural communities, their perceptions of nature, seasons and time shifted. They stopped in one place long enough to see how the world spun around them and how the sun ruled the cultivation of corn and potato with its hierarchy of light, shading to gold or green or the sad rattle of empty brown. They celebrated and suffered this knowledge, with human and animal sacrifice, the sprinkling of blood.

Modern ceremonies still may involve an arch of life, erected in honour of three gods in particular: Mallcu, the mountain deities, also known as providers; Pachamama, the ever fertile, abundantly irrigated earth; and Amaru, the water deity. Together they guarantee the *origin-abundance-distribution of Life-giving Water.** The mummy bundles that accompany the dead are often referred to as *mallqui*, suggesting their role in the cycle of exchange between the dead, the mountain and the fertile earth and water.

Jacobs explains that *When someone dies, a member of the family passes from one state of being to another, moving into a position where he or she is crucial to the protection of the community.*

As recently as the beginning of the twentieth century, death was often assisted, with the dying person being carried into the main room and seated, leaning against a wall, held up by blankets and other woven fabrics. *They then put food, drink, clothes, jewels and personal objects on the table in front of the sick person. The family gathered and celebrated with laments, dances and songs to help bring about a 'good death.'* Influenced by Christianity, the family might then bury the

---

* Juan van Kessel, cited by Jacobs.

dead person, only to recover the body and celebrate traditional rites of honour the next day. They would place the
body at a table loaded with food and drink and spend the
day singing, dancing and crying. Once they'd decided that
the dead person had eaten enough, the mourners would
follow suit, with these ceremonies lasting two or more
days, and culminating, eventually, in a new burial.

The Sacrificer also left his footprint among the tombs of
San Pedro de Atacama. In one cemetery explored by Gustavo
Le Paige, out of thirty-eight graves, three contained disembodied heads. Headless bodies were also fairly common. Le
Paige believed that their condition was the result of rites
that took place after death. But Birgit Jacobs (among others)
does not agree. She cites a tomb containing five bodies, four
of them headless, although their lower jaws had been placed
on their bodies. At their feet, carefully wrapped, sat the four
missing skulls, each one accompanied by the intricate little
kit used to inhale hallucinogens: the tableta, a finely carved
rectangular "plate," the "straws" used to inhale, the pouch
that carried the magic dust. The delicate carvings on each
tableta echoed the rituals enacted with its assistance: each
contained the image of a severed head.

Heads taken as trophies from enemies who died in battle could be viewed as conferring the same qualities of
strength and courage on their new "owners." But the deliberate act of ritual decapitation indicates a far more complex relationship between the belief system and the act
itself. Of all the offerings to the gods, the most valuable and
therefore the one with the most powerful connotations in
the Andean ring of reciprocity was human life itself.

A woman's voice breaks into my thoughts. Grete
Mostny, an anthropologist who travelled the desert in

the thirties and forties, exploring, falling in love with its secrets, the ones she could dig up and the ones she could never decipher, *Ritual decapitation . . . emphasizes the ceremonial context, dedicated to some deity in order to achieve certain favours. We also believe there is a link between the severed heads, human sacrifice, death and a reproductive force. Its culmination combined the magic of fertility with human sacrifice.*

At the time of the conquest, two brash Spanish voices described their meeting with an ancient priest whose *office was to sacrifice humans.* And Gerónimo de Bibar tells of two prisoners being lined up to face the sun, *Then, an Indian dressed as a priest—they specialized in this—came out with an axe in his hands. He turned to the sun, making a speech in his tongue and praising it and thanking it for their victory. With the axe he made gestures over the Spaniards, as if to cut their heads off. Once these ceremonies were completed, he turned their faces back to the sun and went back to his prayers.*[*]

Later practices would substitute the heads of animals for those of human beings. Throughout Chile today, birthdays, anniversaries and any other excuse for a social occasion usually require that an animal be sacrificed. Then it is roasted and shared among the celebrants, creating a powerful bond of blood and satisfaction, death and nourishment: hope.

I had paid my first visit to San Pedro de Atacama in December 1995, discovering a flat adobe-lined village some two hundred kilometres from the coast, where time, as in the old cliché, seemed to stand still. Sparrows hopped among the flowering azaleas planted in San Pedro's central

---

* Quoted in Cervellino's "La Imagen del Sacrificador . . ."

square, flies buzzed in the shadows and above the irrigation ditches. Lizards darted for hiding when I approached.
Water in stone-lined irrigation ditches echoed the straight
lines of dusty roads. Kitchen gardens produced grains and
vegetables, as well as some fruit. In the fields were dainty
llamas in their thick woollen coats, mingling with the
flocks of sheep, and the fleet-footed, agile Andean donkeys—the best mode of transportation over the winding
highways for thousands of years.

For those same millennia San Pedro de Atacama has
been a crossroads, brimming with life in all its manifesta-
tions, a crossroads between the villages of the altiplano, the
bustling cities of Tiwanaku and later Tawantinsuyu to the
north, the Argentine ranches and the Amazon to the east,
and the Pacific coast to the west; expert caravans travelled
the bare high roads of the Atacama, zigzagging from one
waterhole to the next, pausing to draw gigantic figures
on mountain sides, pausing to drink, pausing to dream.
Nowadays the town is still a hub of trading and tourist bus-
tle. Crowds of young Canadians, Europeans and other foreigners stroll through the red clay powder of the streets as if
they owned them, while masses of young men, throwbacks
to my own adolescence of hippiedom, with long hair and
exotic earrings, wild manners and jerky movements crowd
the restaurants, playing guitars and Andean drums. They
wait on tables rather indifferently, as they live out their
own particular dreams of freedom in the wilderness, until
they get bored and return to Santiago or whatever big
city they call home.

Cleave is an odd verb, meaning, as it does, both to "cling
to" and to "split apart." The people of San Pedro cleave
to their past, even as the GasAtacama project cleaves them

from it, snaking huge pipelines for natural gas through the desert, growing abashed at bashing the occasional archaeological site, promising jobs, change, progress, modernity. The explora hotel, too, brings change: a luxury chain that started out in the nineties at the Torres del Paine at the southern edge of the continent, it specializes in hard hiking and adventure tourism. Now they've bought out the Puritama hot springs and are building a two-storey hotel in San Pedro itself, a huge development that rides a field like a battleship, turning its guns of progress on the modest one-storey adobe homes of the town.

The people of San Pedro are descendants of those who first pastured their animals, then settled there and built the irrigation channels, extending the plumed grasses of the oasis far out into the desert. They call themselves Atacamenians. Sandra Berna, the mayor, says, *We Atacamenians have survived two major invasions: first the Inca, then the Spanish. We knew how to survive. Now we face a new invasion. Large-scale projects, especially tourism, bring enormous cultural contamination. Like the Inca—many come to live here, but what's important is that they value our culture and our customs on a daily basis. We can't forget who we are.*

She recalls a time, twenty or thirty years ago, when there was more water in the oasis, more crops. It even used to rain. Isaiah Bowman describes the farms that flourished there early in the twentieth century, selling huge quantities of alfalfa to wandering mule and cattle drivers, along with pears, apples, grapes, figs and quinces sent from San Pedro and nearby Toconao to the miners in the nitrate fields. Even so, he says, landowners could only irrigate once every sixty to ninety days. In 1911, snow fell on the orange trees and vegetable gardens. When it melted, the thatched roof of many an adobe house sprouted, allowing the house-holder to harvest a modest crop of wheat and barley. Curiously, Bowman insists that it was the Spanish who *opened up* the trails of the Atacama, as if they had built them, rather than simply following highways built and painstakingly maintained by others. He and I argue for hours about this, especially when he notes (with some surprise) that *instead of rivalry there is the closest and friendliest relation between the mountain shepherd and the desert dweller.* I say that this reflects customs developed centuries before the Spanish came. I hammer at him with the arguments of Lautaro Núñez and other scholars, who define desert culture as one based on *transhumancia*, that is, a permanent lifestyle that cycles with the seasons from one storey to another along the great ecological staircase of the Andes.

Bowman can be a pain. He has little sympathy or understanding for the native peoples of the Andes. Instead, he is a great admirer of Francisco de Aguirre and his hardworking descendants in Copiapo. And he praises Chile because *Of Indian customs and ways of life, ancient religious ritual, language, and so forth there is not a trace—in contrast to the almost barbaric mixture of Christian and Indian rites in northern Atacama or in highland Bolivia and Peru.* As for the Incas themselves, he admits that their history *shows a certain degree of communication from place to place, but the means of traffic were so limited that this could hardly have had a thorough-going and intimate effect upon the life of the whole plateau.* While the short length of the Incan empire may have reduced its influence, the history of the Andes from Tiwanaku on indicates an enormous flow of ideas, artefacts, customs and products between the main centres and the peripheral areas, however they are defined.

Both Bowman (who visited San Pedro c. 1900) and Grete Mostny (c. 1930) bring to life the people of Toconao and other towns near San Pedro. In late February or early March the men would head up into the mountains to flush out vicuña (a llama-like animal), while the women threaded colourful boundaries across the lower valleys. Herded toward the bright barrier, the vicuñas would not break through it, but rather would huddle, confused, until the men shot their prey. The hunter could keep the skin of the vicuña but the flesh went to the whole town.

For Bowman, San Pedro will always be a town of mule and cattle drivers. The old town is steeped in their flavour, in spite of the modern jeeps and vans that roar through town today. Says Berna, the Atacamenians struggle against Chileans and foreigners alike, to educate young people to love their lands and their culture, to turn water and energy to their own purposes and not to get diluted or swept away in the brutal surge of others' power.

This keeping up with progress is costing us a great deal, she says, her voice gravelly and deep. *The businesses belong to people from outside. Many of our people sold their land, without thinking about where they would go, what they would do. Now they're just employees, where before they were the owners.*

She speaks with consternation of outsiders who try to film rites, such as the town saint's day or other ceremonies, and of the insult of seeing photographs of her own people in the newspaper, labelled simply as "a boy," "man" or "woman of San Pedro," rather than being identified by their names.

Most of the businesses that serve tourists in San Pedro—including the guides—are run by people from outside the town. The people of San Pedro themselves, says Sandra

Berna, face discrimination along with the thoughtless exploitation of their cultural heritage.

Perhaps this ambiguity explains so much of what I saw and did not see in San Pedro—my difficulties finding Tulor, still half buried in the sand, for example. Or the sign on a modest house on the main square, the oldest building in San Pedro, which in July 1998 was still clearly labelled:

House of Pedro de Valdivia:
Francisco de Aguirre built this house
by order of Pedro de Valdivia
before his arrival in San Pedro de Atacama, 1540

In 1540 Francisco de Aguirre (the very same as in Werner Herzog's film *Aguirre, the Wrath of God*) did come to San Pedro, then a thriving desert centre of some twenty thousand souls, to prepare the way for Pedro de Valdivia, Chile's official conqueror. He found people living in homes of adobe and algarrobo wood, eating a diet based on corn, potatoes, beans and quinua, algarrobo and chañar fruit and alcoholic drinks. They stored their food primarily in oven-shaped silos on the roofs of their homes and it was in a sector adjacent to each house that the Atacamenian families buried their *great-grandparents, grandparents and parents and every generation. They used to bury them with all their clothes, jewels, and weapons . . .**

Four years earlier, rushing back to Cuzco, Almagro stopped here with over four hundred Spaniards and thousands of Incans and their former allies, all needing rest and refreshment before they could continue their journey across

---

* Gerónimo de Bibar (Hidalgo, *Culturas Protohistóricas*).

the vast *despoblado* (unpopulated waste, their favourite term for the Atacama). According to another Spanish chronicler, de Oviedo (an older man's voice, fresh and ringing with the conviction of a man used to preaching), they found *the land up in arms and at war, and the people in the mountains, out of their homes and settlements, because the mountains and sierras were very rough, part of which could not be brought to heel. The cause of the uprising was that some of the Christians in Almagro's rearguard had been killed and the Inca seems to have ordered it as well . . . going to war with Spaniards everywhere on earth.* de Oviedo found the Atacamenians *bellicose and vicious.*

When Francisco de Aguirre and twenty-five men came through in April 1540, to prepare the way for Pedro de Valdivia, there was a fierce battle between the Spanish troops and the Atacamenians, who defended themselves from the Quitor fort. The Spanish were forced to struggle up the mountainside through the angled doorways and narrow staircases, finally managing to break down the doors and allow their men to attack by horseback. Aguirre then distinguished himself by brutally slaughtering all the chiefs he could round up and hanging their heads about the town.

"Valdivia's" house was built by the Incas long before Aguirre's visit. Privately owned, it is not open to the public and may never be. Sitting there on the main square, not even a block from the museum and the mayor's office, it gently mocks the credulous visitor, a subtle act of revenge from the overwhelmed Atacamenians on those who run roughshod over their graves.

Even as agencies announce the treasures of the desert on the World Wide Web or in slick advertising brochures, even as they answer tourists' questions, the people of San

Pedro hide as much as they can. Like a potter's kiln, the desert has baked the raw products of many civilizations, preserved them, reduced them to the shrivelled essence of belief. Silent, moved only by the wind, it holds their stillness now, as it once held their hopes and their quick footsteps.

The Pukara (fort) of Quitor stands in abandoned majesty, 2,500 metres above sea level on the peak of a mountain of red rock and clay, part of a range known as the "Hills of Salt," to the north of the town. There is an unassailable sixty-metre drop to the north and east, and a wall one metre wide and two metres high once defended the southeast access. For Gustavo Le Paige, the Jesuit priest who spent most of his life digging up and dusting off the hidden secrets of the Atacama, the Pukara of Quitor remained an eloquent witness to how hard the Incas found it to bring the Atacamenians under their control. His voice is high and chapped, remarkable for the French accent worn to the bone by desert winds: *This is the only possible way to leave San Pedro on the east. . . We find three successive walls each with a sentry box, and 200 metres further north, on the summit of the hill, dominating the whole village, another sentry box. From here, there's no way to miss any movement whatsoever of people down below! The view reached to Atarpe and Guatin in the north, taking in the whole eastern cordillera; Toconao and even further south to Salt Hill; and the whole Plain of Patience to the west toward Calama.*

Bowman loves the ruined stone houses, rising tier on tier to the hill's summit, so *cleverly situated and constructed for defense.* Grete Mostny mapped the Pukara in 1948. It wasn't until the eighties that a team of archaeologists from the

Universidad del Norte participated in its partial restoration. Today, it stands apparently abandoned again, a maze of stone-walled rooms and passages. When I look up from its base, the sky forms a blue crown, with the white gold of the sun shining at its peak.

Most rooms share walls up to a metre thick with the adjoining spaces, forming clusters of living spaces separated by squares and terraces. Mostny says, *Each one of the smaller compounds was in itself a small fortress, and the strength of the enemy, which had to divide to climb to the summit, could be attacked from every direction at once, giving the defenders a tremendous advantage.* Look at the doors to each complex, she says, how they never shared the same access space, so that it was impossible to move quickly from one cluster of rooms to the next—a sign of what she called the *strategic genius of the Atacamenians.* The enemy would have to divide up to enter the complex in the first place, and would soon find itself isolated in a cul de sac, surrounded by defending troops.

There were no windows to let in the light. The people of the time lived and worked outside in the bright air all day. Their homes were shelters from the harsh sun and the biting cold of the night. Windows were not relevant. Some rooms have small, underground chambers attached, used to store potatoes and grain. Most groups of rooms include a small round construction, too small to house a person, which was used as a silo; the grains and other foods that were stored there could be removed using a small opening at the bottom. Many were also used as burial sites, although all traces of grain or skeletons have long since disappeared from the Pukara at Quitor. Although removal of material from archaeological sites is prohibited, this law, like many, is little more than a statement of good intentions. People wander in with eager fingers and out with heavy pockets full of souvenirs. Some of the treasures found in Quitor, Tulor, Catarpe, or elsewhere are now preserved in the museum in San Pedro de Atacama, but many more have been dispersed to the four corners of the world, and will never be recovered or available for study. Perhaps they are treasured nonetheless, and the tender glance of a collector polishes their surface every so often, making them flicker back to life for a brief moment.

We have been unable to find a single grave that has not been violated, said Mostny, devastated and angry, in 1948. *We did find the broken fragments of a burial urn in the ground.* Near the entry of the Pukara, she notes, is a large rectangular building with loopholes, where the guards would have been quartered.

A small tower at the heart of the citadel watches over the empty fort. At the entrance, a sign describes the fort and the efforts made to restore or at least preserve it, but even that has been knocked over. No one supervises the hundreds of daily visitors who roam over its surface, flicking cigarette butts onto the stones, clambering over collapsing walls or balancing on crumbling edges.

Everything seems to be gone, yet something essential remains. The apparent abandonment, the blatant lies (like those in the Aguirre sign) wrap around the truth and keep it safe, steady and vibrant. Standing halfway up the mountain, gazing toward the peak, I catch the sun, still and docile, ready, even, to be touched. It turns the whole sky into a star sapphire. Voices stream down the mountain toward me, like a light breeze, stirring my hair (which the sun sets aflame), making me shiver. If we stop looking

for the remains of the dead, we will find what survives of
the living, still here, invisible, and present as the elements.

Ñusta too is a city woman. (The past is not synonymous
with rural life. In the great city-states of prehistory the
streets were made of finely carved, carefully fitted stones.
She walks the long avenues of Cuzco, their design a drawing, some say, of the magic puma, leaping from the ocean
to the Andes, from earth to heaven, a thunderbolt in reverse.)
Her cities too had some consciousness of the environmental havoc they could, would inevitably, wreak. Otherwise the builders would not have included the gutters and
internal piping to carry clean water to the palaces and temples, to carry the soiled water quietly away. But she believes
in many gods while I believe in none. She lives a life in
which security is the result of rigid order, enforced by manners, above all by dress. (And I, I find even the snobbish
Chilean insistence on having a "good" surname, tedious.
Octavio Paz said the essential difference between the
Americas north and south was that in the North what matters is what you do, while in the South, what matters is *who*
you are, or aren't.)

Rigidity is one response to danger. Natural dangers
still stalked the cities of your time, artificial dangers stalk
ours—the poverty, the powerlessness that wait outside our
doors. Fear of failure, of loss of status. Fear of freedom: that
treacherous water. But my response has been to fling myself into the sea and try and ride the waves. I seldom feel
safe, but amazingly, have somehow managed to create
that feeling around my sons. I don't think they know
how fraught with danger the world is, how important the
rituals we employ to stave off fear. I teach them the rituals,

of course. As Ñusta did. But she had far more rituals to draw upon, to survive. Her rituals were collective. Mine, solitary.

Danger is the flower; fear is the scent, wafting into your nostrils, setting the hairs to tingling along your arms, your stomach's churning lidded down, barely under the breath's control. And the danger, real or not, sends out the fear, like a damp mist, chilling, exciting, calling you out to walk at night when you should be safe in bed.

But for me, that scent, the fear, conjures up the white water of a river, that sense of everything accelerating, the gently flowing water accelerating until it churns white under the canoe. Colouring the steel blues and greens of spring run-off, white water turns the river into a nerve-tingling challenge, the paddle digging and thrusting the canoe through the waves, the fierce eddies between the rocks.

And Ñusta. Here I may meet her at night, but not in the crashing angle of waves, rather under that vast dark chalice of the desert sky, overturned and swallowing up the earth with all its limits. I freeze every night in my cheap room in San Pedro de Atacama, the bare cement walls making me feel like a prisoner or a nun in a cell, putting on layers of pants and sweaters, blankets and jackets until I feel more like a human suitcase than a human being. The shivering splits me apart and I steal out through the streets, longing to belong, to find the warm fire of friendship or love awaiting me in some corner of the adobe city.

But what I find instead is Huillac Ñusta, haunting the ruins of Quitor, caught, as the sun was at midday, on the fort's highest peak, or wandering light as a breeze down its sides, peering into the green depths of the oasis-fed fields at its feet. When I meet her there I can hear the murmur of the Atacamenian defenders around us. For her night is a dark fabric, part velvet, part emptiness. She holds out my hands, makes me feel my way through their long blind wait, the people who first chose this site and built the fort, twisting the buildings together like a skein to tangle and strangle their attackers. On a moonless night, they are reduced to a slight scraping of leather against stone, the chime of a hoof, a sudden cough, a sneeze. I can feel them breathing all around me, the hum of their voices shattered by a stone's ping, a warning of the enemy's approach.

But nearby I sense Ñusta is wringing her hands and mourning. She knows she travels with the scourge. She has looked beyond the night-time's quiet preparations to the battle and beyond even that, she's seen the severed heads mounted on posts or hanging from the charred eaves: all that remains of the fort, the sense of safety, night that once wrapped a silken blanket around us, holding the known world in place.

First the Aymaras came from Tiwanaku. There was some bragging, some threat of violence, but then the sweet fumes of their Amazonian dust bringing the illusion of wings that sprouted from shoulders, the puma's claws, sure and brutal but fleet and therefore infinitely sweet. There were the black shapes of the Andean night blown through the clay vessels they traded into those of San Pedro, the glint of copper, the sun's rays captured and chained to wrists. And there was trade, wheat, corn, the tender flesh of young goats and the endless trails tramped by mules climbing toward heaven, crossing the hell of the high Andes and stumbling down the other side. There were troubles and tension but finally a kind of peace. And there were the stories of the city Tiwanaku, the great, lost Atlantis of the Andes, at its peak a city of thousands of people from the known world—from the Amazon to the east, from the stark mountains north and south, from across the great ocean of the sun's lake, from the eternal glinting snows of volcanoes and the endless gravel and dust of the Atacama, cinched and gathered by the glittering blue river of the Pacific that lay beyond, that grew as you approached until it covered the whole world, a brilliant blue table spread with diamonds for a gods' feast. A thousand years of plenty, the broad fields, the deep channels teeming with algae and fat ducks, the daring green of potatoes and corn slapping the frost away, the laughter of splashing birds and children playing among the crops. The miracle of all that would become impossible, still ordinary then, cloaked in the everyday. (Cities always have hidden corners, angles, where people meet to speak of what's forbidden, to dream, plot, plan, to challenge and negotiate. Cities offer the farmer's son the chance to become an artisan. A woman may find herself a high priest, mistress of the sun, speaker of oracles, occasional granter of mercy.)

Compared to the bloody horror of the Aztecs' sacrifice Tiwanaku's chamber of disembodied heads seems almost a shrine. And yet, I don't believe what they say about people being used to or having different (lesser) feelings for their children. You hold a baby in your arms, you feel it suck your breast, it binds you indivisibly no matter how your culture chooses to parcel out the land or worship its gods. In a land of human sacrifice, you keep your head down, firmly attached to your shoulders at all times for as long as possible. Daydreaming is to be discouraged, as is any other practice that loosens the mind. You hold your children under your skirt, as if they were not yet born. You muffle them inside your poncho, until they break free and there's nothing more you can do.

Compared to the Aymaras, Ñusta's people were new-comers, and short-lived. Oh yes. I know they were great. Or at least had great aspirations, but too little time to realize them all. Wandering from Titicaca west to Cuzco, then looking in every direction. Moving north, then east and south, through their own past and down into this part of Chile. Their roads sliced across the long ribbons of land, chopping them into pieces small enough to control, break-ing up the double kingdoms of the old lords, enough to make peace or, if necessary, successful wars. They took the Diaguitas from the lush valleys of Copiapo and spread them round their kingdom, made those who were loyal their overseers; those who weren't were sacrificed to the gods— just another form of taxation. They watched as those they loved were buried or bled to death or left to freeze on the highest peaks of the Andes, to crouch for centuries as if they were still alive.

There was wandering before. We humans have always wandered. The new part, surely, is the pain, the conscious-ness that I came from *there*, and now find myself *here*, and in the process am not sure who I am any more, *who* being inextricably mixed with *where*, but in such a way that we only realize it once we have left. The strange part really is the settling down, claiming one place for one's own, build-ing fences or walls or simply piling rocks around it. We are a strange animal indeed, when we consider it so impor-tant to—plant-like—put down roots, consider it vital to have roots to acknowledge and seek for and ultimately be proud of.

And when did the pain of exile start? The sense of expulsion, the society that unravels as you, Ñusta, travel southward with Diego de Almagro, as I travel northward into the desert, farther and farther north, seeking the heart of the Norte Grande but not one step closer to Canada, where I came from, who I was. (Sometimes the best approach is to move in the opposite direction. I'm trying that now. When I turn away, I catch a glimpse of you. So different, so hard where I am all emotion, so passionate where I don't give a damn. Something intangible flows between us, a narrow trickle of hope, shining like salt.)

Because in the end, Ñusta, what we have in common, besides this desert where the sky is so much larger than the earth, is this: you wandered so far from home you never quite made it back, and I'm afraid that will happen to me. The empty desert forces us together, two moving specks of longing for warmth, for something we both fear to lose, something we can't quite give up even though we sense that really it's long gone. A dog barks behind a white adobe wall of San Pedro de Atacama. I feel your fingers' warmth, a dry scrawl, etched in mine. And then I find my fist is empty, my eyes staring at where I know the wall will be when I wake up tomorrow morning.

Eventually, I do manage to find the Incan *tambo* (inn) still known as Catarpe, another ruin of carefully mounted stone walls, abandoned on a plateau above the Vilama River, up the valley beyond Quitor. I stand and lean my elbows on the rounded stones from a river bottom and gaze northward toward the high road, dreaming of visitors and movement stirring at the base of the triangles of huge mountains. The Andes here are composed of wrinkled rocks the colour and texture of flesh left too long in warm water. The Vilama River winds between them, surrounded by salt-encrusted grasses stirred by a gentle breeze, and the occasional bleat of a wandering band of sheep.

A narrow path leads up a gully between two hills, and eventually I follow a guide up that crevice, listening to stories of graves pillaged and treasures stolen. Now, only the smooth, grey rock walls remain, embracing roofless rooms and framing a view of mountains, endless A's in an alphabet that never got past its own beginning: an endless wait, broken occasionally by the passing of troops or functionaries, an Incan governor.

Mostny's voice is in my ear again, *like the other sites, not only in Catarpe but throughout the region, the entire contents [of the cave] had been moved and sacked. We could still see some skulls, most of them already broken and mixed with other bones. There were none of the usual elements to accompany the dead in the cave. Apparently, this had been a communal grave.*

So, like the purloined letter, they are hidden by being left on view. The Pukara of Quitor and the Tambo of Catarpe are sacrificed to the tourists, and we can study models of the geoglyphs and other wall-carvings in the museum, to keep us away from the original caves. I find this oddly reassuring, as if by accepting what they have to offer I have joined a conspiracy to defend something I can only sense, its breath tickling the hairs on the nape of my neck.

For the Atacamenians, this time-honoured strategy is not going to be enough. Mirta Solís and others like her know it, are trying to figure out what to do. In 1998, when we spoke, she was president of both the San Pedro de Atacama Neighbourhood Association and the Council of Atacamenians, an elected body representing all the

neighbourhood associations of San Pedro and the surrounding desert towns and villages.

This is a poor town and we need water, Solís says. *In the fifties
and sixties it used to rain, regularly. We had a lot of wheat and
alfalfa. But over the past fifteen years there's been no rain and the
flow of water has dropped noticeably.*

The indigenous communities are divided over what
to do about major projects like the explora hotel or
the gas pipeline, whose builders in June 1998 shattered a petroglyph that marked the Incan highway (*the
kings' highway*, an elderly craftswoman called it). In the
heat of debates, marches and confrontations, Mirta led
negotiations that have ensured that the Atacamenians
will hold on to their water rights and perhaps some
control of what *development* and *progress* will mean to their
community.

In 1994, the council took over a boarding school in
Calama that was about to be closed, keeping it open and
providing subsidies for native children to continue their
education. Mirta herself suffered years of separation from
her parents in order to get an education, and she watched
her hopes of going on to university shatter on the sharp
edge of reality.

Today, she says, large companies filming advertising for
Ford cars or Coca-Cola come to the desert. *First they speak
to the city government, then the community through the council.
There's more respect for us now*, she says. *We accept their presence
if they make a contribution to our development plans and commit
themselves to preserve our heritage and to take away all their
garbage.* In some towns, this has brought a connection to
the electrical grid or paved roads to facilitate communication with the rest of the world.

But it's far from easy. In the case of the Puritama hot springs, the council reached an agreement with the explora hotel that will put the council in charge of running the springs for two years, a unique, though controversial, experiment in native control of a native resource. But other indigenous leaders question why they had to negotiate to administer something that was already theirs.

Another issue is language. After the conquest, the Spanish administrators in San Pedro cut out the tongues of anyone who spoke the Atacamenians' original language, known as Cunza, *our tongue*. Only a scattering of words from Cunza survive today, although some are preserved in the songs and chants that accompany traditional ceremonies, such as the cleaning of the irrigation channels, which takes place every year. Now, well-intentioned government policy, inspired by the new Indigenous Law and the large Mapuche population in the south of Chile, requires bilingual and bicultural education. Scholars and elders from the communities have combined to try to prepare a dictionary of Cunza, but Mirta asks, why learn Cunza? Why not learn English instead? That would give the Atacamenians access to the wealth of knowledge and connections available, for example, through the Internet. She wonders if links to native organizations in North America, the chance to study abroad, wouldn't do more to further her people's interests today. The debate is a difficult one and it pains her to see divisions among the Atacamenians.

Being a woman leader is also difficult. In fact, San Pedro, with a woman as mayor and a woman as leader of the council, is unusual. Mirta, who is over thirty and still single, faces constant questions about the appropriateness of her role as an administrator at the first aid post in San Pedro.

She tells of the diplomatic difficulties of attending the canal cleaning ceremony, in which as a woman she has a specific traditional role and must sit in a specific place, while as a visiting dignitary she is required to sit among the men. When four schoolchildren died in a fatal car crash, shortly after the election of a woman mayor in another Atacamian town, near the Argentine border, some elders blamed the deaths on the community having elected a woman as their leader.

We talk until late, a strange kinship stealing its tendrils between us. It's quickly torn away, uprooted, when we walk back outside into our differences, me the red-haired foreigner, just another strange tourist wandering the streets, she at home in the dark, amidst the adobe. She walks a few steps, is gone in a moment.

Then it's night again, and I'm alone, shivering in my cell. Thoughts about Ñusta, and whether I will ever find her, take me back to Catarpe. I want to talk to Grete Mostny, to tell her (I know she knew, she felt it, in spite of her complaints) that the treasure of the Tambo de Catarpe is still there, still guarded amongst the carefully piled rocks of those walls. Their most important secret remains, disguised, yes, but safe—protected by the trappings of neglect: the sense of waiting. It roils like smoke between them, twisting like a puma's tail, its tongue hot and dry, sharp and fraught as the cliff's edge where the stranger stands, the man in Incan clothes, who stares up the valley for hours, watching the unchanging brown A's of hills, their march frozen, the air still. The trees in the valley below, the feathered grasses of the wetlands may shiver in the wind, but here everything he perceives is as still as time: the absence

of movement and marching feet, the lack of the low grunt
of the mules. He takes the occasional sip of water, paltry
and modest in his mouth, emptied of fish and fire and
the fierce leap off mountain ridges, the long, frigid drop
through their bowels. He holds their memory on his tongue
for a moment, then swallows it sadly, aware of all he has lost.

The reluctant member of a tour, I come up behind him
five hundred years later, catch him with his arms leaning on
a window sill, his weary head resting on their bony flesh.
His back is to me. I cannot see his eyes, but mine follow his
gaze, strain past his shadow in the window frame. My eyes
and his, fixed on the stillness of the mountains. One small
movement—a frightened hare, a sparrow's flutter, a falling
rock—and he would be released to his time, and I to mine.

Perhaps he went into battle and had his throat slashed
or his head bashed in. I may comfort myself with the delu-
sion that I came back to Santiago, to sit at my office window and watch sparrows peck at the seeds I've scattered on
my balcony. But really we are both still caught there, here,
forever, on time's pin. I can feel the rocks cool and smooth
as a fish's belly under my arms, his bones, cool and naked,
in mine.

He's waiting for her; or if he's not, would still be glad to
see her, wouldn't care that she didn't really come this way.
And I too am waiting for her and grieving, because I know
she has come and gone and won't be back. Like a child lost
in a forest or a mall, I have come back here, to stay and
wait. I hope to repeat a meeting that never was.

The next day, I stand in the centre of a perfect sphere. Two
planet-sized glass bowls, one blown from the earth, the
other from the sky, touch the perfect round circle of their

lips together to form the flat illusion of earth on which my feet rest. The eastern curve of the bowl has captured the blue flare and ice-tipped pyramids of the Andes, while the west encloses the Domeykos mountain range, the boundary between San Pedro and Calama, where a yellow lamp burns, lit by the setting sun.

Yesterday I stood on a crest of paved highway and watched a wall of storm clouds converge, engulfing the Lasca volcano's blunt tip. As they rose above the rigid crests of the mountains, the clouds blasted apart, then collapsed in ropes of mist trailing across the slopes. I could feel the wind driving at my back, pushing me on and up toward their most sacred gods, whether I believed in them or not: Goddess of Earth, God of Water, God of Thunder come to heal the wound between heaven and earth.

Now the storm has cleared and stilled. I stand on a road crusted with salt, two perfect half-circles of shallow sea lap at my feet, spackled by water bugs that are sought by hungry birds. Tall and matchstick thin as spare trees, leafless and pink.

Bowman, on his trips during the early 1900s and later in the thirties, must have stood here too. His ghost whispers in my ear, addressing the *salars*—salt fields, salt lakes—with the precision of the geographer. High up in the Andean *puna*, the harsh flat plain along the roof of the world, the weather is *too dry to rain*, the air so dry that *it takes an immense amount of moisture-laden invading air to . . . furnish moisture enough to offset evaporation in the lower air even when there are local showers in the upper air. The rain in such cases sometimes actually fails to reach the ground.*

I can see the clouds hovering over the earth, raindrops gathering and trying to let themselves fall effortlessly toward the earth, only to find themselves thwarted and sent back without ever sinking between the stones, mating with seeds, coaxing them to wear rebellious green. I can see the farmer whose seed lies in her fields waiting, the songs rising from her throat calling the rain down, promising the rain its leading role in raising the dead and making them walk again through the rippling fields, watched only by the yellow eyes of corn. What word could you ever use, what sacrifice cure the horror of watching the falling rain vanish before it caressed the fields?

And down below, the salars crunch underfoot like snow, the fruit of mountain-born streams racing downhill into the valley, then spilled wantonly across the plain, losing the long war of attrition against evaporation, salts concentrating far more quickly than the liquid can gather.

Poised at sunset in the midst of the salar, I sense both menace and celebration here where you can see for hundreds of miles, but nobody's watching.

In the still, shallow sea, all but the moon has doubled to face the night. The earth is composed of cloud, the sky a mirror of water. The pink arrow of a flamingo shoots through that sky of water, flying through the air lapping at my feet.

I could spend the night here, learn to worship new gods, frozen, white as ice, awake in the morning with a new name. But there's no way to leave this place, no way to make it mine. It has already claimed me, turned me into just another black speck, crawling across the colours of the light.

There is a moment and a place where every thing becomes its opposite. The excitement of arrival is mingling with the moment of departure. The whole landscape seems to flow through me and I through it, and yet my thoughts stray back and forth, between San Pedro and Santiago.

At this point in my life, in my fifth decade, I seem to have developed a taste for dead men. Perhaps it's simply that unlike their living counterparts they can be reduced to a phrase that spins in my head for months or years, delighting and dizzying me, filling my eyes with amazement in the midst of the most boring daily routines. Luciano Kulczewsky, the gifted Chilean architect, did that, when I read his phrase about the entrance to San Cristobal Hill: that it was the work of his that he loved most, because it had made the most people happy. I'll never forget the day in the Parque Forestal, rolling with three-year-old Jaime in piles of leaves, when Pato suddenly called out and I looked up, up through the tangled telephone wires, past the bare branches of horse chestnuts, the muddy smell of cut grass in fall and saw the huge winged cat crouched on a roof seven stories above me, preparing to pounce, its eyes fixed on us. Gargoyles in twentieth-century Santiago! And the building was pink and inappropriate as the salar, with stained-glass windows, squeezed modestly between two others, a delicious urban treat for anyone with the eye for it.

Lautaro Núñez too. I hadn't intended to seek him out, but the only real study of Huillac Ñusta that I could find was his. As were the book on the history of San Pedro itself and several other studies. When I prepared my trip to San Pedro I discovered he was also the director of the museum. I looked forward to meeting him, but in spite of my calling for weeks in advance, there was no way I could make prior contact. *He's away, He's sick*, the secretary would say. My faxes went unanswered. My time was running out. I went anyway. The first time I ran into him in San Pedro he was just leaving the museum. We arranged to meet the next day at four. When I got there, he was busy. Ten minutes' worth of conversation and I was out the door, with barely permission to use the library. I wept.

So I did my interviews and wandered through the small town, watching the foreigners take over the streets, the Atacamenians themselves living parallel, under-the-surface lives, the way the everyday machinery of any town is mostly hidden. In Tulor, amongst the partially rebuilt cluster of adobe homes, the spirit of its discoverer, Gustavo Le Paige, clings to the walls like torn paper, the way his eyes must have searched and sifted through the sand, catching their shape—the tops of walls turned into footpaths beaten into the ground. A priest for whom it wasn't enough to marry and teach dogma, who insisted on pioneering archaeology and anthropology in this part of the desert, which perhaps at that time seemed particularly deserted. A generalist (like me), he overstepped the limits of his calling and beat his own path through another profession's territory. More and more shocking these days. Soon this may be more taboo than sex or money. In Chile today you're not even allowed to practice as a journalist if you don't have an almighty degree. This is not a system meant to further knowledge, but rather to exploit it, like any other monopoly.

Perturbed, I walk for miles, walk and wonder and keep my eyes open and my mouth mostly closed. Anxious to avoid land mines and still follow paths beaten through the desert for centuries. I don't go back to the Valley of the Moon. I don't know why, exactly, except that it was so much, so exactly what a desert is supposed to be, a great mound of shifting sand, to be scaled and admired from below and above. It struck me as too essentially obvious and contradictory, too, to treat the desert as if it were the moon, ignore the essential, extraordinary facts of how heavily inhabited it has been for several thousand years.

In Tulor, when I finally find it, what amazes me most is how its walls and ceilings have become the ground beneath our feet. And what touches me most isn't the flapping jacket of the priest, or even the ghosts of women from a thousand years ago squatting by their heavy stones, grinding the wheat, or going out with the men to trap the wild flesh of vicuñas with the frail spun wool that froze their thundering flight. It's the children, whose spirits I sense, heavy-bellied, spindly-legged and running, letting their laughter sail behind them like kites, soaring into the hot white air all around them. Their voices and the fact that the river will one day simply change its mind like any fickle neighbour and move away, leaving the village too far from its brackish necessary waters. So the children will watch, perplexed, as their parents pack up what little can be carried, swing it onto their own backs and the animals', and begin the long hike away from their history, moving away to become the roots of San Pedro de Atacama. Those children—how often must they have looked at the river, and their children's children after them, worried that this river too may decide to move away. They will sing this fear, this knowledge, pouring it into the high taut notes of a song and add a ritual to keep it from happening again.

Hence, the songs in Cunza (*my tongue*), the precise rites every spring as the people of the town gather to feast, but mostly to clean out the irrigation channels, to welcome (tempt!) the water back, persuade it to stay where it is most welcome. And yet, the water dwindles. All the modern works have not been able to keep it. On the contrary, the water is enticed away like the men, diverted to work in the mines and the cities.

I feel most connected when I am alone in San Pedro de Atacama. Like someone waiting on a street corner for a friend, I acknowledge the other people around me, but my eyes keep turning away to look up the road, the old Incan road, not the asphalt highway. Like someone on a blind date, or worse, a substitute sent because the real person couldn't make it at the last minute, I fear (know) that Ñusta will be disappointed. Like Núñez she will hustle me out the door and send me on my way. I am above all a commoner and not a priest, no aristocratic ways or means clinging to my old blue jeans or the bright, almost Andean greens and pinks and purples of my Indonesian tie-dyed jacket.

She, or rather the landscape (the salar!) where I wait, will teach me colour during the hours that I watch and scan the horizon for her trail of dust, or flash of metal. She, or they, will teach me to see all over again, to sink my gaze into a tiny green plant, floating fat and stubborn as a lily pad on desert grit, to lift my eyes, inhale orange and purple, yellow and pink, green and blue all blended together, to value the clear, sharp air they paint onto the walls of my lungs. (I remember a friend who exclaimed once how you could always judge a person's character from the colours she wore, and noted that I, for example, always wore grey. I was horrified, this being the result of my always wearing my mother's cast-offs rather than buying my own clothes. I felt as if I'd been caught living someone else's life.)

For you, Ñusta, colours bright and harsh as the Andean landscape, vivid and contradictory and then, suddenly plunged into the subtle pearls of mist and iridescence. For me the greys and blues of English rocks and leaden skies, the pewter surface of the north Atlantic, the bright brittle blue of sunny Georgian Bay, the deep dusty khaki of its shadows, the green needles of the pine, tinged with teal as if the water stained even the air, even the needles and the leaves floating high above the land. The Anglo-Saxon and the Inca. The woman who could never fit in and the woman who rose to the pinnacle of her society. The anonymous nobody. The legend and the saint. Caught in this journey together and to what end? If we don't relive our history it dies. Who are we then? Someone else's invention, someone else's thing, as you became, Ñusta, but whose were you in the end? Can you be reclaimed?

History places Huillac Ñusta with Diego de Almagro, and then forgets about her. Her father and Paullu escape, part of the first round of Incas to disappear off into the mountains, heading north and away from Diego de Almagro's southern thrust. I believe, however, that she remained with the Spaniard, making the gruelling trek along the highways of the Andes, then over the high plain, weaving her way through Bowman's whirlwinds, *lifting their yellowish-white columns of dust to altitudes of a thousand feet or more.* But even as she moved closer to Chile, to San Pedro, the desert, me—she was slipping away, moving out of real life, out of history into literature, before her final leap into legend and the absurd sainthood in which they hold her to this day.

Is she really coming? Has she already escaped?

A young woman bred for beauty and service, to be the companion of a king or nobleman, is a sacrifice any way you look at it. The brash, rude soldier, cruel and hot, power made flesh, so warm and tangible she could hold it in her hand. Like Malinka in Mexico, some of the Incan women did join the Spanish invaders, creating new bloodlines, many of which still dominate Peru to this day.

Diego de Almagro had already established one profitable (for him) liaison with an Incan noblewoman, Marca Chimbo, sister of Manco Capac (their parents were Huayna Capac and his full sister). If she'd been a man, if the Spanish had not come, she could have ended up ruling the whole Incan empire. Instead, she gave Almagro *a pit in which there was a quantity of gold and silver tableware, which yielded eight bars of 27,000 silver marks when melted down. . . But the poor creature was not shown any greater respect or favour by the Spaniards because of this. Instead, she was repeatedly dishonoured. . .*[*] Later she married another Spaniard, lived out her life and died a Christian.

My eyes search the bare surface of the desert. I could despair. I am writing about a desert where it never rains, but when I look out the window I see Georgian Bay in northern Canada, a gentle mist creeping out through the pores of earth, spreading itself around trees and over the marsh, gently erasing the landscape, turning it into a blank page, a palimpsest where much is written and much has disappeared. I can stare at whole forests, a road, sail and motor boats, which fade under the vanishing magic of the mist.

For Ñusta the present was a kind of cliff she could stand on and gaze out over her past, the broad plain before her. Much of our past, as a species or as peoples, is known. In theory, I know my own past, but when I try to look at it closely, it begins to fade like the marsh and the lake, yielding

---

[*] Cristóbal de Molina (Hemmings).

to the mist with a kind of mocking visual laughter, slipping away from me without moving.

Heraclitus said you couldn't bathe your foot in the same river twice. You can't visit the same country twice either. The country I came from no longer exists. Change is so rapid, *pachikuti*, which means the world turned on its head, flipped like a coin and falling toward its opposite. Ñusta journeyed and longed for the country she had left behind, but the Spaniards and their native allies were erasing it as quickly as the mists erase my own.

I am here but I can't see where here is, so my imagination fills in the gaps, traces the lines of buildings, the silhouettes of pine and cedar, invents the cry of a jay or the rustling of a chipmunk by the water's edge. Perhaps Ñusta too thought she could rebuild and re-create it, breathe her own stubborn, bold life into buildings of clay and stone, draw strength like water from the twisted tamarugo trees and nourish the dead dry mineral dust that rose in clouds under their feet, turn it green and edible, raise the flat horizon and turn it vertical, so it too could reach toward that great blue bowl of sky. And splash its face and drink.

I once thought exile a relatively simple thing. Or at least its definition. Exile is forced. I was not exiled, I thought, because I left my homeland by choice. But many exiles don't return, even when conditions in their countries improve. What are they then? Exile is no longer their official definition, but it has become their identity and even the mist can't erase what they see with their inner eyes, the shades and shapes of who they were meant to be, fighting it out with who they are, like shadow puppets, tracing births and murder, journeys, harvests and sacrifice on the bright walls agleam inside their minds. Living in foreign lands, forever foreigners, more comfortable feeling strange in a stranger's land than in their own familiar territory whose every sign and scent and voice speaks of what's gone, all that exists no longer and yet lingers forever, the old furniture stuffed in the mind's attic.

Children honestly don't see the difference; adults believe we're immersed in what's real, even as we trace our own lives in the fabric of our world, twist it and tie knots and dip it in dyes of our own making, then marvel at the colours and shapes, the whirling patterns of our lies (or was that lives?).

Definitions allow us to spread things around, attach specific words to people, herd them together, differentiate. But when the exiles were expelled from Chile, or I went to live in Chile, there was a possibility of choice—for them, stay and risk death; for me, stay home safe and risk missing something both dangerous and extraordinary, a creeping of the mist up the post of time, a fraction of them or me that lingered behind, was lost, the person, they, I, Ñusta, was meant to be. Seventeen and a half years of the regime for the exiles, eighteen years in Chile for me. Ñusta might have barely a generation to build her new world in the desert.

When I said yes, and got on a plane and travelled, I didn't know what came with me: that part of me that screamed *no*, that clung to the familiar shadows and colours of my world, that even now—now more than ever—has lodged in my bones, demanding the familiar smells of damp mown grass in summer, the bite of pine underfoot and in the nostrils, the scent/sense of lake-soaked air billowing around me, mist on a day in early fall, the leaves like winking lanterns of gold and scarlet. Or the cold chill of winter, its dry scent, the crisp smell of snow about to fall and erase summer, the bright dry autumn leaves flashing their last message across the seasons, an SOS, a promise, both.

But all this is meaningless to Ñusta. Her life expectancy was perhaps forty years, less if she had been chosen for the sacrifice. Perhaps that's why it was so easy for her father to leave her (if he left her).

When Ñusta and her father and her father's men were herded along and forced to join Almagro's expedition, most of her must have screamed that same *no!* reeking of blood and smoke and the deadly thud of skulls crushed in battles under stone, the mocking sigh of the owl, the drowning gurgle of sword-pierced lung. But surely some subterranean part of her murmured *yes*, to see the high plateaux, to know the vivid peoples of the Atacama, to stretch the distance between herself, the bright Sun God and his implacable servant, the Sacrificer.

Because when you leave your own landscape behind, the terror and the joy, you lose your own shape, what it forever bound and held in place. In the open reaches of the Atacama, you must define your own form or go to pieces, dissolve into a handful of bone, blown sand, dust of glass, sparkling and avid, but silent under the glaring sun.

4

UNDER THE
BLACK RAINBOW

➤

*The Journey
Across the Andes*

August 1535

L IKE THE BACKBONE of some monstrous planet-
sized creature, the knotted peaks of the Andes curve
down the Pacific coast of Latin America, the central
organizing feature of the Andean empires that ruled here
for thousands of years. Peaks stretch from near Panama in
the north over 7,000 kilometres southward all the way to
Cape Horn at the tip of the continent. For Bowman, they
were *a great lava-covered volcano-studded wall*. For Ñusta and
the people who came before her, the Andes articulated
their homeland, served as a highway, not a barrier. They
explored every cliff and ravine to discover the narrow
mountain passes at dizzying heights that would allow passage from one ecological system to the next. Because of
the volcanic eruptions that heaved great chunks of the

range skyward—sometimes as high as 1,500 metres during their 20-million-year existence—most of the passes float well over 4,400 metres above sea level, some even higher.

As Ñusta turns her back on the holy city of Tiwanaku, lost amidst the crowds, she greets the young servant girl who travels with her, her eyes following the Spaniards on their quick-footed horses. She has only a vague idea of what these aliens are like. But by now she has heard many details of Atahualpa's death, had time to learn his elegy by heart, to repeat it like a sad, hopeless prayer. Still, she has no idea of the society that spawned Almagro and his men, must watch them, always and closely, for clues to her future.

What she sees is the result of the reality that to be poor in Europe is like no thing she has known: it is to be worse off than a stone, because the stone feels nothing when pummelled by rushing feet, when crushed to yield up its dust of gold. But men and women need to feel they have a place, love, food, respect. When a beggar's eyes fix on a lighted window, her whole body travels along that gaze. When the slick fingers of a child steal into a rich man's pocket, he's after more than the man's wallet. And when a wealthy lord flicks an insult like a gob of spit into a poor man's eye, it can sting for a lifetime, can burn through one generation to the next. So it is with Almagro and others like him. They are driven as much by the Europe they've left behind as the landscape laid out before them, promising riches.

Fierce, with nothing to lose, the Spaniards use the Incas and their captive peoples as they've been used, and worse. They know no limits, fail to see the borders and edges that sewed together the ancient empires of the Andes. They're blind to the Andeans' uncanny ability to shade from one epoch to the next, then mark the sharp twist of change that ends an epoch with their word. These men are pachikuti, a word they do not know, could not pronounce if they saw it written in parchment or across a hill; it means the world turned on its head, hell thrust skyward into heaven, heaven into hell. They travel through layers of time as translucent and complex as any in Europe, but they see only green fields of ripening corn and bright futures, not the ancient past that spreads like an abyss before their feet.

At first, the journey falls within the predictable. Huillac Uma, Ñusta's father, and Paullu, Manco Capac's brother, travel ahead, in theory to announce the coming of the conquistadors and prepare a welcome, or at least prevent rebellion, among the Incas' subject tribes. Behind their smiling faces, the empty reassurances, Ñusta knows that a small voice chants a Quechua song that the Spanish might steal if it ever reached their ears.

We'll drink from the enemy's skull,
we'll make a necklace of his teeth,
we'll make flutes of his bones,
drums of his skin,
and so shall we sing.

They blow southward, clouds bearing bad weather from Lake Titicaca, toward the newly founded town of Paria, near Lake Aullagas. They rest for a while there, gathering strength during the month of August. Ñusta, like the Spanish, gorges on corn and meat, watches how the men go after the native women. Pachikuti, values stood on their heads: *A Spaniard who was a good raider and cruel and killed many Indians was considered a good man with a big reputation. Anyone inclined to treat the natives well or to stand up for them*

was despised, Cristobal de Molina, a priest travelling with
Almagro, notes in his diary. She has tried to remain at
Almagro's side, challenge him even as she receives his
caresses. The commoner in him loves the royalty he perceives in her. He finds his arms embracing the untouched
quality of the aristocracy at home, trying to mark it as his.
Beyond the power of their embrace, Ñusta looks over his
shoulder and sees how the Inca's subjects suffer, driven
southward by whip and club. Occasionally, she wakes to
find another party has escaped, retracing the trail northward, back into the Incan/Spanish heartland around
Cuzco, and the rumbling of rebellion beginning to buzz
along the Incan highway. Occasionally, Indians surround
the Spaniards' scouting parties and kill them. But mainly,
the Spanish gather plunder, and their slaves stagger on
under its growing weight, in ignorance of what lies ahead.
The Spanish voices that tell the journey's story start off
swollen with certainty but gradually fade, grow hesitant.

*Any natives who would not accompany the Spaniards volun-
tarily were taken along bound in ropes and chains. The Spaniards
locked them up in very rough prisons every night, and led them by
day heavily loaded and dying of hunger*, Molina writes, his
conscience beginning to trouble him. He goes on: *When
the mares of some Spaniards produced foals, they had them carried
in litters as a pastime, leading their horses by the halters so that
they would become good and fat. . .* de Molina, Ñusta and
others watched as *one Spaniard on this expedition locked twelve
Indians in a chain and boasted that all twelve died in it.* Disembodied heads again, sacrificed to the journey, to individual
greed, not to a society's quest for advancement. What meeting was possible between a society in which beheading was
the greatest possible sacrifice to life and these Europeans,

who, as de Molina painfully records, would cut off a man's head *to terrify the others and to avoid undoing their shackles or opening the padlock on the chain*?

She marches to the jangling of their weapons, she serves Almagro in his tent and in his bed. All the while she threads the known and the unknown part of their journey together, with the bright bleeding beads of elegy.

What is this black rainbow
soaring above?
For the enemy of Cuzco a horrid arrow
dawns.
Everywhere the sinister hail
strikes.
My heart foresees
with every instant,
even in my dreams, assaults me,
at rest,
the blue fly announcing death;
endless pain.

The order of the universe is gone. Her tongue feels its way over the words, the way Catholics finger their rosaries. She mutters. *The earth refuses to bury its Lord . . . as if it feared to devour its champion. And the rocky heights tremble for their Master, chanting dirges. . .* The gods to whom we prayed, the ancestors we cared for, marching the husks of your bodies through crowded streets, year after year—none of it has worked! The grief, tears, rage that swell like a child within her. *The yellow sun shrouds Atahualpa and his name. The Inca's death reduces time to a blink.* Such grief, pushing feet forward, holding them back, and under the grief, doubts, spouting like the blood of their beheaded companions, great fat drops falling and congealing on the ground. *A mirror from the wellspring of his tears reflects his body! Everyone! Bathe in his great tenderness to your waists.*

She knows Manco has begun to plan his great rebellion and she believes it will succeed. Many of those on Almagro's march will eventually join and die for him. She cannot believe she will never see Cuzco again. But nothing can stop the pachikuti once it has been unleashed, not all the songs and rituals of centuries. Doubt and loss whisper holes in the hymns that have always granted her sanctity in the recent past.

> *Within his multiple, powerful hands*
> *the caressed ones;*
> *within the wings of his heart*
> *the protected ones;*
> *within the delicate fabric of his breast*
> *the clothed ones;*
> *call out now,*
> *with the pained voices of sad widows.*
>
> *The chosen nobles have bowed down together*
> *all in mourning,*
> *the Huillac Uma has put on his mantle*
> *for the sacrifice.*
>
> *All men have marched*
> *to their tombs.*

If the Spanish could kill Atahualpa, then whose life could be secure? *We weep*, the elegy whispers at her heels,

with no one and nowhere to return to. . . Will your heart, Inca,
bear our wandering life?

When she raises her eyes, she sees them all wandering,
as lost as their dead king, southward, backwards, unwind-
ing the twisted threads of creation, retracing the steps of
Incan troops who travelled and triumphed under their
leaders, guided by the Sun. Now the Spaniards, proud and
cruel, stumble along beside them, clumsy, yet in command. And under the rhythms of their marching feet, they
sense the uneasy echoes of the songs of the people they
thought they had conquered but had only silenced, oh,
so briefly, with their victories. Now these foreign songs
insinuate themselves through the gaps in the Inca's de-
fences, crying out in strange languages, quick to rebel,
quick to reclaim memories, plant them and coax them
to grow again. The Incas' former captives, eager for freedom, are oblivious to the Spaniards' sleight of hand. The
Spaniards manage them as well as the Incas had manoeu-
vred the shining trays of gold that caught the sun's light,
so they could make it pour from the centre of the Inca's
heart.

Almagro himself is the son of a labourer, the circumstances
of his birth so obscure that Ñusta would have laughed if she
had heard a contemporary's comment that *he was born of*
such low parents that it could be said that his lineage began and
ended in him.[*] But it would have been a bitter laugh, and for
now it is I, not Ñusta, who peers over the old Spanish
chronicler's shoulder, looking into the mass of men, horses,
slaves, searching out a face that I have never seen, am not

---

* Pedro Cieza de León (Barros Arana).

sure I would recognize. Born under the black rainbow, condemned to wander. This fate is more common than we think, perhaps in some way happens to us all, although for some people it is more terrible than others. We live in a world of refugees, our doors closed, our curtains blinding the windows to this essential fact. I too, without realizing it, have joined the ranks of those who stand like children with their noses pressed against the bakery-shop window of the developed world, yearning for the sweet breads and cakes within, but with little chance of entering and buying.

Short, ugly, in awe of his king, Almagro distributes wealth as liberally as the swear words and blows that accompany his hot temper, possesses none of the social graces, but he is also considered a bold fighter, a hard worker and a loyal friend. For the first time, Ñusta watches a different kind of power in action, born of force and an unseen authority (really the flouting of an unseen authority, because he replaces God's will with his own). This is a man out of his class and thriving on it, abusing with all his strength, exercising the authority he has always fought against.

He is almost sixty by the time she is forced to travel with him. He's brooding over Pizarro, his lifelong friend and partner. In recent years, envy has eaten away the trust and easy friendship between them, and turned them into reluctant rivals. Just before the journey it almost exploded into civil war. He's trying to put that behind him now, but this whole journey grates on his blistered soul. He feels trapped. Was it just a ruse to get him out of Cuzco and steal away the kingdom he wanted for his own? Just before leaving, Ñusta went to the Christians' temple where she watched Almagro and Pizarro kneel together before the altar, making vows of loyalty, a marriage of sorts. A marriage of convenience that would not last. Almagro had only three years left to live.

He'd lost an eye fighting in Panama and suffered from a venereal disease that his doctors had been unable to cure. (The people of the desert through which he was soon to travel had discovered a cure, but he was never to know this or receive its benefits. The Atacamenians would bury a man with syphilis up to his neck in hot sand and leave him exposed to the blinding light and scorching heat for a full day, keeping him hydrated with blackberry tea. Although the Europeans studied this method—and later included infusions of blackberry tea in their treatments back home— their ministrations never worked. The secret of the cure was the high fever, over 40 degrees Celsius, that burned the syphilis bacteria out of existence.)

By the time he set out to conquer Chile, Almagro already possessed a huge fortune, and, after considerable manoeuvring before the king, he even managed to have his son with a native woman from Panama declared legitimate and therefore his rightful heir. Nevertheless, stories of wealth and fine lands farther south tempted Almagro away from Cuzco and the scheming of Pizarro and his brothers. He spent over a million and a half gold pesos on preparing the expedition, buying horses, military supplies, clothing and food at the inflated prices then prevalent in Peru. It was a grand gesture from the man who'd grown up practically a beggar. It would not pay off.

Almagro's expedition marches right past the silver-laden mountains that would eventually become Potosi, so eager to find sparkling chalices and golden mirrors spilling out of temples that they miss the mines that would eventually produce two billion dollars' worth of silver, enough to fuel much of Europe's economic activity for the next century, paving the way to industrialization. Another conquistador, Juan de Villarroel, will discover it, after a llama herder tells him stories of glistening metallic rivers flowing from his fire one night. South of Lake Aullagas the generous fields of corn and cattle give way to the high peaks of the Chichas mountains, still covered by winter snows. Almagro pushes ahead, the rest of his expedition straggling along behind him.

By the end of October, Almagro has reached Tupiza, a small town near what is today the Bolivian-Argentine border. Munching on *enormous loaves of bread made from algarrobo, which was the common provision of the infidels,*[*] he pauses to take stock. Four months on the road and he isn't even halfway to Chile. Already his friends in Cuzco are sending him messages, urging him to return. Father Tomás de Berlanga, Bishop of Panama, has reached Peru and will be considering the conflict over Cuzco. Almagro hesitates, drawn by his ambitions to own Cuzco in the north, and the hope of founding an empire to the south.

In Tupiza, he lingers, torn by conflicting ambitions, illness and his own nature, hard and blind as iron, forged in the crucible of hunger and abuse that sixteenth-century Europe reserved for the poorest of the poor. Rebellion was brewing back in Cuzco even before Paullu departed, with his brother Manco Capac at the head, harassed and distrusted by the Spanish (except Almagro), troubled and angry at their lack of respect for his imperial self. There must be moments when Almagro considers throwing in his lot with Manco, his brother-in-law, instead of the Pizarros.

---

[*] Mariño de Lovera (*Culturas Protohistóricas*).

But the poverty of his past drives him on. Stories of wealth to the south must have come from the Incas themselves and must have been greatly exaggerated. The Incan conquest of these lands is less than a century old, but even far away in Cuzco they had a clear view across mountains and deserts, brought to them by their *chasquis*, the messengers who crossed the plains in relays, like the buzzing wires of a telegraph, carrying quipus, the Incan abacus of string and knots that computed the kilos of grain, the heads of sheep and llamas, people themselves, decades of tribute trickling into their coffers.

If the Spaniards get that far, the Incas know that at the end of the seemingly endless trails across gravel, over mountains of crystal and salt, way beyond what is today the city of Santiago, where the Incan empire ends, the Spanish will meet the Mapuche, fierce, proud people who blocked the Incan empire's ambitions at the Maipo River, just as later the embrace of the great Itata and Bio Bio rivers would defend the entrance to Mapuche territory, a potent natural border that the Spanish will never permanently cross or change.

And the Incas know that the vast barren plain of the Atacama could prove a more forbidding enemy to the brash Spaniards in their heavy armour than even their strongest army. How to get them out of the way, tempt them, keep them travelling south, though, through the hardships of the lingering Andean winter?

As Almagro dithers in Tupiza, Paullu and Huillac Uma return from a sally southward, bringing taxes in gold and silver from the subject peoples of Chile, piled on the backs of llamas and mules. It is only 90,000 golden pesos, nothing compared to the million and a half Almagro spent getting his expedition off the ground. But it is enough to convince him that treasure beckons, south and west over the mountains toward the desert and the setting sun.

Even so, he can't leave right away. The shoes on their horses have worn down to the bone, and there is no iron to forge replacements. Almagro orders his men and slaves to hammer new horseshoes out of copper, a metal too soft and pliant to resist Andean granite. While the forced wait continues in Tupiza, Almagro's fierce eyes contemplate the mountains beyond which his future waits. He is tired of the petty squabbling of conquistadors, tired of politics, he likes the feeling of a sword in his hand, a horse between his legs during the day, a woman at night. He likes to take great strides across the stage of a battlefield. Above all he likes to win, the unequivocal victory of the enemy lying dead at his feet and the booty his for the taking. These divisions, the petty betrayals that have festered and swollen with the pus of conflicting ambitions, trouble his soul. He once loved to fight beside Pizarro, trusted the sense of the man's broad shoulders at his elbow, glimpsed out of the corner of his eye. He'd felt safest then, in the midst of battle, the one place where he always triumphed. The rest, the letters to court, the elegant pleading to the priests, the endless nights of negotiations, perhaps it was really these that were driving him away, driving him toward Chile and ultimate failure. He might have confessed it to Ñusta one night as they lay, trusting she would not understand his tongue, his old rough flesh, hers young and tender, braided together, slick with their own heat. But more likely she simply sensed it. *I would rather die fighting*, he might have told her. *I can't stand the waiting, the endless defeats of administering a town or a fort, my only salvation lies in movement, action, giving and eventually receiving sudden death*. There is no comforting him then, but she doesn't necessarily want to, enjoys the dark paths of his suffering, even as it moves her, the great tough-talking man who will one day be taken, who more and more consciously seeks that moment when he will be taken and it will all be over and he can rest, his feats and defeats recorded in a history he won't have to write.

One night, Paullu and Huillac Uma slip away with hundreds of their followers. Perhaps their task, of luring part of the Spanish force southward, has been completed. Perhaps they could simply stand the Spanish and the journey no longer. Whatever the reason, they disappear up the lost paths of the Andes, retracing Kon Tiksi Viracocha's steps to Titicaca and back along the path of creation to the highlands of Collao. There the second major Incan rebellion against the Spanish is bursting into flame.

Almagro makes a half-hearted effort to find them, but already his eyes are fixed on the Atacama's plains of gold, or so they look from this distance.

Ñusta, the city woman, the convent woman, the protected woman now travelling on horseback or on foot, climbing the endless, Escher-like stairways of the Andes. Perhaps it's my turn to haunt you now, to watch over you, like an old witch from your future, anxious when I see you flagging, pained to see your pride shredding under the steady abuse, like a silk scarf blown against thorns. You had almost convinced yourself that you were more like Almagro than the Indians he beat and killed. But then that morning when you woke, threw back the llama skin, and felt at once their total absence—the willcas, your father, Paullu—all hope of rebellion on the road had vanished, and without you. You thought you were a party to all their plans, but now you see you were nothing but a pawn, a bright coin tossed at the Spanish soldier to deceive him, tempt him on. You owe him. And you have watched him, ugly, crude, brash, yes, but leadership, strength, above all power, are always attractive. The more powerless the watcher, the more attractive the power he wields like his sword. You would step closer to it, finger the sharp steel of his blade, wonder at the coldness of its temper, hard where copper and gold are bright and soft. Full of its own mean light, where the metals you have known until now look like the sun, bask in its beauty and spread it around.

You were always the public one, the visible symbol of a ceremony that was supposed to last for millennia, but now the ritual objects of those ceremonies are being melted down in the crucible of European greed. Stripped of that public persona, who might you become? A woman born and bred to serve in a church, now plucked from the altar and headed for the vast open temple of the skies over the Atacama. And as you travel, above you like a dark cloud new stories gather and dog your steps, shaping your destiny.

Ñusta, the Atacamenians tell a story that I think is about you, about what you are facing and what could happen to you. Ñusta, whoever invented the rules governing the lives of ghosts decreed that ghosts could not speak, move solid objects, or communicate with the living except in very limited circumstances. Today, I who am living attempt to reach you and comfort—warn!—you and find myself bound by the same rules. Thus do the living become ghosts in the territory of the dead. I watch over your journey without being able to touch your face, throw you a quilt, lend you a fleece jacket. Perhaps as you dream I may whisper this story in your ear, because I am sure it is about you, could help you, warn you. Be awake in your dreams!

Story of the condenado (Atacama)

Like you, Ñusta, the main characters are running too, but this is a love story of sorts, or at least, that's the way it starts (perhaps you think whatever is starting between you and Almagro is a love story too, and that what I think doesn't matter). The story tells of a young man and woman, the daughter of the village's wealthiest family, who want to marry, but her family refuses permission, so they run away. They're in such a hurry, however, that they forget to carry food, and the youth must steal back to his parents' home, where his father surprises him and, thinking him a thief, beats him to death. The next day the horrified father finds his son's body. He lays him out on the table and soon friends arrive, bearing offerings of food. They follow the death rites and finally bury him.

Meanwhile, on the path far from the village, the young man rejoins the woman and they go on walking until they reach a lonely house where a family offers them food and rest. The youth, however, cannot eat, and the woman of the house identifies him as a condenado *(condemned man). She tells the girl to visit a wise woman who lives alone by the river. The young woman convinces her companion that she must go, and during a brief moment alone with the wise woman the girl confesses her problem. The woman gives her a comb, a strand of wool, a mirror, a* sagraña *(some cactus spines also used as a comb) and bread.*

"When you cross the river pretend you've forgotten your package and come back as if to get it," the woman tells her. The girl does

as she is told. As she returns across the river she throws the mirror into the water, forming an enormous lake. Then, she throws the sagraña near the water and a dense forest springs up. She goes on and on until she's thrown everything down that the woman gave her, but still the condenado chases her, shouting and throwing fire. She throws the white strands of wool upward and they turn into white clouds that billow around her. She throws down the comb, cutting deep ravines into the landscape.

Still she runs and still he follows her. Lungs bursting, feet bruised and exhausted, she's about to admit she can go no farther, when a man on horseback appears, a rosary gleaming on his chest. The young woman throws herself on the horse's neck and holds on for all she's worth. When he sees the rosary, the condenado collapses, leaving only a pile of bones.

The horseman dismounts and gathers together wood to burn the bones. The girl leaps onto the horse and refuses to get down, clinging all the harder to the horse's neck. Finally, making as if he's given in, the rider insists he must adjust the saddle and she dismounts. The man leaps onto the horse and disappears off down the road.

So the girl finds herself walking back to her parents', nibbling constantly at a piece of bread that the woman gave her. At the door of her parents' house, the girl too falls to the ground, leaving only a pile of bones.

The rider who rescued her was God.

When I was a child I read fairy tales more fervently than the Bible and all my life I have resorted to them for strength in harsh times. One generation's Bible is another's myth, a third's fairy tale, a frail skein of explanation to guide us through the blind night and back to freedom. Ñusta. You are running away from one reality and into another. Either way there is only death and the piles of old bones that mark both beginning and end of your journey, but how you run and whatever compromises you choose to make on the way will change the stories we inherit. Run cautiously! Run fast! Try to write your own story!

I see you trying to write your own story and I see the writing corrupted by winter run-off, letters erased by the cold wind of realities we don't control. I see you struggling to use Almagro, who uses you. Fleeing from the Christian god until your only way out is the Christian god. I am here, I'm here, at least in your dreams let me reach you . . .

Small as lice exploring the vast skin of the Andes, Almagro's expedition winds its way down the Jujuy valley in what is now northern Argentina, its inhabitants all vanished, in hiding, because somehow word has reached them about the Spaniards' ways. In Chicoana, the last village before the Andes, they wait for the snow to melt and the first wave of corn to ripen, then pile these provisions onto the backs of their slaves. They are already worried about the tumultuous river roaring before them. It takes them more than twenty-four icy hours to stagger across the usually tranquil Guachipas River. Caught in the fierce throes of spring run-off, its frigid waters crash down the narrow gorge, washing away their pack-animals. When your turn comes, Ñusta, you plunge in riding a horse, the child, your servant, high on its haunch behind you. Her small hands reach forward around your waist. A girl who has dared to follow you out of your past. You feel a flash of unwanted tenderness. But even as you think perhaps you should pull her around before you where you can hold her more firmly, the horse loses its footing and the icy waves smack your side, almost knocking you off. When you right yourself again and the horse finds its footing, she's upside down, her legs still clinging to the horse but her arms flailing in the water over her head. *Let her go*, says the gruff voice of a Spaniard who's passing. And you try to pretend you can. For a moment, you do. You try to nudge the horse on with your heels, forget the girl as if she were of a different species. The girl's head pops up to the surface for a moment, you see her choke on her own cry for help. That silent cry catches in your throat. Her gasp for breath. Clinging with all your strength to the horse, your right hand gripping the saddle, your left dives of its own accord through the foam-streaked waters, plunging and slicing its way through ice until your fingers meet her hair and pull her gasping to the surface.

On the riverbank at last you stare at her, at what your left hand has declared, the truth you have been ignoring. You are not like Diego de Almagro. You come from somewhere else. You hold her as if she were a part of you, tears hot as the river is cold dripping onto the moss around you.

Of those who manage to survive the crossing, many collapse on the other bank, wet and exhausted, their strength swallowed forever by the raging waters. Almagro pushes on. Copying the locals he and Ñusta spread their bread with the sugary pulp of the algarrobo tree and munch their way down the valley to a place called Quirequire. There he fights battle after battle with the Incan messengers, the chasquis, suffering losses but pressing on, leaving a trail of atrocity behind him. Still the memory of the trials behind them will shrink in the perspective of what lies ahead. The expedition straggles across the mountains of Gulumpaja, then crosses the plain of Laguna Blanca, passing salty lakes of shocking turquoise, the remnants, some think, of a prehistoric sea that once covered the region.

Finally, they reach the plunging ravines of the San Francisco pass, which will carry them across the mountains into what is today Chile and what was then the dual empire of the Atacamenians to the north and the Diaguitas to the south. The ragged line of men and animals worms its way across the surface of the Andes, a fragile trail of dots, inching slowly southward, toward illusions. As the wind whips ice into their faces, Almagro raves about rooms piled with golden cups and ornaments, temples sheathed in gold, tall men wearing breastplates and diadems that catch the light of the gods and transform it into earthly treasure. More powerful than a magnet, the rumours of pure metals winking in the depths of the Atacama pull him forward, blinding him to the treachery that huddles beneath the ice or dances among the snowflakes, as blizzards lash the flesh of men more used to striking others than being tormented themselves.

Knees bent, groaning, they pull themselves over rocks and up cliffs, grinding distance like glass under their aching feet. Sometimes Ñusta will glance up and see the silhouettes of other travellers who have passed before them, huddling behind rocky outcrops, trying to get out of the wind, their animals frozen in misery around them. Bibar, the Spanish chronicler who followed in Almagro's footsteps a few years later, is muttering something to me through frozen cheeks, sounds so drunk I can hardly make out what he's saying: *The winds of this unpopulated place are sharp and cold, and it's common for a passerby to shelter behind a rock and remain frozen and standing for many years, so that they look alive and thus you find abundant mummified flesh in these parts. [The expedition] ran into many of these bodies huddling under cliffs and along ridges, so many that they served as signposts so you wouldn't get lost, all of them looking as fresh as if they'd just died, rather than 300 years old, as the Indians tell it.*[*]

If she turns to look back, she will see that they too are leaving their own trail of lifeless statues behind to mark their passage. Bibar says, *I saw many bodies of Indian men and women, of sheep and horses, black people and a Spaniard who died and some other bodies left behind from when Diego de Almagro returned with his people from Chile to Cuzco . . . the temper of this earth is such that the dead body lasts many years, becoming completely mummified, so it doesn't spoil or rot, nor diminish, nor fall apart, but rather remains whole as if recently expired.*[†]

Ñusta follows the same road as the Spanish but the signs speak differently to her, for she is trained to read them. They pass buildings surrounded by fences over a metre high, and in vain she hopes for the innkeeper to come bustling out, a lonely man anxious to offer food in exchange for conversation, to report on his part of the empire and learn of its conquests and its wealth, add new knots to the delicate patterns of the chasqui's quipu, to ensure that he will remain part of the accounting. These shelters began during the empire of Tiwanaku and the Incas have revived

---

[*] Pedro de Mariño de Lovera (Hidalgo's *Culturas*).
[†] Gerónimo de Bibar (Hidalgo's *Culturas*).

them, anxious to spread their influence to the limits of the four directions, their three-dimensional cross.

The Spanish may write in their journals of strange caves where lazy Indians lay down and unwittingly froze and died. But Ñusta recognizes the tombs of ritual sacrifice, knows where the human and animal remains lie, carefully dressed and staring at where the sun will rise, their frozen gaze guiding its course over Incan territory.

Ñusta, I can see you alone when night has fallen and the exhausted Spanish huddle by paltry fires or swallow the brief flame of a mouthful of liquor before tumbling into sleep. You steal away from the Spaniard's tent, a black figure, flickering with the fire's gold. Confidently, you lead me along the narrow paths that climb up from the low stone buildings where the Spaniards crouch, consumed by hunger. In the moonlight, amplified by the glittering snow, you can make out the rounded houses of the priests, those three semi-spherical shelters, their walls of neatly piled rocks like those at Catarpe, where I am still standing leaning on a low wall, looking out for you with a man I have never met, who has somehow become part of me. But here, you insist, the priests and their servants brought their sacrifices during the winter equinox and summer solstice. I look through your eyes and see the pilgrims walking from distant villages. How their hips sway, their limbs remembering the steady rhythm of the nomad still, although they settled in their villages centuries ago. You can lift your eyes and see beyond the people walking as far as the circular lodges of adobe bunched tight and fat as juicy grapes on the stark branches of desert paths. You've seen men and women like these stroll nonchalantly into Cuzco, their animals sweaty and thin, their packs hefty and rich with the treasures of the Andes. You can see, with the wisdom of those sacrificed, how this epic journey of the Spanish in which you have somehow become embroiled would be little more than a normal day's work for those others, and these teeth of ice gnawing at your warm, heaving lungs an accustomed companion.

Once, as the expedition shelters in the buildings de-signed to house worshippers, I follow you as you pick your way up a narrow path and then vanish into the warm mouth of a narrow cave. Claustrophobic, I hesitate, before plunging after you into that darkness. By the time I am fully inside, beside you, there is a small lamp lit and I hear your voice for the first time, small and rough and musical as the antara, lonely for the other voices that usually combine to form the chorus. Special prayers, I can tell, by the way your eyes don't wander. By the blue light of the lamp and the reflection off the snow outside, I watch your fingers, short, smooth and brown as clay, trace shapes, painted on walls and I move forward to make out the outlines of llamas and birds—earth and flight, the two mercurial borders of your world. Then, as your eyes dig through the darkness, your fingers follow, raking through the surface of gravel, specks of blood staining the tiny stones. You pull a duck-shaped vessel from the earth, stop for a moment, cradle it in the palms of your hands as if it emanated warmth. Is this sacri-lege or worship? Hope or despair?

Your fingers plunge farther and farther into the earth, pulled by the warmth of ancient fires preserved in the ashes. You know that like tissue paper they wrap and pro-tect the outlines of something the priests left buried here. Ñusta, even I can tell that in the strict rigour of your faith this is wrong, but will pachikuti make this right? Is this the only way to find a new path out and away from this disaster?

Now it is your touch I feel as it re-creates the dull gleam of a silver mask I can barely see, but I feel its expression, proud and cruel; the reddish glow of a face carved from an ocean shell gleams in your mind's eye. You blink as the emerald and ruby of iridescent feathers flash in your hands as if you'd caught the bird itself rather than a silver statue's cloak made of feathers torn from an Amazonian parrot. For less than a hundred years your fellows have passed this way, building these shrines and invoking your gods, planting, they thought, the seeds of success as they followed their own path toward the conquest of Chile. Now you hold their hopes in your hands and try to imagine what you should do with them.

In the cave's still silence, you tilt your head as if you heard the murmur of their words. They flow like melting snow through the rock's dark veins. Outside, past the thousands of tons of rock above our heads, the peak of this mountain still fumes. Like the sacred fire at the height of a ritual, it blows thin pillars of smoke skyward, connects earth to heaven. You lay your head on the mountain's chest as it heaves. These are its last. Soon it will sink into sleep and silence. I can see that you dream and in that dream the narrow smoky ladders break and fall, and finally lie beside you, chained forever to the earth.

I can smell your despair, the dark bitter tears, even though you rub your face vigorously with snow. It reappears, flushed with fear and shame and anger, like a reddish harvest moon. They've handed you over to someone else's god, and you know it. You also know that the old gestures and prayers performed for the wrong deity will bring unpredictable results. I reach out to you but my fingers are transparent, comfortless as the ice that surrounds you.

Often after this, when you pause on your journey and the Spanish seek at least the illusion of shelter, food and rest, I watch your anxious fingers pick out the remnants of crystal arrowheads, the blunt fists of stone axes, the head of a stone hammer, or fine, delicate weapons of obsidian. Occasionally you find stockpiles of firewood and carry them back to the camp below. More often, you coax your own small flame into light and crouch over it; despair overtakes you, turns your proud memories to dust. The antara is never played alone, but once I catch you evoking the words of the song called *Arawi*—they swirl like autumn leaves around you, press the sharp edge of an arrow into the smooth skin of your palm.

> *My mother between clouds*
> *and rain conceived me,*
> *to see me wander through the clouds,*
> *to see me cry like the rain.*

> *You were born in the cradle of martyrdom—*
> *she said in her pain*
> *and as she wrapped me in diapers*
> *like a swollen river she sobbed.*

> *It's impossible for the world to know*
> *a being as unlucky as I.*
> *Damned, damned forever*
> *the night that I was born.*

Afterward, you turn wearily back to the cold light of the Spaniard's fire, the tiny devils of its flames crushed and malicious, licking the cold ground with their passion for destruction.

Finally, the high peaks of the Andes flatten slightly into a broad plain, almost 150 kilometres across, 4,000 metres above sea level, dry as the desert below, the ground covered with loose gravel, split by the abrupt heat and the plunging temperatures of night, sharp as tiny knives. The travellers find no food beyond what they carry. As their horses struggle to find their footing on the gravel, their riders grow ever hungrier, but they deceive their stomachs' clamour, chewing on coca leaves.

Their lungs, too, cry out for nourishment. For Ñusta and the other people of the altiplano, adapted to the oxygen-depleted air of the Andean heights, the thin air is enough to keep sane. But for the lowland Spanish, to climb toward heaven is to enter a delirium amounting to the wild spiral of energy and release brought on by alcohol, shadowed by hangover, but longer-lasting. The head thickens and starts to spin, then throb. They long to vomit, to lie quiet while the universe spins around and below them. The solid peaks of the Andes turn into pulsating visions, swirling among clouds and wind, rearing up before them like wild stallions, then vanishing among veils of snow that twist into thick ropes of wind, rake across their cheeks, thrash the breath out of them, turn their flesh white and hard.

Desperate, determined as ever to survive at any cost, Almagro gathers together twenty of his strongest men and leads a fast-moving advance party down into the valleys of what is today Chile's "Little North," the Norte Chico, centred around the mining centre and port of Copiapo. There, in a few short days, he collects 4,000 bushels of corn, the dried meat of 4,000 llamas and guanacos and 15,000 partridges, and sends the provisions galloping back up into the mountains to save what he can of his tattered force.

Almagro and his troops rode down from the Andes into a continent of sorts in which the Incan conquest had left many of the original cultures intact. The "countries," if we define them by their peoples, consisted of the Aricans at the northern tip of present-day Chile, the Aymaras in a narrow territory on the border between Bolivia and Chile, the Atacamenians in a huge territory, and the Chango fishing people occupying a narrow line of coast. Farther south, along the line of the Copiapo River, and marking the path along which Almagro travelled, the Atacamenians' vast and complex territory gave way to that of the Diaguitas, followed by the Picunches at the Rio Aconcagua (near where Santiago is today), the Chiquillanes in the mountains, and the Mapuche, Pehuenche, Huilliche and Puelche.

As the landscape fragments into islands, the people increasingly live their lives out not on earth but on the water. The Cuncos of Chiloe, the Chonos, Kawesh'kar and Yamana who divided up the southern islands, fragments of snowy lands sprinkled like bread on the Pacific Ocean, culminating in the Ona on Tierra del Fuego Island and the Tehuelches riding the peaks of the southern Andes on both sides of what is now the Argentine-Chile border.

The northern desert when the Spanish arrived was dotted with the ancient cities of the Atacamenians: Peine, Toconao, San Pedro de Atacama, Toconce, Ayquina, Chiu Chiu and many more. Centuries of labour had tamed the winter run-off, the "lying" rivers that ran only for a few brief hours every day, tempting them into towns and fields that grew rich with the now-domesticated llama, quinua, the protein-rich Andean grain, algarrobo, chañaral and other gnarled trees bursting like fountains out of sand, rich with protein and juice, ready to ferment into ritual drinks or to be dried like nuts and ground to flour for the flat breads of the Atacama.

These towns and their lords were part of the fine knots of pre-Incan fabric woven before their arrival, their secret numbers recorded in the quipus that were created to re-member the details of trade and travel between the Pacific coast, northwestern Argentina, the Andean plateaux, Bo-livia, Titicaca, Cuzco and beyond.

Europe at this time was a checkerboard of delicately weighted powers, jostling to maintain authority without allowing any single entity to hold sway over all the others. Much of what would become modern-day Europe was slowly taking shape—there were the kingdoms of Portu-gal, Spain, France, England, the Netherlands, Switzerland and then the vestiges of the Holy Roman Empire, the Ottoman Empire, the Kingdom of Poland that would shortly be broken into the three territories of the Mus-covite Dominion.

Earlier, the two continents, like two planets whirling unaware of each other, followed parallel paths, where the difference in the details made all the difference. Eight to ten thousand years ago hunters and gatherers had explored these reaches, their bare feet tracing the first roads through the Atacama. Farther north, around Lake Chungara, the Chinchorro people had poured their grief and loss into

the world's first mummies, three thousand years before the
Egyptians. Today, the San Miguel de Azapa Museum in
Arica still serves as the unblessed shrine for the mummy of a
six-year-old child. Her limbs of wood and muscles of straw
frame a startling black face of clay, eyes and mouth round
with astonishment.

As Europe reached the end of the Palaeolithic Age,
Paleo-Indian cultures arrived in the Atacama; these nomadic groups of hunters and gatherers roamed the desert,
watching both the llama and the water for clues to
survival.

As people in Europe's Neolithic Age (3000 B.C.) began
to tame the land, shaping the first tools and techniques
necessary for agriculture, the Atacamenians were discovering how to domesticate the llama and so gain an edge
in the battle for survival. Along the edges of the Salar de
Atacama, the people of Tulan began to build temporary
settlements of circular homes, living on the results of their
hunting and gathering, and developing complex rites to
bury their dead. On the hard stones of the desert they
scratched their victories and mourned their defeats in
circles and squares, the slim figures of people and animals
telling of the importance of the llama and its wild relatives
the vicuña and the guanaco, describing the birth of cultivated seed. They travelled from the altiplano down the
deep ravines that mountain rivers cut, as they flowed from
summer snows into the sand, then vanished into air.

As the Phoenicians (1000 B.C.) entered the Bronze Age,
the pastoral communities of the Atacama started to weave,
invented pottery and began their own metallurgical experiments, thanks to the rich minerals of the desert. Past the
Iron Age and into the time of the Romans (two thousand

years ago) the desert's villages were producing enough of a surplus to generate ever more complex handicrafts and societies, until, by A.D. 1000 more or less, they had formed towns that thrived on local mining, crafts, sheep-herding and crops, along with the endless exchange of goods between the coast, the Andes and beyond. Small towns bloomed along the Loa River, around the present-day town of Chiu Chiu and up into the rich marshlands of Turi, which produced a corrugated ceramic in villages like Pochoche, Coyo and Tchaputchayna. As the towns and the herds of llamas grew, so too did the need for pasture, and ever more complex irrigation systems. As they cared for their animals, the herders slept in caves like those in Tulan, where generations carved the pictographs that would mark the layers of rites and ceremony for succeeding generations, the birth of collective memory, history written not across the pages of a book, but across the landscape of the desert.

Five hundred years before Christ, living populations dared to settle, forming lush green islands amidst the despoblados, vast empty spaces of the Atacama. With these, the culture of San Pedro de Atacama spread along new ravines and created new marshlands through the development of ever more intricate irrigation systems. The town of Tulor grew up south of what is today San Pedro de Atacama, its round thatched huts forming a tightly knit circle of circles within a low mud wall, its people cultivating corn and raising llamas, collecting algarrobo and chañar fruit until for some reason, around the time of the first contact with Tiwanaku, the people decided to move away, closer to the villages of present-day San Pedro, leaving their town to sleep for centuries under layers of sand.

When, between A.D. 400 and 900, the first caravans began to arrive from Tiwanaku, the San Pedro culture of the Atacamenians was just reaching its height. People buried their dead in cemeteries near their villages, another layer of history and of hope, near the clusters of trees and crops that kept them alive, while roving eyes searched skies real and metaphysical for explanations and guides. Lautaro Núñez says that *The inhalation of psychoactive plant dusts from the eastern jungles allowed initiates to experience the colour and scent of the gods, the shine of silvery lagoons and the birds' eye vision of condor-men . . .*

During the Quitor phase, shiny black clay figures with broad hips and mocking faces became the maximum symbol of the Atacamenian culture's development, often mixed with religious and cultural icons from Tiwanaku. Complex rites accompanied the inhalation of hallucinogens to the wild chorus of the antara and the chanting of the priest, who could become condor or puma in his quest for mastery over the natural elements that ruled their lives—the key to the people's loyalty and ultimate power. The most sacred celebration culminated at that point where the priest, hugging the sacrifice to him in one final, fierce embrace, flicked his hand deftly across her throat. The knife, like a pen, drew a single red letter, her last cry or gasp an offering in exchange for eternal triumph at war, a plea for mercy to implacable nature, an incantation to ensure the fertility of women and crops, a blow to strengthen the priest's authority.

High priests named and rode the gods like the howling winds of the high plateaux, struggling to control the supernatural powers that rule life and death. It was not an easy office, it was hard to keep ahead of people, keep them convinced of the magic the priest could convoke and control at the end of a hollow straw, in a tiny pile of dust: the power of flight, the power to see the future, the power to turn the people's will to theirs (and those of the powers that be), demanding they work hard, lacing their daily activities together with conviction, festivals and rites.

Núñez notes that *Thus the strength and spirit of the mountain became the condor and penetrated the body of the priest. Water took the form of the snake and physical strength and intelligence adopted the body of the puma. All of these were embodied and spoke through the mouth of the priest, who as the intermediary between the powers of the underground, the earth, the mountain and heaven, could transfer to the community the necessary rites, duties and benefits of religious nature on determined days of the year.*

During that harsh summer of 1536, the Spaniards and their Incan guides walked to the border of what, if we were capable of viewing them through the same glass as we view ourselves, we might have called the Atacamenian archipelago, human islands linked by the constant movement of the herdsmen and traders. Like an ocean of sand, the desert both set apart and connected the modest cities of the Atacama, clusters of gently rounded homes with thatched roofs, where people were successfully coaxing the rare rivers into their fields of crops, hugging the water with their beaten paths and trading posts, celebrating the lightning and the peaks that carried that water from the cloudy heights, all the way to the salt fields and gritty tracts of dry earth. On a nearby height, the *pukara*, the fort, stood guard, marking the tensions between the desert's different lords.

Five hundred years before Ñusta, colonists from Tiwanaku had also made this trip, offering polished ceramics, elegant ceremonies, poetic words to dress up the scarlet craft of the Sacrificer and persuade the people of the Atacama to open their doors. Like Ñusta they carried the *siku*, an Andean wind instrument related to the Atacamenians' antara, which had reached the desert long before.

For two thousand years, its clay throat vibrated with their stories—the startled bellow, the trembling song, the weeping protests of mourners and celebrants. In 1997, a researcher at the Pre-Columbian Museum in Santiago produced a spectral analysis of the "torn sound" (*sonido rajado*) of the antara, comparing it to that of a classical flute. At the first trill of the flute, the hertz and milliseconds on the left side of a 3-D graph rise sharp and pointed as a mountain range, then drop abruptly into foothills, settle quickly into plains flat as the Atacama before they fall into the sea. In contrast, the peaks of the antara's hertz and milliseconds rise high and sharp as the harshest Andean peaks, and continue to pulse, punching toward the sky. Like razor teeth or sharp knives, they slice upward, they splinter and stab, they tear to ribbons any effort at order and peaceful harmony.

To play the antara, the musician must blow with the full force of his lungs, much harder than with any European instrument, a tribute, again, to the hefty lungs of those who inhabited the altiplano, a relic from that border land where oxygen-starvation leads to a mad dance of delirium or strength. What's more, you don't play the antara alone. Instead, the musicians form two rows, and must move as they blow the sound out of their very marrow, leaping and bowing low, skipping and humbling themselves, turning into mere shadows cast by the music's flames. Like fire themselves, they play the ancient sounds of death and sacrifice, take comfort from the life they hope will burst from seeds of bone.

Diego de Almagro may have felt that this music was *extremely strange and anguished, wild, like anguished seabirds*, flat as the cry of goose or swan, monotonous, dissonant, *deafening and at the same time, strangely captivating*, as some of his contemporaries put it. From one generation to the next, boys and men formed eternal lines, competing like teams of football players, thick, heavy drums pounding a connection thin and strong as wire between them, binding them together, to the earth, to some central unity that they must never lose to chaos. At times, like bumper cars, they drove into each other, banging thighs against elbows, balance against disaster, trying to leave their opponents sprawling and shamed on the floor. Occasionally one of the groups of dancers would admit defeat and pause to reorganize into the complex equilibrium, the dance of their beliefs.

The antara, when it first appeared in the Norte Grande between A.D. 400 and 1100, did not travel alone. It was part of the cultural and economic revolution wrought by Tiwanaku as it spread its influence among the mighty lords of the Atacama. The great city-state was producing a religious revolution as it spread its powerful ideology among the vibrant cultures of the desert islands, the oases. In the Atacama, a privileged class, roughly one out of every four or five people, not only had access to the consciousness-altering hypnosis of the music, but also to the magic of the fine dusts of desert plants containing mescaline.

With the drugs came rites, a subtle dance of beliefs that burned like a cherished flame within the shamans. While the music played and the dust danced in their brains they journeyed beyond their skin and the rough barriers of the

mountains. Their last view of reality on takeoff and their
first view on landing were of some version of their own
faces, carved into the finely crafted tablets from which they
inhaled flight. Small chips of turquoise marked their eyes
as deep, blank lakes, as empty of life as the desert itself. In
one hand, the carved figure on the tablet usually held an
axe, in the other, a severed head.

The Sun and the Sacrificer, the two hands of God, followed by their retinue of wildcats, travelled from the Gate
of the Sun to the land where the sun ruled, along with
lightning and the Pachamama, the earth. The antara's tubes
became part of the lord's funeral ensembles; they were built
into the foundations of temples and figured in each culture's most important rites.

Today the wild, dissonant cries of the antara still echo
in Christian ceremonies, and with them, the Ñusta's
shadow, grown large as the Yacana, overwhelming, omnipresent, bright. But then, as she crossed the desert, a prisoner of Diego de Almagro, she felt only how the empire of
the Inca was crumbling under her feet, how the antara
seemed to sing it to destruction.

Ñusta gazes with amazement on the lands that have long
nourished her empire, without being known by it. She can
sense the centuries of settlement and exchange, the familiar panorama of towns and states, each governed by their
two lords, the duality of heaven and earth reflected in the
human patterns that give meaning to this world.

Although the nights are still shot through with ice, during the day the sun massages her bones, bringing them
back to light, warmth, strength. In the evening she sips the
foul water from the scarce waterholes known as *jagüey*

(only the desert thirst makes the water from these jagüeys bearable, stored as it is in the leathery udders of recently killed llamas or seal's bladders, roasted flour poured in to try and cut the unpleasant flavour) and turns her back to the road that might one day lead them to the coast. She gazes longingly at the great blue pyramids of the Andes, an endless line, tempting her to turn back.

Sometimes she gathers her people around her, a small human knot cut loose from the ancient city, loose and alone in the wilderness. In her own language, the flowing of words that the Spanish don't yet control, in the midst of the desert she tells them about *Yacana, who descended from the world above to drink water. Of this, and the other stars we must speak, and of what their names are.*

They say that this Yacana, the one I have named, is like a shadow of a llama, this animal's double that walks through the centre of the sky. We men too, yes, we can see it coming, dark. They say this Yacana, when she reaches the earth, walks under the rivers. She's very large, yes; darker than the night sky bearing down upon us, her neck has two eyes, and tall, she comes. People call her Yacana.

A man, in an instant of joy, saw Yacana fall before him, then as she reached the earth, how she went to drink from a nearby spring. At the same time, the man began to feel himself crushed under flakes of wool that other men were shearing. This occurred at night.

As the next day dawned, the man went to see the wool they had sheared. It was blue, white, black, dark yellow, mixed colours; it looked like everything that has a colour. And, since he had no llamas, he sold all this wool immediately and, in the very spot where Yacana had fallen, he worshipped her.

Then he bought a female and a male llama. And from this pair alone he came to have two or three thousand llamas.

*They say that this Yacana descends at midnight, when it's no
longer possible to see or hear her, and drinks all the water from the
sea. They say that if she didn't drink all that water, the world
would be buried. The dark stain that goes ahead of this shadow
called Yacana has the name of Yutu ("Partridge"). And they
say that Yacana has children and when they start to suckle, she
wakes up.*

*There are also three stars that shine almost together. And
they're called the "Condor," the "Chicken Hawk" and the "Fal-
con." And when Las Cabrillas appear, very large, they say: "This
year we're going to have excellent ripening of the fruit," but when
they're small, they say: "We're going to suffer."*

During the day there is nothing to do but think, as their
walking tries to consume an apparently endless distance.
They chew on the corn and the dried fruit that Almagro
sent back from the oases and the fertile valleys he found.
Gently, gradually, the sweet juices of the desert fruit pour
the sun's energy through her. The steady swing of her
arms, the muscles rebuilding in her legs gather new
strength. She enters ever more deeply into the unknown,
leaving behind her a landscape she will not cross again.
Occasionally, as they pass a hill of slate, an excited murmur
shoots through the crowd. Mostly, the Spaniards don't see
them, but Ñusta and her people do: carefully scratched and
scraped into the dry parchment of the earth are the shapes
of crosses, arrows, wildcats and llamas, birds in flight and
people walking, leaping, standing with arms waving, eyes
and mouths open to shout a welcome or a warning. These
symbols and maps crack jokes or make their readers cry,
suddenly rich and wise with the experience of others,
stories of courage and laughter, even songs, etched on the

desert's sloping walls, tell them of travellers who've passed before them, who in the passing of Ñusta and her people now pass again, shadows lingering inside the living bones. A river of blood, they pulse and throb on their way from the mountains to the coast, as people have done for thousands of years.

Ñusta walks and thinks, thinks and walks, the pictures dancing before her eyes even when they are closed. With Almagro far ahead with the advance party, she feels relief. She sees him as a distant point, provider of food and drink, but also a pain sharp as a thorn deep in her bones: his pain, his unease, his quest, which she can feel will lead him to death on the battlefield. For him this journey through the desert can be reduced to that single, final destination he barely knows he's seeking. She has both loved and hated him, but now she must choose. To return to Cuzco with him is not to return at all, but to take her life across the border into the Spaniards' camp. Forever.

Ñusta thinks and walks, the desert a book, each page a poem or the voice of an oracle, subtle and brief, hard to comprehend, but necessary. As the coloured layers of sky, hills, gravel plains begin to tinge with green, they approach the rich valleys of the oasis of Copiapo, a tiny emerald paradise on the desert's edge, artificial, perfect, rural, no city in sight. Now they walk amidst *lovely farmland, all the watercourses are hand made, and each valley looks like a beautiful, well-planned garden, where, the natives tell us, never a drop of water has fallen from the sky, because it doesn't ever rain on these flat lands, but neither was the water from the earth lacking, because in every valley there's a hot spring that always carries water and where there isn't one, they irrigate their lands and kitchen gardens with the water from underground springs. The* valleys, still separated by fields of sand and *despoblados, unpopulated reaches, of ten, fifteen, twenty leagues* are heavily populated by people prosperous and graceful. Still, to reach Chile they will have to cross another *despoblado, a hundred leagues of sand, without a single green thing anywhere.*[*]

The motley assortment of men and women who bathe themselves in Copiapo's river are a far cry from the proud columns of Spaniards and slaves who set out from Cuzco some six months earlier. The Spanish, better clothed, consuming the best of the food and carrying the least of the burden, have fared much better than their native "servants." Almagro and his chroniclers have kept the records that mattered to them: *one hundred and fifty horses were lost.* Historians will estimate that Ñusta may have seen the deaths of as many as five thousand of the expedition's native men and women, a few black slaves, more than thirty Spaniards. Far behind her, invisible in a future Ñusta will not know, the Incan writer Garcilaso de la Vega will write in Spanish that ten thousand turned from flesh to ice on the narrow stony paths of the high Andes, human statues left to mark Almagro's prowess.

Almagro continues to rob and raid, ostensibly seeking wealth, but his true goal is really death and a peace he will not find in life. He and his men advance down one valley after another, the occupants disappearing, hiding their crops and leaving their homes abandoned. What little Ñusta sees of the Diaguitas people of these valleys can be summed up by the broken pottery scattered among the ashes of fires that are often still warm when she arrives in the rearguard of the scourge that Almagro has become.

---

[*] Cristóbal de Molina (Hidalgo's *Culturas*).

She squats in the ashes, burning her fingers on the hot shards of what was once the delicate white, black and red geometry of the Diaguitas' pots, the ducks poised to fly away, the dancing women whose bellies held precious water, keeping it fresh and cool. She searches the burnt remains of villages for food.

Ñusta knows she is looking at a trail first cut by the Incas themselves, who turned the Diaguitas into *mitimaes*, an odd combination of slave and trusted administrator, whole peoples that the Incas collected like taxes, settling them elsewhere in the empire to labour or control, selecting the finest of the women, like odd change, for the sacrifice. Sometimes the mitimaes were particularly rebellious peoples, sent into exile to prevent further uprisings. At other times they were docile and passive, and therefore served as good administrators for the Incas. Many of these Andean lords *awaited any chance to shake off the Incan yoke. They allied with the Spanish without imagining that behind them rose the presence of another state*, wrote another historian.[*]

The roads through these valleys reflected the Incas' engineering feats, but also proved strategic from a military point of view, cutting across the valleys, breaking up the Diaguitas' interlocking fiefdoms into the meaningless fragments of a scattered puzzle, making it easy for the Incas (and the Spanish who followed) to scoop up the pieces. For sixty years, troops flowed down from the Andes, crossed the desert and invaded the peaceful coastal valleys, taking them over and bringing an estimated 30,000 people under the Incas' sway.

---

[*] M. Rostworonsky (Stehberg).

The Diaguitan people lived in comfortable unfortified towns in times of peace, retreating into the stone forts known as pukaras in times of war. Their lords enjoyed the free labour of their subjects on a rotating basis, along with the results of their work in the local mines, carried out primarily to benefit the Incas. The valley El Huasco had *two lords, both named Sangotay . . . who were conquered by the Incas. They wear fine clothes of wool and cotton . . . harvest corn and beans, quinua and squash. . . They have no idols, nor houses of worship. The rites and ceremonies of these Indians are the same as those of Copiapo. They're people with fine bodies and good fighters and very attractive. Their parties and celebrations are great gatherings. They drink wine from algarrobo and corn and get drunk. They do not consider this a loss of honour.**

In the valley of Copiapo, Almagro formed an alliance with one of the local groups, but he also revenged the death of three Spaniards by rounding up the main Indians from three valleys and burning them alive. He distributed their people among his men as slaves.

Ñusta knows she cannot travel with the Spaniard much longer, but she stares out into the desert around her and sees no other road.

Still her eyes burn through the green valleys, raking the gravel and the dust beyond, looking for answers. She may not know the full story of the Atacama, but there is enough of her own past here, in these Incan roads layered onto older roads, trampled by the feet of the peoples who laid the foundations for the entire Andean world. Her eyes are shaped by the same extreme horizons, the infinite

---

* Gerónimo de Bibar (Stehberg).

plains rising abruptly to treacherous heights. Her copper skin is the colour of the desert itself, her feet strong and muscular, as accustomed to walking as were theirs. She feels the lines of messengers, ponders for days the stories she's read scrawled across the hills. Gradually they blot out the hope of *rescue* and begin to spell *escape*. Flight will take her not only out of the hands of the Spanish but beyond the control of the Sacrificer or the kings, but perhaps, she thinks, comforting herself with lies, she will stay within the traditions that gave meaning and direction to her life. *In a river of blood, Atahualpa walks, dividing into two currents.*

But she knows of the lying rivers, the ones that run in the morning and vanish by afternoon. She puzzles over their meaning as she walks the banks of the Copiapo. Do these refer to Atahualpa's two warring sons, his time, their time, split into two streams of blood that ran uselessly into the desert, and are at this very moment evaporating under the hot sun of the Spaniards' attack? Lying rivers. Promising the cool relief of the oasis, they vanish when you bend to drink.

For all she's travelled and come through, she no longer knows what lies behind her. The Spaniards' hunger has sucked every familiar meaning out of the wise old words, emptied them, or worse, filled them with a meaning that is slowly being revealed to her, spelled out in the headless bodies of men who die in chains, of women used and torn and thrown away, a legacy of brutality. The Incas are harsh, too, in their own way, but this was senseless waste. This was not the horror of sacrifice to benefit a higher social order. This was murder, one crime after another slashing the delicate threads of reciprocity that have woven the Andean peoples together for thousands of years. Even when they war against each other, they know the rules that govern their conquests, their defeats. After war, there is always peace. But this time she is not so sure of what will follow.

One night, as her feet are tracing the cold shadows of stars across the pitted surface of the desert, a coldness pierces to the marrow of her bones and she gazes out at the blank landscape over which she has come. Sanded and polished by the light of the moon, it looks blank, pale and empty. No city reaches the majestic heights of its temples and pyramids skyward. Not even the Andes are visible. There is nothing left, she comes from a vacuum. *With no one and nowhere to return to. . . Will your heart, Inca, bear our wandering life?* Even if she could bear to retrace their steps and walk again, the high roads of the Andes are in thrall to the Spaniards' rough fists, devoured by their diseases, interred by their weapons.

It's not just the Inca Atahualpa who roams alone now, with no one and nowhere to return to. The Spanish have brought with them cataclysmic change, the pachikuti, turning a united people into a diaspora, scattering them like drops of water on a hot grill. They have returned to the dawn of time, to a time of birth, of new gods, new ideas, new empires.

She looks around her, blinking, as if awaking. Then gazes out at the desert the way in Europe people gaze longingly out to sea. There could be something waiting just beyond the horizon. Here in the desert, people have lived for thousands of years. Survival is possible. Human islands. Surrounded and separated by sand and salt. Free to do as their own history and hearts dictate.

More and more the survivors of her own people crowd close in the evenings. Almost absentmindedly, as if in a trance, she tells them stories, helping them to lose themselves in the hopes and victories she can conjure up for them. She is young, a priestess, and strong. The past is waiting for her, amidst the shifting sands that surround them.

> *Then he bought a female and a male llama.*
> *And from this pair alone he came to have two or three thousand llamas.*

From a small village the Incas built an empire. Surely, given a chance, under the guidance of the right gods, they will do it again.

One night, she gathers as many of her people to her as wish to follow, and steps out of the circle of the Spanish camp, following the coast and the desert stars northward, stopping briefly for water, then hurrying on, fearful of the Spanish at her heels. A terrible hunger of her own, for something she only partly understands, drives her on.

She hasn't heard the story of the condenado. I haven't reached her, not even through her dreams. And yet I can see it adhere to her like dust. It dulls her shining.

5

WHITE GOLD AND CRIMSON

The Nitrate Era

I sing the Pampa, the sad earth,
reprobate earth of curses,
that never dresses in green
not even at the finest season's peak;

Where birds never warble,
nor flowers grow,
where the river never laughing winds
free and fleeting.

— *Francisco Plazo, El Pueblo Obrero, 18 April 1908*

Oh, Iquique, up to the gills in cognac and the vivid
afternoon filling the crystal goblets of melancholy!

— *Andrés Sabella, Chilean poet*

La Tirana (Chile), July 1998

I QUIQUE SITS on the Pacific Coast, its back to the steep cliffs of sand that threaten to slide down and cover its patchwork quilt of buildings with a uniform mantle, smooth and beige and warm as the flanks of the animal desert, drowsy as a giant cow, barely aware of the humans it would crush. An anonymous dot of a fishing village on an endless sandy coast before the conquest, Iquique languished until 1730 when the Huantajaya silver mine once worked by the Incas came back to life, hungry for candles, flour and wood. I arrive by plane in July 1998 with Patricio, my husband, and Camilo, my fourteen-year-old son, on a new leg on my journey in search of Huillac Ñusta, her elusive trail through the Atacama. I will find signs of her at every turn, but it will take me a while: first I have to lift my eyes from the books I've been hunting through for traces of the past—her present—and listen to the voices whose words are written on the hills.

The city itself is a child's wild collage of tattered port stitched to tacky shopping centre, the elegant frame houses of the nitrate era pasted back to back with square cement hotels, a high-rise or two like architectural ink blots, Chinatown trapped and trussed in a tangle of telephone wires, all crowded around a windswept square surrounded by the pretentious but still lovely Club de la Union, the Cathedral newly painted, a gaggle of skateboard fans surfing its angles, walls and stairs, making Camilo, who left his board at home, sigh for the easy comradeship of its adepts.

The city reeks of car fumes and ocean debris, but nevertheless offers up an air sharply etched in salt, making its breath sit damp and cool. I inhale deeply, clearing the

Santiago sludge out of my lungs, and Bowman's voice floats through me: *It is only the rare downpour that gives Iquique anything at all to average through the years. It is as nearly like a rainless land as any known on the earth today.*

Here in Iquique as the twentieth century twists away from the nineteenth into the twenty-first, it is hard to find traces of a deposed Incan priestess, who lived when speed was still measured in terms of animals and distance by the human stride, when the seemingly endless leagues of desert could be crossed only on foot or horseback, when cars and electricity were still the ludicrous objects of an undreamt-of future. I find I can't take the movement of time seriously, the animal part of me remains convinced that everything is going on here, now, all change captured and held in the present instant, the rush and hum and crackle of information-laden air, abuzz with radio waves, voices from a world away shouting in my ears, the tapping of computer keys, the purring of Internet, the news of Clinton's affair with Monica Lewinsky just breaking, a new bombing expedition of Iraq still in the future, Pinochet about to be arrested in London, Kosovo about to explode, cellular telephones jangling or squeaking like electronic crickets. Everything is *now* to me. Why take notes? I'm here, awake and watching. Can't conceive of this scene falling prey to the *camanchaca*, that tantalizing ocean mist that never yields rain, seeping into memory, dulling its sharp edges.

As we pull together a supply of water, sandwiches, chocolate and toilet paper—our basic requirements for a day's outing—I have no idea what waits on the tabletop of desert above us, but I'm eager to find some key to the codes that encrypt its secrets. First we visit the town museum. After Calama, it is a wonderful surprise, the faithful reflection of a bustling city that somehow remembers and celebrates its past, even when it doesn't fully understand it. The building itself, a gracious airy mansion of wooden pillars and siding, dates back to the nitrate era a hundred years ago, when the desert was mined for the main ingredient in both fertilizer and explosives. It has been lovingly restored, the museum on the main floor, and some of the town's administrative offices above.

The displays themselves are modest, the artefacts simple but lovely, each one a powerful incantation, transporting us through time. Officially restored in 1987 at the height of the military regime, it tries to censor, but can't resist the truth.

Each room is designed to capture a period. Drawings in watercolours and pastels, of breathtaking simplicity, show people using the items on display in their natural context; I've seldom seen an attempt to breathe life into the clues death leaves behind it that succeeds so well. Our visit to the museum becomes a stroll through sunlit layers of rock and time. In one room, a skull from Tiwanaku, painstakingly bound and deformed to reach that civilization's view of perfection. In another, a finely woven piece of cloth, which I long to finger. Composed of heavy wool stripes, it contains all the colours that stretch away to the Atacama's mountainous horizon, including the mirages. A watercolour shows a priest inhaling deeply from a hallucinatory instrument similar to those I've seen in Atacama, changing from man to puma as he breathes. Fine pottery, harpoon tips, neat woven bags covered with diamonds of red—the Aymara room depicts that people taking refuge in the highlands, *surviving on the roof of our territory, sustained by strong cultural traditions, with the wisdom to maintain life, their economy and towns in one of the world's highest altitudes.*

Another picture illustrates a group of Incan miners and functionaries travelling from the altiplano along the Tarapaca ravine, to find and exploit the silver mine in Huantajaya, which they dedicated to their god, the Sun. Just a few years earlier Huillac Ñusta might have run to them and found refuge from the Spanish in her own familiar culture. A little farther along, a display of silver and copper jewellery reveals the Christian cross amidst vicuñas, llamas and alpacas, condors and eagles, stones and coins enshrining conflicting beliefs.

The "nitrate room" is really a suite, displaying an amazing range of objects—elegant ladies posed on postcards with delicately tinted roses in their hands, the yellow petals of pansies on one side of the cards and messages from the harsh reality of the nitrate offices on the back. The only clock has stopped at one minute before midnight or noon, while the huge worn shoes offer a glimpse of barrel-chested men, their skin burned black as old leather, muscles swelling as they swing coarse wooden mallets and metal scoops to break loose the *caliche*, the salty crust that hid the nitrate, and heave it into the rough wheelbarrows, which are also on display. Signal lanterns speak of work stretching long into the night, and as in many a New-foundland museum the remains of the "first" telegraph announce the presence of foreign owners. A photograph shows a group of men sinking narrow poles into the earth. And in one room a miniature nitrate town echoes the urban tracings of the desert's first modern cities, streets laid out in rigid grids, workers' homes lined up along them, the administrators' more elegant quarters set slightly apart from the other residential, service and industrial areas. These towns that sprang up all over the desert, tiny bright constellations shining well into the night, were always called *oficinas*, offices. Odd that Chile's first industrial cities should be referred to thus. I stare at the model for a long time, entranced by its details, not suspecting how much of Ñusta's spirit lingers along those narrow streets, in the flimsy shacks of corrugated iron.

For a while I study the demonstration model of the Shanks process, which was developed in 1878 by a man called Santiago Humberstone. The caliche was first steamed, reducing the desert crust to gravel to produce a liquid saturated with nitrates that was then seared away by the sun, leaving a white crystal to be packed into sacks and hauled by mules to port for shipping overseas. The process was used through to 1945 and took advantage of even low-grade ore. Two oak buckets with their respective cranks, *for making ice cream*, speak of elegant picnics, Scottish shawls spread out on the rough desert face, for the women who refreshed themselves constantly from the perfume bottles, or the men who dipped their pens into the elegant bronze inkwells and sent reports speeding back to England. They sipped their tea from the porcelain cups imported from Europe. Glass chimney lamps, rolltop desks, old cigarette packs, a family photo album covered in flowers and showing a spectacular lineup of women dressed for the opera. Like San Pedro de Atacama's graves, one of four embellished with beads and other symbols of wealth and power, here the remains of comfort speak of a way of life that floated on the desert's surface, fragile as a lily pad. As we will discover on our journey, the pleasures of life in the nitrate offices were easily disturbed, rent or sunk by illness and death.

And there's a seemingly endless display of the *fichas*, that is, the buttons that the companies used to pay the workers instead of money. Rafael Quiroga Zegarra, who lived out his last years in the town of Huara says, *The fichas from La Palma were aluminum. The fichas from Santa Laura were prettier, they looked like nickel. . .* For many years he fingered the raisins, walnuts, olives and crackers that stocked the company market in Humberstone where he worked, receiving the omnipresent fichas in payment for the over-priced goods.

An American traveller and writer named Theodore Child visited this part of the desert, known as Tarapaca, in 1890. He stopped for a while at Primitiva, one of the most modern nitrate offices, belonging to that industrial Almagro, John North, an Englishman. When it was in full production, some 1,400 men worked here for $3 a day, their homes of thin boards contrasting with the sober solidity of the administrator's house. Nearby a camp of women and children was vibrant with the barking of dogs, the movement of burros, Bolivian women selling their wares. Child describes the company store, operating out of a building or truck, as the only enterprise allowed to sell merchandise to workers and their families.

The workers lived in patched-together shacks with corrugated tin roofs that sizzled all day like pots on a stove, but the administrators lived in electrified comfort. Child describes the wives dressed in whites playing tennis and sallying out on horseback to explore the desert, the men in the Kipling-like precision of military-style jackets, immaculately creased pants and polished boots.

Labour has always been a major problem for mining operations in the desert. In 1615, the Count of Montes Claros, Viceroy of Peru, ordered an urgent shipment of 668 quintals of copper from the Atacama. Fulfilling the order took almost ten years. Vicuña Mackenna notes that in the early 1700s a labour shortage had caused the price of copper to rise from 4 to 8 pesos in the mine and from 16 to 20 pesos in Lima. This, because the *mitayos or Indian slaves ate nothing but their own tears, the salary of the wretched. . . For this same reason, they gradually disappeared . . .*

All the colours are deeply stained with the sepia of old photographs. This might seem an illusion, but it's not. The desert's own shades are soaked in nostalgia. Even today, when most of the nitrate offices are ghost towns, scattered in lonely abandonment by sand-covered train tracks and stations, some uncaptured sense of what life was to the men and women who thronged here from the lush green south and the arid heights of the Andes to the northeast lingers among the old buildings that still stand, cracking like seed pods under the hot sun, waiting for those few drops of rain that fall every hundred years or so.

There were bitter strikes here, and bloodbaths—we'll travel into them like storms as we explore this part of the desert. Yet something else happened here, too, something far more important. The air is charged with it still. We are filled with it every time we inhale.

It takes the better part of an hour for our rented car to climb the sandy flanks of the mountain that squashes Iquique against the coast. Cars, trucks, buses are strung together like gaudy beads across the mountain's flesh, as ample as the prostitutes that once strutted along the fancy streets below. They zigzag back and forth, skyward to leave Iquique, earthward to arrive. When we reach the top, we spot high-flying parachutes that blow backward like bright kisses. We turn our backs on the Pacific Ocean and head into the giant sandbox of the Atacama. Shrunk to child size in its vastness, we will spend the next few days wandering and wondering among the cast-off machinery, truck tires, small houses, trees collapsed like brooding, dusty hens. We will stare in confusion at the tracks of endless trains that run no longer, a giant tic-tac-toe, criss-crossing the sand, potent with its own existence, yet meaningless, played out, abandoned.

I suppose, the Pacific being the world's largest ocean, it had to have a worthy beach. Here, the Atacama stretches its vast silence from sea cliffs ashriek with gulls a hundred miles inland to where it crinkles gently upward toward the lashing winds of the Andes. You might think this empty beige blanket of a place would have nothing in common with the insolent green of the lake district. You might think it could spawn no common culture, no shared beliefs. And yet, a thousand miles to the south, above the sea, the lush greenery of these same cliffs follows rows of neat iron or wooden crosses marking graves with no bodies. In this cemetery, in Los Lobos near Talcahuano, lies only the memory of the fishing people who disappeared without a trace, the idea of their lives wrapped in their families' anguished search, then laid in a tiny coffin dressed in a set of clothes, to be prayed over and buried, all that remained, all that matters.

Here, as in Los Lobos so many landscapes away, as we drive past dunes under a sky the deep cobalt of old bottles, we pass other bodiless tombs, modest shrines, stained by the waxy puddles of candles that seared the recent dark. *Animitas*. The desert's dead. They refuse to be forgotten, lurk in the shadows just behind the gates of their homes. These may be sumptuous and overblown in marble, or humble, their territory staked out by rubber tires from giant trucks. Paper flowers rustle in the wind above the mute offering of a cigarette, a few drops of water, the dry skeleton of a tree.

In the high Andean passes, travellers leave echoes of the animitas, piles of stones called *apachetas*, in which they place their offerings of coca leaves, whittled sticks and candles.

Where do they all come from, this motley parade of spirits who refuse to die?

On 8 December 1935, with the nitrate industry in deep decline, three thieves ganged up on a railway worker, Hermogenes San Martín. They beat him about the head, used his own belt to choke him to death, then emptied his pockets and stole his clothes. They dumped his body in the cemetery of Iquique, where *many people, moved by the horrible crime, began to visit the spot, until an Animita appeared and the belief took root and faith sanctified him*, notes Oreste Plath, untiring researcher and reader of the unwritten past. In 1952, a legally formed society took over the care and development of the site, and by 1989 it offered benefits, including home-care visits, mortuary fees and social activities, to some 250 members.

A little farther south, in the port of Antofagasta, a similar society marks the grave and the memory of three railway workers, blown to pieces at dawn on 16 July 1924 when a boiler exploded just as the train prepared to pull out of the station. The devotees of the three men still visit to ask for favours, and they have lit so many candles that the walls are stained with smoke, and puddles of melted wax flow like lava onto the pavement under bright heads of flame that may burn all night. Plaques mark the gratitude of those who've been helped:

My sincerest thanks to Evaristo Montt for healing my feet.
A Circus Artist. Mercedes Aguirre, 1970.

Help us so that there are no more fights at home. Thanks.

Help us to find our happiness. JRC–CAO

Thanks for listening. Keep helping. GHV

According to popular belief, the spirits of those who die violent deaths linger; their eyes watch over the living while their lips whisper in the ears of gods, begging for favours. Each animita marks sudden death by accident, murder or massacre. These roadside shrines cry out in protest at a brutal death and, often, at the lack of justice for the victim. They may be children like Marina Silva Espinoza, a three-year-old girl whose stepfather slashed her throat and left her under a tree in a Santiago park on 24 May 1945. Or fourteen-year-old Elvirita Guillén, who shot herself after being entrapped and raped by three soldiers. She was buried in the Limache cemetery in southern Chile on 17 March 1937. Her attackers, including two women who held her down for the men, received jail sentences of one to six months. Another animita recalls the *Adrianas* of Copiapo, the modern city in the oasis once visited by Diego de Almagro. These three women, according to a newspaper report published in 1990, carefully clipped and saved by Oreste Plath, were forced into prostitution during the economic recovery that followed the collapse of the nitrate boom. They died between 1936 and 1937, one shot, one stabbed in a jealous quarrel, the third of unknown causes.

Other animitas recall the lives of mentally disabled persons, like Pepito, who won the affection of the townspeople of San Fernando. They protected him and showed up en masse for his funeral, because they considered him *innocent* and *simple*.

A newspaper report of his funeral said: *He reached our world the product of a broken marriage, a mixture of incomplete genes, but he grew up well and in the countryside he learned the murmur of the wind, the richness of its earth, he made the birds' innocence his own. . . He sought out adventure in contact with the city and discovered the goodness of its citizens. . . In exchange, he provided news. His childlike mind could capture any tidbit of interest to others, through the blinks, the nervous gestures, leg movements like those of a rooster in heat. That is what he gave: communication.*[*]

Still other animitas shelter the spirits of murderers themselves, duly executed after trials considered unfair by public opinion in general, particularly the poor. Of these, perhaps the most stunning is the case of José del Carmen Valenzuela, who stabbed Rosa Elena Rivas to death, then chased her five children around the farm until he managed to catch and kill every one of them. They had given him shelter barely a month before. He had spent his childhood living in caves, eating roots and wild plants. While in jail he became a Christian, learned to read and weave baskets, and sent money to his mother so she could visit him.

Valenzuela became known as the Animita de Canaquita, widely recognized for his miracles. A popular song protested his fate: execution in spite of rehabilitation.

All over Chile, along highways, in cemeteries and train stations, set into walls or by sidewalks, modest shrines mark injustices and unexpected deaths. Many are covered with plaques with thanks for favours granted, some garnished with crutches, dolls, the detritus of physical handicap, the

---

[*] Sergio Morales (Plath).

joy of release from limitation. They mark a way of remembering people who would otherwise be forgotten. They mark a way for the powerless to reclaim their right to enshrine the ordinary, to protest abuse, to declare their own saints when the Church is too entangled with the powers that be to notice or care what happens to its humbler servants.

They mark the way ordinary people of the desert have always marked memory, choosing their own heroes. Just as electric power lines reflect the grid of power that binds and serves the desert, so do the animitas hold in place an invisible net of influence that covers the desert, tracing the endless circle between living and dead. This custom may have something to do with Roman Catholic or European culture, but to me the modest structures lining the highway, embellished by traffic signs, the bright colours of warning, the sudden cross that tags the spirit's new dwelling place, are huacas. They mark the gateways through which spirits pass, the "dead" who connect the living to the essence of life itself.

If I could, I would have searched through them one by one, stopping the car every few miles as a new one came in sight, checking to see if there was some trace of Huillac Ñusta. Easier to trace the concrete shape of human construction than search the scarred horizon for her path.

In the old mining town of Humberstone, eighty kilometres straight up and inland from Iquique through the flowing dunes of the desert, five stark wooden crosses mark the graves of what turn out to be pets, probably dogs. But empty buildings, broken machinery, rusted iron skeletons, the buildings staggering from old age, neglect and wind, seasoned with broken glass, mark another kind of memorial—to the end of the nitrate cycle, the white gold that drove Chile to war with Peru and Bolivia, the fertile dust from the world's driest desert that made roses bloom and wheat flourish elsewhere in the world.

Humberstone began in 1872 as a nitrate office known as La Palma, under the ownership of the Peruvian Nitrate Company. It became a new stop on the ancient trails of the Atacama, as men and mules zigzagged from one waterhole to another, carrying fruit and dried meat from Pica and Matilla to mines in Victoria, Huatacondo and Collahuasi, for Bowman, a week's journey away over a steep trail, for us, an hour's drive from Iquique. At the time, all that is today northern Chile belonged to Peru and Bolivia.

Over the years La Palma worked 130 stakes scattered around in the surrounding desert; it went through different hands, suffering its first strike in 1932 when it was owned by the Gibbs Company. In 1934 it was taken over by the Compania Salitrera de Tarapaca y Antofagasta, which built most of the main buildings still in existence today: the church, the market, the hotel, the theatre, the hospital, school, pool, bosses' homes, sportsfields, company stores, etc. On 21 November 1934, La Palma was reinaugurated, now under the name of Santiago Humberstone in honour of the chemical engineer who brought the Shanks process—and with it the Atacama's first major boom—to the nitrate industry.

We peek inside the married workers' small houses—a row of rooms, a hallway-sized kitchen, a postage-stamp-sized back yard—and then I wander away from Patricio and Camilo down the dirt lanes, through passageways and doorways that still seem impregnated with the smell of smoke and sweat, the shrill whistle of a young man strolling along after work, the grinding teeth of machines.

In one old building our voices echo hollowly. I thought it was a chapel, then realize it is actually the toilet room. In the warehouses where the raw desert crust known as caliche was boiled down to extract the nitrates, which were then dried and packaged by the sack, we bang our heads against old conveyor belts the width of a callused hand, and have to step carefully around the black ruins of shelves and storage rooms.

Light blazes through wooden slats that, far from rotting, seem to have dried and shrivelled in the heat, while in the still air of the theatre we can still smell the thick grease of the actors' make-up, feel the whole audience lean into a woman's husky song. In 1909, a visitor to the region describes a performance in a theatre similar to this one:

The theatre profusely adorned with flags, pennants, bouquets and two artistic trophies formed by material from ladders, hoses, hard-hats and axes from the Dolores fire department provided a supreme blow to the sight. A compact audience of distinguished gentlemen and nice elegant ladies in the boxes and the stalls, formed the most enchanting scene ever witnessed by the neighbours. . .

The introduction of the Drama Club, by its director Mr. Luis Ponce, who gave a speech on the different schools of Art and its great civilizing influence, was magnificent and his luminous literary play, worthy of being heard by an audience of intellectual artists. . . With each scene, the audience exploded into applause for the novel artists who behaved like real veterans of the stage, wrote one enthused reviewer.[*]

---

[*] Enrique Valderrama, in *El Pueblo Obrero*, of Iquique, 8 January 1909 (Elizondo Bravo).

A typical evening would follow a program of *Schubert, Reminiscences by LaFertte,* poetry by someone named Ilya Gaete, a talk *Thoughts about the working press,* March, *The New Roads,* a poem by Francisco Pezoa, and a play *by Adolfo Boyer, presented by the Art and Revolution Theatre Group.*

Some of the books circulating, at least in the early 1900s, included Kropotkin's *Country, Factory and Workshops,* F.S. Merline's *Socialism or Monopolism,* Proudhon's *Moral Sanction,* Darwin's *Origin of Species* (translated as "Origin of Man") and Victor Soto Roman's *The Christian Lie.*

In 1970 Chile's ministry of education declared Humberstone a national monument. Nonetheless, by 1998 it was a ruin. Its constant visitors seemed bent on dismantling it piece by piece, every one of them walking off with a souvenir from the moment it was officially closed down in 1960, after a formal ceremony by the pool with its three-storey diving board.

But like the hundreds of other "offices" whose skeletons still dot the desert outside its walls, Humberstone, the last of the offices to close, still has a story to tell.

Open pampa. . . Nothing can hide from death's eyes. Along the ground you can see traces of the harshest times. And in the firmament, the sun collapses in a furious shout of laughter full of fire, writes Andrés Sabella, as he sings into being the north where he grew up. *If the devil had a handkerchief, it would be the desert.*

In 1886, writes Sabella, Alfredo Ossa, Juan Zuleta and Martín Rojas are camped out on the *macabre table* of the *pampa.* For years they've been searching the desert for their fortune. Behind them winds a trail littered with failures, five in total. Alfredo Ossa uses a bit of the white stuff on the ground to light a cigarette. To his surprise it crackles into flame, revealing the presence of the white gold known as nitrates that at the time composed the world's best fertilizer and were a major component of gunpowder. Without realizing it, in the flaring of a match, the glow of a cigarette, the three men have *become the key to an epoch; from their callused hands Love and Drunkenness, Streets and Monuments, Misery and Betrayal have just emerged at a full gallop . . . All they recall is that in every chunk of raw ore a smile sleeps, an impossible woman peels away her clothes, all doors are breached without a protest . . .*

There are some forty nitrate offices and stations still marked on the map in our Turistel guidebook, most of them scattered haphazardly around the pampa above Iquique, strung together by the rusty thread of the old railway that supplied and served them. We turn north along the Pan-American highway, travelling farther into the patchwork quilt of time preserved by the dry air, lit by the sun, half disguised by sand and gravel. A sign flashes by on the right, announcing, *Soquimich, Oficina Mapocho: Here our dreams begin.* I catch a glimpse of an animita, like a small blue doghouse with a marble prayer book open beside it. At a crossroads near the village of Huara we turn and drive thirteen kilometres west toward the Cerro Unita, a lonely hill rising in the midst of a gravel plain. On the western wall of that hill a tall figure, eighty-six metres high, strides or perhaps dances, with an axe in his—or is it her?—left hand. To the left floats a circular figure that could be the sun, a severed head, or a star. The Sacrificer still rules over this stretch of desert.

These are my first geoglyphs. *Arte rupestre.* I've seen the term in books and museum flyers, but until now it meant nothing to me. Now the three of us stare at the graffiti giant carefully carved on the desert's "wall," narrow paths cleared of rock and surface shale until the white bone of the mountain appears, thousands of years ago, part of a ritual or simply a road sign, now hedged in by the wild scrawls left by four-wheel-drive vehicles that have roared up and over the hill, directionless and destructive. Above all, blind.

Returning to the highway, we continue northward, seeing the gigantic flat "cakes" of waste ore (*tortas*) left behind by the nitrate offices. Occasionally an old chimney rears its battered rusty head to announce the Oficina Peñasol, Baquedano, Mapocho, Ramírez, Santiago, Constancia, Valparaíso, Primitiva, Germania, Agua Santa. Like the names of ships they breathe stories, these offices that were really small, inward-looking, self-referent towns, small vertical stains on the horizontal desert—I try to make sense of the names but only end up with more confusion: Primitive, German, Holy Water. Empty names on the map, empty buildings on the landscape, emptied of human voices, populated by ghosts of wind.

We stop again, parking beside the highway to gawk at more geoglyphs. No single figure, this massive outflowing of art and sentiment explodes in rectangles like jugglers' props, staircase up and down, over the head of yet another Sacrificer-like figure, a lonely (severed?) head, the sun atop an entire adjacent hill, a small thread tying a circle (the moon?) like a pet dog to its flight.

We—Patricio and I, with Camilo a quiet passenger in the back seat—are following the map in Turistel, our favourite guidebook (Chile's only guidebook). We argue with the text, jabbing our fingers at its spotty pages. The detailed information it offers omits as much as it includes, ushering us through the official version of the story, the official landscape, trying to tempt our tourist dollars out of our pockets without compromising its stitched-together version of the past. But its delicate and ambitious one-sided fabric is torn over and over as we flash by a geoglyph or an animita, and the oral culture, the memories of silenced peoples, battling with the written word.

Past the Pampa del Tamarugal, past the ghosts of yet another office, Zapiga, and the turn-off to Pisagua's port. The Tiliviche Ranch still literally holds the key to the British cemetery, one room full of secrets in this mansion of the past. After a few misses we find a road to the left of the highway that winds down into a modest oasis, with a trickle of clear water nourishing bright green at the very bottom. A sad man with blue eyes haunts the old house. He's descended from the first Brit to "own" this oasis, who planted it with acres of alfalfa to feed the mules that carried the nitrates from the offices to the ports, and wood, grain, even water, from ports to offices. He loans us a large brass key and points us across the creek to the cemetery.

Great wealth. Great hardship. Women came here, and children were born. Children who never left. James Thomas Humberstone, died 1 June 1939, aged eighty-nine, *Peace, Perfect Peace*, lies under a marble tombstone, *Deeply Loved* by family and friends, who have long since died themselves, his lifetime spanning the great booms and the final bust of the nitrate business that both made him rich and chained him to the desert. His wife lies here too, Louisa Irene Jones, died 27 August 1942, along with Maira Jane Jones (her mother?) who died in Iquique on 27 February 1926, aged ninety, widow of Captain Lewis Jones. She too was mourned by her children, long dead; her grandchildren and great-grandchildren, scattered survivors, pepper the world. Tiny tombstones mark the greatest griefs, children's graves, in the marble garden, an almost endless supply of hope briefly embraced, then buried: Amy Agnes Humberstone, 11 February 1881, aged one year, five months; sister Irene Cecilia, 24 November 1882, aged one year, three months; brother, Arthur Edmond, died 11 April 1885, aged one year, three months; brother Horace James Lewis, died 3 May 1885, aged one year, nine months. A very un-Chilean pine casts a piercing, fragrant net across the graves, gathers them all in.

Further along, Janet Hall, wife of George Seton Steel of Iquique, died here in Tiliviche on 9 October 1877, less than a month after their infant son, George Seton, died in Iquique. A stone recalls the life of Henry North, who died at the age of thirty-eight in Pisagua (but wasn't buried there; we will visit that cemetery later this afternoon), on 9 June 1883—perhaps he was a son of Colonel John Thomas North, the nitrate king.

A good place for a library or at least an archive, I think, but of course there is no such thing: the landscape lies bare, struggling to drink and breathe, nourished by a scant trickle of water, the acres of crops once ruffled by the wind gone silent now, as they shrivel and turn back to clay and gravel.

Humberstone, Steel; North, whose name became synonymous with the northern desert where he made his fortune. The names match the place, as if the whole desert and its history were the cunning creation of a novelist . . . And as if our presence here were part of the novelist's design too, we stand gazing at the graves as another century prepares to turn, studying the ciphers of events a hundred years ago, a hundred years from now, pages flipped forward and back, the Andean cycle hard spun, time moving like a weaver's card advancing through the warp, then turning back to leave another line, another layer of the same, unchanging pattern, repeated through the work.

Are we, then, always facing the same disasters? Marrying the same decisions for better or for worse?

For John Henry North, *London was a courtesan kneeling at his feet*, says Andrés Sabella, the northern poet. Although Sabella buys into the official story that North was a down-at-the-heels Englishman who struck it rich during the nitrate boom, Harold Blakemore, the historian (a clipped British voice that hides his passion under a layer of cool control) describes him as the son of a prosperous coal merchant. North was educated in a middle-class school in Leeds and apprenticed to Shaw, North and Watson in Huslet, *builders of mills and boats, one of whose partners was a cousin of his father's*. North teamed up with Maurice Jewell, appointed the first British vice-consul in Iquique in 1879, and together they ran a prosperous business importing machinery, tools and other merchandise for the nitrate offices. They developed strong ties with the new, steam-powered shipping lines that were beginning to ply the coastal waters off the Atacama desert. While most of the other foreigners were trying to cut their losses and avoid the war, North was developing a system to bring water to Iquique from Arica. In 1878 he rented storage and other facilities from the Tarapaca Water Company. When its owners fled the war, the new Chilean authorities recognized the company as North's. You win some and lose some, he might have added, since the Chileans sank his ship, the *Marañon*. But North eventually turned a profit from that disaster too. With the help of his friends Robert Harvey and John Dawson, North ended up holding most of the certificates of ownership of the nitrate offices. In 1880, with only 2,848 people employed in the nitrate industry, the Chilean authorities appointed Harvey inspector general of the nitrate offices, while Dawson was a banker based in Valparaiso.

According to some observers, North used these contacts to ferret out the Chilean government's intentions vis-à-vis the nitrate offices, and then proceeded to profit from his insider information. For others, he made an astute bet on a long shot of his own. Either way, he won the jackpot. By 1882, nitrate exports were on the rise,[*] and at the same time, the Shanks process was reducing production costs. When rising production threatened to depress prices, North and other industry leaders began to form combines to limit shipments and bolster prices.

Throughout the rest of the eighties, North, who had resettled his family in England, founded company after company to exploit Chilean nitrates, paying his shareholders generous dividends.[†] By 1888, as demand and consequently profits peaked, London's stock exchange had become the international centre for the business of extracting Chile's nitrates and selling them to the world.

Newspapers in Liverpool and London praised North's astute business sense, his brilliance and above all his results, although North quotes one Stephen Williamson who told a friend (an intelligent voice, soured somewhat by envy's wisdom) from Liverpool that North was a *typical charlatan,*

---

[*] To 492,000 metric tons, up from 359,000 the year before.
[†] 25 per cent in 1885 and 20 per cent in 1887.

although smart. He's currently the most important man in Eng-land, except perhaps Gladstone! Just adding North's name to a share issue could increase its premiums 300 per cent. For a decade North bought and sold certificates for the nitrate offices, sometimes for ten times the price he'd initially paid. *The Economist* questioned the legitimacy of North's claims for his companies' values, and Williamson continued to criticize North's methods in his private correspondence.

North, Blakemore's clear, controlled voice tells us, played the role of Nitrate King to the hilt, building a palatial mansion on Avery Hill in Eltham, Kent (my grandmother's childhood turf), and organizing fabulous parties and outings in its extensive grounds. At Christmas, he invited the whole town to share a roast ox and enjoy fruit, candy and other presents. He restored ancient abbeys, raised racehorses and became the most popular man in London. In the meantime, however, Williamson and *The Economist*, like a Greek cho-rus, complain about the unjustifiable proliferation of nitrate companies, worrying symptoms of speculation, harbingers of over-supply and therefore dropping prices.

As North bluffed his way through London, the Chilean government enjoyed its own boom, thanks to export taxes of 27 to 45 per cent on North's and others' nitrates. Thus began Chile's traditional dependence on mineral exports for a sizeable chunk of the money in its national treasury. Miners turned their back on other, hitherto profitable areas (like copper), and glutted themselves on nitrates. Copper production plunged, nitrates soared from 60,000 metric tons in 1879 to 1.46 million in 1900. During the last two decades of the nineteenth century these lonely offices of the Atacama produced 18 million metric tons of nitrates, worth some US$3.575 billion (in 1975 dollars).

Hand-painted draperies from Italy, fine carved furniture with delicate insets of the finest pearl from France and England: much of the nitrate bonanza went to importing luxuries from Europe. The now tiny port of Pisagua and many other nitrate-related towns acquired elegant homes, waterworks (mostly owned by North), banks (mostly North's), railways (North's too), and luxury theatres attended by dignitaries dressed in (almost) the latest fashions from London. Sarah Bernhardt herself played in *The Lady of the Camellias* in the elegant municipal theatre of Iquique.

North may have been the king of the Norte Grande, but a Chilean, José Manuel Balmaceda, was still the country's elected president. His government (1886–1891) chose to invest the windfall profits from nitrates in public works projects, transportation and education. In March 1889 Balmaceda, a liberal in Chile's very conservative political world, travelled to Iquique by ship. There, his voice still echoes off the rocky cliffs, along the sandy beaches:

The industry's problems stem from two sources: first, the foreign monopoly that attempts to raise the price by limiting production, and secondly, the prohibitive prices charged by the Nitrate Railways Company, which also tend to stop nitrate exports . . . Private ownership is almost entirely held by foreigners particularly of one nationality. It would be preferable for this property to be held by Chileans also . . . but if national capital is indolent or hesitant, we shouldn't be surprised that foreign capital fills this gap with care and intelligence. . .

The monopoly of nitrates cannot be held by the State, whose fundamental mission is only to guarantee property and freedom. Nor should it be the work of private [firms], be they Chilean or foreign, because we will never accept the economic tyranny of the majority or the minority. The State will always have to hold on to enough of the ownership of nitrates in order to safeguard, through its influence, its production and sales.*

Toward the end of that same year, as the nitrate industry began to show a surplus and another producers' cartel planned to artificially reduce exports and thus boost prices, Balmaceda moved to cancel the monopoly held by North's Nitrate Railway Company. North reacted by joining forces with Balmaceda's political opponents in congress, who accused Balmaceda (shades of Allende) of violating the constitution.

Although it's true that nitrates brought incalculable fortunes to the country, says the mining historian Alexander Sutulov, in the dry cold tones of someone who works hard at being objective, *it also put it in the unsustainable position of excessive dependence on one product, a dependency that was almost fatal, when the natural product was suddenly replaced by a synthetic version.*

In 1890, the bottom fell out of the demand and prices collapsed. Chile's first major strike in the mining industry and, a year later, its only civil war ensued. Balmaceda died an abrupt and violent death, committing suicide rather than relinquishing power in the midst of social conflagration.†

---

* José Balmaceda (Blakemore)

† Interestingly, the Chilean military has always tried to argue that the coup of 11 September 1973 was actually a civil war, and that the four thousand or so people who died or disappeared during the seventeen years that followed had died fighting. The report of the Commission for Truth and Reconciliation, published in March 1991, and innumerable reports by human rights organizations, including the United Nations, Amnesty International, Human Rights Watch, the Chilean Human Rights Commission and the Committee for Defence of the People (CODEPU) indicate that only a handful of those killed died as the result of fighting. Most were executed, disappeared after arrest or died during torture.

In the decade just before the war, workers flocked to the
Atacama's nitrate industry, to the space and the illusion of
freedom (a.k.a. wealth) of the Norte Grande. Between
1880 and 1890, the number of workers employed in the
nitrate industry rose from 2,848 to 13,060. Many came
from the lush fields of southern Chile where they had been
little more than slaves. For them, the desert *shone . . . like
an abandoned sack of gold.* Sabella's voice, rich with poetry
and fine red wine. It is the job of the recruiter, dressed in
his elegant English suit with a gold watch pinned to his
breast, to wave that sack of gold before the eyes of peasants
entrapped on southern farms or the unemployed who had
flocked to the city of Santiago, the port of Valparaiso. He'd
walk into a southern bar and ask, *My friends, aren't you
drinking?* And he'd order drinks all round, tossing his down
and asking for another while his companions nursed theirs
tenderly all through a lengthy evening. A gold ring would
flash on his finger as he described the marvels of the nitrates lying on the ground just waiting to be picked up, the
women dressed in silk, looking like queens, the generous
wages. When his bewitched listeners asked how to get
there, he generously provided transport on a ship from
Valparaiso. So they stepped out of small, secure lives
within a tight social framework into the sucking vacuum
of freedom, complete with all its betrayals.

The reality, as Basilio Osinaga, a former nitrate worker,
told historian González Miranda, was somewhat different:
*. . . There was no minimum wage, you worked and earned
according to the material you extracted. If you did badly in
the* calicheras *where you were working, you earned nothing . . .
[If this went on too long, the worker simply] left with the*
camanchaca.

Between 1895 and 1917, the workforce in the desert doubled again, to 56,378, and the nitrate offices spread long fingers of activity from the ocean to the Andes and beyond, into Argentina and Bolivia. For many the Atacama must have seemed like the long memory of a teardrop, shed centuries past, stretching from north to south, squeezed between sea and mountain. But the caravans cut across the Atacama, feeling their way along narrow ravines and through river valleys lined with the subdued green of vegetation forever under siege. Vegetable gardens and wheat began to cede to the temptation of alfalfa as the demand for forage for the mules made this the easiest and most profitable crop to grow in the oases. Today many of those same fields lie abandoned, as the mules no longer ply the routes back and forth across the desert, no longer lace salt and snow together with the ceaseless rocking of their gait.

In February 1911, furious snowstorms high up in the Andes caused flash flooding down below in the nitrate towns of Pozo Almonte, Huara and Pisagua. Many workers' camps were destroyed and nitrates processing suspended. June of the same year brought rain and violent thunderbolts steaming out of the sky toward Antofagasta, while Calama's noisy streets were temporarily hushed under a miraculous mantle of snow. Throughout July, San Pedro de Atacama lay under ten inches of snow for the first and perhaps the only time in its known history. The phenomenon could only be compared to 1885, when forty days of rain brought flooding to the tamarugo forest.

Most of the time, however, there was no such thing as rain or snow in the Atacama. Along the coast, fishing villages turned into thriving towns and fancy cities in miniature, sucking up the moisture from desert oases, as they shipped nitrates out and luxuries in for their English owners. In the Andean foothills, up the Tarapaca ravine and in the small oases of Pica, Camina, Huatacondo and others, the newcomers stimulated agricultural production as they battled over scarce water, buying all the fruit, beans, meat and wine available, and when that was not enough, bringing in supplies from southern Chile.

The system, the harsh, lonely life, the sense of possibility, sparked two major national strikes, in 1890 and 1907. It's shocking to read the two virtually identical lists of the workers' demands, formulated almost twenty years apart. In the time between the two strikes their bitter struggles seem to have achieved very little real change. Above all, in both 1890 and 1907, they wanted an end to the ficha system, an end to the monopoly of the company stores, stable salaries at a fixed conversion rate, safety measures on the job, respect for their right to elaborate petitions and hold assemblies, and schools in every office. In 1890 they also fought for an end to alcoholic beverages in camps, an end to the charges on drinking water and an end to company control of their correspondence.

Sergio González, a modern sociologist, calls the nitrate period *the heroic period of Chile's workers' movement, the epoch in which men and women . . . built a cosmo-vision based on rationalism, but they believed in it with the fervour of an Amerindian mythology.*

This is the living Bowman's time. He was enthralled by the drivers as they hollered, prodded and pushed herds of up to a hundred cattle from the fertile alfalfa meadows of Salta in Argentina, up and over the Andes and down to the hungry nitrate mines on the desert below. *Finely bred stock would perish at once; but these hardy beasts are able to go two or three days without water,* he says. *The cattlemen are Indians or half-breeds from the Salta region or the bordering valleys. They know all the trails and watering places, and they know what the cattle can stand.* The men themselves lived on dried meat, *chuño* (dried potatoes), some rice and a meagre soup. They slept wrapped in saddle blankets or ponchos, and spent the thirteen or so days that it took to reach San Pedro de Atacama, rest and food, herding the cattle together against the wind, hoping they'd miss the gales of snow and dust known as the *viento blanco* (white wind).

In San Pedro de Atacama, men and animals would feast and rest for a night or two before completing the last three days of their journey, across the desert to the nitrate fields, where the men were paid 45 pesos for the entire journey.

The wisdom of the traditional routes, says Bowman, was demonstrated in 1912 when the Abaroa brothers tried a more northerly route through Chiu Chiu and Calama. They lost twenty-eight of their sixty cattle and the journey took twenty days.

Sabella describes the mules: *They were beautiful in their breadth, when work had painted only the palest grey clouds in their eyes. But as the calendar progressed, they started to collapse, to turn into a sad hide, becoming nothing more than a creaky skeleton, covered by a bloody, scraped ferocious layer [of skin].*

The nitrate era, with its wild ride of boom and bust, wealth and want, changed Chile forever, turning a small agricultural country with an all-powerful oligarchy into a semi-industrialized nation with a significant working class. The nitrate workers were aware of events in Europe and Russia, and enthusiastic debates raged over anarchism, socialism and other utopias, and how to achieve them.

Until one day, like a lament
from the heart's deepest chamber,
along the streets of the encampment
a rebellious note resounded:
they were the proud-chested kings,
theirs a clamour of many angers,
the trumpet blast of the rights
of poor working people.

We drive through a landscape marked by tortas, the giant, tomb-like cakes of waste left behind after the nitrates were extracted. In the distance we see the occasional chimney or rusting barracks. These are the hieroglyphs of the nitrate era, a language we can still decipher if we take the time. The theatre at Humberstone once rocked with music, applause, dreams. Among the plays performed were many written by workers themselves. They had their own newspapers, which travelled the pampa with the caravans, were slipped from hand to hand, contradicting official versions and calling on workers to become major players in their own lives.

Newspapers, plays, popular poetry, much of it originally published in the newspapers, an explosion of debate, literature, a questioning of life's harsh contours, a deep longing that created fertile soil for the foreign ideas that arrived daily with the ships in the harbour. Perhaps at no other time in its island life was popular Chile, as opposed to its powerful elite, so connected and so anxious to follow the ideas that were transforming the outside world.

Thus northern movements like the *mancomunal*, the union movement, gave birth to political leaders who cut their teeth working in the nitrate offices or the workers' newspapers of Iquique, then reached southward, joining forces with similar movements in the capital, Santiago, or beyond.

Luis Emilio Recabarren, writer, journalist, publisher, and eventually founder of Chile's Socialist (later Communist) Party, wrote scathing editorials criticizing conditions in the nitrate offices, as did another founder of what became one of Latin America's strongest communist parties, Elias LaFertte. In his memoirs, LaFertte wrote, *I spent two years working in the offices of Argentina, Resurrección, San Lorenzo and Santa Lucía. At the beginning of 1910, I ended up unemployed and went back to live in Alto de San Antonio with my mother.* The Heights of St. Anthony in Iquique, named after the patron saint of lost things.

Like the conquistadors people went north, twentieth-century historians say, *to make money and not to put down roots.* But as the nitrate industry rode out cycle after cycle, profits soaring to the heights then plunging into the depths, it took the economy along with it. In 1890, on the eve of civil war, the nitrate workers organized Chile's first general strike. In 1901, Iquique's mancomunal organized its first strike. In 1902, trolley operators in Santiago went out. In 1903, the mancomunales of Tocopilla did likewise, followed by coal workers and longshoremen whose movement ended face to face with a regiment. In 1905, a famous *meat strike* in Santiago protested the high cost of living and ended in riots, with 70 dead and 300 wounded.

In 1907, the country still had no labour laws at all, in spite of the enormous industrial growth that came with the nitrate industry, Santiago's growth as an urban centre, the coal mines in the southern towns of Lota and Coronel, and the widespread development of railroads connecting the far-flung towns scattered throughout the gangly country Chile had become.

Companies did as they pleased, and while there was growing tension between foreign interests and the Chileans themselves, the foreigners had the capital and the technology to develop Chile's new "properties," and the national treasury was glutting itself on taxes, creating a strong incentive for the country's oligarchy and its politicians to keep the nitrate operations running very much as they had for the past thirty or forty years.

But hunger was blowing like wind through the desert cities and nitrate offices, breathing its heat into the seething frustration fanned by the company stores. Pedlars, some of them former nitrate workers, roamed the pampa, trying to break the company's stranglehold. Like the ubiquitous dust, the rhetoric of revolution and sacrifice was in the air too, carried by the pedlars and workers as they drifted from one office to another.

Sabella: *Unemployment pulsed like a macabre bee. The workers watched the pampa turn into a horrible pit of hunger. It was a bitter time of tears and anguish. Children tried to smile and horrible grimaces shattered their faces. . . The days seemed longer, under a sky blackened by blasphemy.*

In early December 1907, strikes began to break out like pox, starting with 300 nitrate railway workers, spreading quickly to urban railway workers and then port-workers anxious to earn the same raise (16 pence) as the nitrate railway workers had been promised. By the tenth of December, workers in the San Lorenzo office had gone on strike and on the eleventh, when the administrator refused to consider their demands, they began to march across the desert toward San Antonio where, rumour had it, the governor himself would speak. The desert was suddenly alive with people walking or riding the trains headed into

Iquique. Their cause was just, the need great, their hope wide and open as the desert sky. Exhausted, they settled down for the night, rolling themselves into a blanket beside a dying fire. Mostly they zigzagged across the desert from one nitrate office to another, relying on their fellow workers for a bite to eat, some wood to feed a fire, or steaming hot tea to warm their callused hands and help them to forget their blistered feet, their weary, aching bones.

When the governor failed to appear in San Antonio, the workers and their families poured over the cliffs and down into Iquique. Leoncio Marín watched the marchers from a moving train: *In the very centre of the column we could see the colours of the Chilean, Peruvian and Bolivian flags waving in the proud wind, as they led an international army, marching under the shield of the sun of justice, which lit them up and called to them, not from Iquique as their imaginations suggested, but from eternity itself. . . They went, then, an army to clamour for the bread torn from the homes of its soldiers.*

The train stopped for a while and the marchers rested.

The machinist gave them all the water he was carrying and passengers provided them with fruit, bottles of beer and so on. Once this was done, the strikers, without shouting a single subversive slogan, said goodbye with many thanks. Immediately the train set out and they continued their pilgrimage.[*]

On Sunday, the fifteenth of December, the strikers gathered at Iquique's racetrack to present their demands to the Chilean authorities, who agreed to intercede with the nitrate company owners on the workers' behalf. They wanted their fichas converted into pence at the going rate of the currency, with no discounts. They wanted the scales

---

[*] Leoncio Marín (Deves).

at the company stores checked for accuracy and they wanted low-grade ore evaluated for its nitrate content instead of flung from the reception ramp, depriving them of payment.

The newspaper *La Patria* describes the *strange aspect* of the racetrack, more accustomed to *elegant and lovely ladies*, but now full of *husky, corpulent rogues, their faces toasted by the pampa sun*. A lengthy rally ensued, with high-sounding speeches from the local authorities, occasionally drowned out by the response of the crowd, and loud shouts of *Yes* and *No*. Julio Guzmán García, the acting regional governor, and Antonio Viera Gallo, a local lawyer, failed to convince the workers to return to the desert, and they set up camp around the city.

Rallies filled Pisagua and Zapiga too with the hurrahs of workers, while the strike spread and thousands more marched on the port. In the city, the workers organized domestic life in the Santa María School and a strike committee distributed food, limited drinking, controlled traffic and provided public services. Other committees approached local merchants and unions for support, which they generally received. A letter to the president of Chile was signed by nitrate workers, merchants, owners of foundries, nitrate railway workers and others.

As the days passed, thousands of workers continued to descend on the city, and soldiers disembarked in the bay. Altogether, some 26,000 people moved into Iquique and camped out at the Santa María School.

Accounts differ sharply on what happened as the weekend approached. A parliamentarian, Malaquias Concha, in port at the time, would later tell the chamber of deputies that he saw a peaceful, orderly strike. Negotiations broke off at the nitrate-office owners' behest, in spite of a government offer to pay for half the increase the workers were requesting.

The regional governor, Carlos Eastman, declared a state of siege, and ordered the nitrate workers to stay in the Santa María School. Notes and emissaries flew back and forth, but the strikers refused to return to the desert. The commander of the ship *Ministro Zenteno*, then in the port, commented that *The alarm in the city was great and all the families began to leave their homes to . . . take refuge in the ships in the port*. Rumours flew that strikers were going to torch the city.

Eduardo Deves writes that *The coast and the interior, enemy worlds, just as the cosmos and chaos are enemies, one open to culture and temperate climes . . . the other closed to thought and its products, segregated and coarsened by a freezing climate . . . The upper class conceived of the worker and especially those from the interior in such a way as to make it reasonable to expect the worst excesses and atrocities from him.*

Unless they are pathological killers, people tend to murder only when convinced their own survival is threatened. In 1973 (and again in 1999 during Pinochet's extradition trial in London) the military and its right-wing supporters justified the slaughter of their opponents with the story of *Plan Z*, a nonexistent hit list of important Chileans marked for murder by the Allende government, which they claimed to have discovered. Undoubtedly, many Chileans believed in this list.

Perhaps some of those involved in the *resolution* of the *situation* at the Santa María School in Iquique genuinely feared the workers. For whatever reason, the workers wouldn't yield to their demands. They had to find another way to get rid of them. All Sunday afternoon strikers converged on the school, following the governor's orders.

Just before 2:30 p.m., a fully armed unit of the army formed near the school, under the command of General Roberto Silva.[*] He estimated there were some 5,000 people inside the school and another 2,000 milling around outside. For the next hour, the workers continued to make impassioned speeches as the general's emissaries tried to persuade them to leave. Four hundred striking stevedores joined the nitrate workers in the school. The general then went in himself and ordered them to leave. By 3:00 p.m., even some of the strike leaders asked the crowd to disperse. The crowd shouted back: better to leave Chile than return to the pampa as slaves. *Viva Argentina!*

A few minutes later, Silva decided: . . . *as head of the troops, exhausted by an enormous responsibility for future outbreaks, I ordered them to shoot the agitators or I would shoot myself.*

Minutes remained.

Commander Aguirre made his way through the crowd, shouting that they would be shot if they didn't leave. No one moved. He left. Over the next few minutes, some two hundred people uneasily made their way, amidst derisive whistles, toward the street. But Silva issued his final order.

An army picket and a navy picket fired. Silva said that the strikers shot back, injuring three soldiers and two sailors, and killing two horses. The terrified crowd surged toward the entrance onto Montt Square. The troops, panicked by falling bodies, and convinced the workers were

---

[*] General Roberto Silva Renard. I will use only his first surname here, for simplicity in English.

charging, blasted away, then charged, lances raised, into the crowd.

According to some, the guns only fell silent at last when Vicar Rucker rushed into the square, plucked a baby's corpse from among the dead and threw himself between troops and workers, begging them to stop. Afterward, Javier Ovalle Castillo watched as the police wagons drew up and men . . . *threw the dead, the dying and those with only slight injuries into the back of their wagons, to rush them off to a common grave. . . The injured coughed up parts of their intestines, [or] clutched severed arms and legs to their bodies torn apart by bullets, and fought sadly against thieves after watches, rings, chains and purses and the gravediggers themselves, who were under order to take them, with what little life was left them, to the common grave.*

Nicolas Palacios, a contemporary physician and chronicler, says the massacre was referred to as a *battle* and celebrated *as a victory in the Chilean and English clubs, [where] abundant champagne was drunk to celebrate the day's success.*

Blessed victims who descended
from the Pampa, full of faith,
on their arrival, all they found
the vile machine gun.

Eternal insult for the beasts
who massacred without compassion!
Forever stained by workers' blood
the visual stigma of a curse!

How many died remains the eternal conundrum of Chilean history, with estimates ranging from 200 to 10,000.

Their memory still burns today. We think their deaths are what matters, but we're wrong, we've stumbled over the truth and not recognized it. That's what pushes Ñusta on, what she mutters between her teeth as she struggles across the desert toward the forest of tamarugos, eagerly searching for a well that will make the foundation of a new city possible.

This is really a work of science fiction, I said. *First you must build the world, and then you must inhabit it. . .* Ñusta, this is really about being nobody, long centuries of untold stories that don't matter to anyone who writes things down. Your story. My story. Their story. How ordinary people have found ways to write themselves into their own history, if no one else's. The animitas are such small, concrete parentheses in the midst of the desert, who would take them to be temples of resistance? Not necessarily raised against the actual, current world, they are rather memory's cry, bent on piercing forgetfulness, the oblivion history condemns us to.

I exist, each one says, we join in saying, when we stop to refill a jar of flowers or water the tamarugo tree. You existed and I am reaching across time to take your hand and offer you this chance to speak. But my hands come up empty. I have not found you yet, may never find you. All I've found today is the whistling of a ghostly youth as he strolls along an empty lane in Humberstone. He tells me there were moments when they bore you along on their shoulders, like a boxing champion. Because in the end (did you whisper this to me last night?) what mattered wasn't the massacre at all, but rather the fact of their uprising, Chile's first, their daring to challenge, their movement beyond the control of the nitrate owners, their own government, the sheer joy of banging on a door, flinging it open and marching through. No matter what the cost, they could never go back. They never did go back.

In the spark of their resistance, their bid for a freedom that was beyond their reach, that looked as close and remained as distant as the Andes themselves, Ñusta found new life. Not in the nostalgia of the nitrate owners, the Diego de Almagros of another epoch who came to make themselves great and succeeded or went mad in the desert of their attempts. No. At first she came closest to them at night, infiltrating the stories the women told as they put their children to sleep. She returned in dreams, then carried on in the songs sung by Bolivian miners, whose festive costumed dances repelled the owners but attracted the miners and their wives.

Far from the green fields of the south, amongst the dry salt that might one day fertilize them, their spirit, your spirit, darts with the desert wind from one abandoned office to another. Perhaps freedom is always relative, can only be understood in contrast to what went before, the great haciendas where the farmworkers remained virtual slaves, their women the subject of the owners' bridal right, the labour of woman and man and every child tithed to the folks who lived in Buenos Aires or Europe.

To work for a wage, even as an exile in the desert, meant that a worker could turn his back and slip away, guided by Ñusta's moon through the desert night, rising with the next day's sun to labour in another office. These were choices that had not existed before. They changed the faces, bent to work, bent to avoid the sun. They changed the thoughts behind the faces.

A youth still whistles as he walks the streets of Humberstone, but he whistles his own song. Even if the next day his limbs will work to another man's rhythm, he whistles his own way down the decades to the present. The smooth flow of his hips pursued by his shadow moves between the walls formed of gravel sacks, the steady flow of his stride just before me where I walk, anxious and waiting.

6

NORTE GRANDE

The Desert in Flower

To fear the worst oft cures the worst.

— William Shakespeare

The Tamarugo Forest (Atacama) 1536

YOU WALK, you think and thinking brings change. But when you're running away from something, everything is different all at once. Fear blazes in your mind more fiercely than the sun itself. Sometimes you hardly know what scares you most, as you gather the water skins, the sacks of food, the thick woollen ponchos and the copper tools that you had carefully hidden away amongst the Spaniards' supplies during the easier weeks of the journey. If you look before you, there are only the lifeless stretches of the Norte Grande, the Great and seemingly endless North, a land ruled by the total absence of life, a tyranny harsher than any you have known so far: freedom.

But if you look behind, you sense Diego de Almagro stalking the bare prints of your flight, stamped into the desert's surface now and forever. He sniffs at them like a dog, then points, gesturing his men onward toward you; they brandish their iron swords that clap like thunder when they hit a shield. At night, the fires burn low, but the flames leap, lighting your mind with their sizzling orange as if it were a cave. Almagro is galloping toward you dressed in the bloodstained robes of the Sacrificer, congealed gore at his wrists, a necklace of human skulls at his throat, and behind him long trails of chains crossing the desert like the Incan highways, each town marked by a headless body or a disembodied head.

Still, sometimes in your sleep you find yourself turning back to him, a terrible longing in your throat, a yearning to wail. Cuzco, glimpsed over his shoulder, is calling you back to the quiet world of the Acllawasi, a room filled with the shining black hair of lovely young women selected for their physical perfection, the chatter of gossip and laughter, the finely woven fabrics of the gods growing and flowing like water from the light touch of their fingers. You would go to him and seize him again in your arms, your eyes squeezed shut until he carried you back and you were gazing into the golden eyes of Mama Huaco, combing her long tresses with the light gossamer of a cloth, prostrating yourself before her first thing in the morning, then bringing her the Empire's best corn and chichas to help her break her fast.

Ñusta is thinking, strangely, in this wall-less, building-less place, of the stones, the way they were carved and fitted to form the smooth and solid walls, the foundations and temples of her existence, how she loved to run her fingers over their coolness when the sun burned hot and steady over Cuzco, and there was the shout of strange voices and a myriad of tongues hawking their wares in the open plazas. She remembers how during the siesta hours if she was anxious and unable to sleep her eyes would pretend the lines between the level rows of stones were highways and she was walking them. Now her callused feet hurry over real highways, barely touching the ground. The murmur of woollen robes around her is the only sign that she is not alone, all breath saved to fuel this desperate bitter flight toward a disaster she can feel pressing in around her. During the day she huddles together with her motley group of followers; they cover themselves with desert-stained wool and try to sleep. When night falls, a hasty fire marks a moment for food and then they're off like chasquis, racing on. But those Incan messengers were retracing the boundaries of the known empire with their feet, renewing each border and strengthening the lines of their connection. Ñusta is running through emptiness, seeking to cut away the ties that bind her to Almagro. Those ties that also bind her to her own past. The man who saved her life, even as he destroyed her world.

Because there will be those who whisper that she isn't really Incan but came like so many others from some captive people, part of the tithes paid, that the man who would one day become the Huillac Uma picked her out of a new flock of young girls with smooth skin, eyes as brown and full as the dark earth nourishing the fields of corn, and that he ordered her to be taken to Cuzco and raised with the other girls in the Acllawasi. There, the story goes, she was initiated into the mystery of the Incan ceremonies, serving the Incan Queen, the Coya Mama Ocllo and her line of ancestors, whose ancient mummies were carefully preserved and tended in the temple, and once a year carried out to survey the cities and the fields.

A Spanish conquistador's voice, impressed in spite of himself: *There were to be found in the city certain temples containing many figures of solid gold and silver, in the shape of women* . . . *I saw more than twenty that must have been replicates of dead ladies, because each one had a court of pages and ladies in waiting who served them as if they were living; they offered them food and cleaned them with such obedience and respect as if they were living flesh, and they prepared such exquisite foods as if these figures would really eat* . . .

She dressed them in the finest robes of her weaving and spoke to them as if they were alive, and when the Spanish came she watched Atahualpa's men carry the least of them out of the temple and toward the crucible where her future was being forged. But she didn't know that at first, when the rough Spaniards erupted into her world, eyeing the women of the Acllawasi as if they had discovered the world's finest whorehouse. She tried to go on with her duties, she pushed the women around her to continue in their labours as if all were normal, as if by carrying on their rites they could weave time back into order, place the Spanish in a small corner of the ongoing world and keep them there. They all tried to keep everything functioning as they believed it always had. But this was doubly difficult for Ñusta. Her servants were treating her as if she herself were a queen, preparing her for the next Inti Raymi, the great ceremony to the Sun.

For years, like all the women, from the great Coya, the Inca's wife, on down, Ñusta had worshipped and tended to the Sun's wife, Mamaquilla, the Moon herself, while others who followed her tended the long line of Coyas who stood mummified and saintly behind them. The Coyas as carefully chosen as the Inca himself. No one inherited, all those chosen had to earn the honour and glory of ruling the Incan empire. There were no guarantees. When Capac Yupanqui's Coya went mad, the Sun ruled he could marry someone else who would really help him to govern. When the Inca was away, the Coya ruled, and when the Imperial Council could reach no decision it was she who broke the ties of their inertia. Ñusta waited anxiously like every woman in the Acllawasi for the Coya's decision on the future. She dreamed of the greatness that might come to her down the path.

From the outside, the Spanish saw that *In the great palace was the great Coya, almost as great as the Inca himself. There were temples, bathrooms and gardens for her and for her ñustas, her ladies in waiting, and there were more than two hundred of them. She was in charge of marrying them to the gentlemen who served in positions of honour in the Inca's house; it was wondrous when the great Coya emerged from her palace and she was always served with the same majesty as the Inca.**

At first, life was joyful. She woke every morning wondering whom she would marry. Would she serve the Inca, perhaps even become one of his secondary court of wives? The great Father had chosen her and watched over her education with great jealousy and care—or would she remain forever in the temple? She refused to contemplate the third option, a refusal that became more difficult with every day that passed, as the four-year cycle advanced relentlessly, and each day thrust her forward to the next religious feast, known as the *capacocha*. Its approach, the preparations, forced her to recall the last, when *Four young girls . . . were*

* Martin Murua (Silverblatt)

chosen, pure and unwrinkled, the essence of beauty, daughters of royalty. . . From the four corners of Peru they came, from Colla-suyo, Antisuyo, Contisuyo and Chinchaisuyo. People emerged from their towns, marching out to join them, their local gods, the huacas, held aloft on their shoulders, riding above the ocean of dark heads and strong hands, along the Incan highways toward Cuzco where they merged and met in the central plaza. There, where the Inca sat on his throne, they marched around him twice and then paused, bowing low before the Inca. He greeted them cheerfully. Once they were all gathered together he spoke directly to the Sun in dark terms saying . . . receive these chosen ones to your service. He raised gold goblets on high and toasted the Sun with chicha many years old especially prepared by the Coya for this purpose. The high priest slit the throat of a white lamb, sprinkling a white corn dough with its blood, calling this sanca *and sharing it so the Inca and all his court thus took communion together. They shared what was left of the meat of the ram sacrificed to the Sun. The feast lasted for days. One hundred thousand llamas were sacrificed.**

The first time this happened to Ñusta she was a child running among the legs of adults dressed up in their Incan finest. They raised their golden goblets to toast some event that was occurring high above her head and far away. But for the second Inti Raymi, which included the capacochas, she was fourteen. She still remembers the beauty of Tanta Carhua as she marched into the capital at the head of a procession that included virtually everybody from her home province, the village of Urcon. Small and lovely, her features perfectly balanced, her hair oiled and shining dark and blue as deep water on a moonlit night. Even the huacas of her town stood second to her, as she walked proudly toward the central plaza

---

* Hernández Príncipe (Silverblatt)

and the Inca on his throne. Ñusta worshipped the ground
she walked on, could not imagine her ever being destroyed.

A few steps behind her, her father Poma walked, every
bit as proudly, no hesitation in his long strides, nodding to
people left and right. The Inca himself received Tanta
Carhua, holding feast after feast in her honour throughout
the Inti Raymi, nodding and laughing occasionally at
something that she said. Was she to marry the Inca, Ñusta
wondered, would this be a wedding feast? There were
honours too for Tanta Carhua's father and his court, above
all her father, about to become governor of the entire
region where their village was located, a man who'd paid
the highest price, willingly, a perfect example of the kind of
citizen the Inca liked to conquer. (Ah, yes, because we can't
speak of just one Conquest in the Andes, but two. Both
exacted a high price. Both tended to accept payment, full
or partial, in the currency of women's flesh.)

The story of Tanta Carhua would be told everywhere
throughout the capital, wind its way through the intricate
knots of memory and along the messengers' highway, her
life the price her father paid to obtain his governorship.
After the feasting in Cuzco, she and her retinue returned
to Urcon. When the procession reached her home town,
Tanta Carhua once again marched at the head, followed
by her father and other chiefs. The chasquis later said that
seeing the food laid out to welcome her, she told them all,
*Enough feasts! The ones the Inca held for me in Cuzco were more
than enough, and they carried her from Aixa to a high peak,
where they dug and lined an underground chamber for her and
placed her in it and buried her alive.**

---

* Hernández Príncipe (Silverblatt)

During the capacocha Inca Raymi, the Inca, wined and dined (so to speak) dozens of women, including Tanta Carhua. *And when the feasting was over, they took all the women* capacochas *assigned to Cuzco to the temple of Huanacauri or the House of the Sun and put them to sleep, then lowered them into a waterless chamber where they buried them alive. The Inca sent the rest back to their own land where they met the same fate, the living currency in an exchange that left their fathers members of the privileged caste, governors. For each dead woman the priests administered a cult every year, worshipping and imploring her to care for the province of her origin.**

For ever after, Ñusta, you tried to console yourself with this, that Tanta Carhua too joined the Incan divinities, became a protector of her people and her lands, arbiter between earth and heaven, worshipped by her people, receiver of sacrifices, healer of sickness and pain. This was the way it was, the right and only way, but even when you were hidden deep within the thick walls of the Incan nunnery other voices would sometimes reach and torment you, the voices of those lamenting the other, earlier, conquest, in which the Incas were the proud conquerors and the myriad peoples of the Andes had been forced to submit. There were those few who cried out, who tried to protest: *Foreign tyranny bangs at the doors of our homes . . . if we let the Lord Inca in he'll take away our old freedom . . . the best of everything we have, the most beautiful women and girls and . . . our old customs will be exchanged for new laws. . .This tyrant will make us live forever as servants and vassals.*[†]

---

* Hernández Príncipe (Silverblatt)
† El Inca Garcilaso de la Vega (Silverblatt)

You tried to lose yourself in the endless ceremonies, as
the daughter of the high priest. Your father was bent on
moving ever higher, ever nearer to the Inca's elbow, nudging those who stood in his way, oh so politely, edging them
away until they slipped out of sight and vanished, sent off to
head foreign missions or found new temples and dynasties
in distant lands. You stood, you knelt, you marched amongst
the lines of women serving the goddesses and dead queens,
just a few feet from the parallel lines of men, you spoke in
their name, interpreted, advised, controlled your own small
court. . . You too prepared the bread for the *situa* communion, mixing the blood from sacrifices with flour, placing a
small piece in the mouth of every non-Incan subject who
visited Cuzco for the ceremonies, and sending small bites
to the Incan Federation's leading chiefs, among them Tanta
Carhua's father, so they would continue to swear their alle-
giance to the Empire.

You too were sacred, a wife of the Sun, the Inca's adopted
sister, perfect and beautiful. Sometimes when you went
out walking, the peasants would recognize you and fall to
their knees. You watched as the Empire grew. With each
new town the first building to go up was the Sun's temple
and the house for the women priestesses known as the
Mamaconas. Some of your companions would be moved
out and away to the new provinces, taking on new duties,
spreading the Incan faith, watching over the local huacas,
although for every newly conquered people, the main
huaca was always removed away to Cuzco where it could
be properly cared for, watched over, a sacred hostage to
the Empire.

When the two brothers, Atahualpa and Huáscar, went
to war over who would become the new Inca, fighting

their way through the empire, they finally reached Cuzco, where the only buildings to survive were the Sun's temple and the Mamaconas' house. By then the old ceremonies were already fraying, but none of you could stand it, could accept this, could imagine how you would fit into a new order. After the battle, you stood in the doorway and gazed at the ruins all around you, then turned your back and re-entered a world still whole, untouched, in order. You tried to forget, but the sound of weeping from all around you (it was as if the very walls were weeping) wouldn't let you.

And as you continued to grow, so too did your longing for the Coya's decision on marrying you. All around Cuzco the conquered towns and peoples insisted that woman and man lie down and know excitement and joy together, essential for life to continue. But here in the Mamaconas' house under the finery, fed by the rich foods, the carefully aged chicha, your nipples grew taut and your juices flowed as you watched the men pass by, pass through, choose wives and carry them off, scaling positions of power in the Incan hierarchy, taking their women with them. In the midst of the confusion, your father assumed the post of Huillac Uma, the highest position in the Incan faith. You breathed a sigh of relief and waited for word of your future. It could only be brilliant. In a way it was, although when the messenger came knocking at the Coya's door and the Coya passed the order down through the hierarchy and finally it reached you, you could hardly believe it. Amidst all the change, with the Spanish already settling in and dividing up the treasures of Cuzco, another capacocha Inti Raymi was to be held, a crucial one that would probably decide the fate of the

Incan Empire, the power of its gods to withstand all that
was to come. Among those to be supremely honoured, to
honour the Supreme, you were to be sacrificed.

From then on, you wore the finest woven cloths, ate
the tastiest of delicacies, drank the rich wines of the Inca
and the Coya themselves, waited on by your former companions, distanced from former friends. You watched some
of them leave the Acllawasi to marry Incan royalty, but increasingly they left the cloister to cement agreements with
the Spanish adventurers, ignorant of aristocracy, eager to
screw themselves into a royal position. Perhaps that's when
you noticed Manco's friendship with the Spaniard you
came to know as Diego de Almagro, watched as it acquired
a force usually reserved only for the most royal of the Incan
lords. Perhaps it was just coincidence that led him to come
upon you alone one day in a palace courtyard, your guards
hastily dispatched to perform some useless mission. You let
him catch only a glimpse of you that time, but from then
on you tormented him—a breath of your perfume wafting
through the hallway just as he entered, the swish of your
robes when your paths crossed so fleetingly he didn't even
see you, the sudden peal of your laughter through the open
window as he met with Manco. In the end, it was enough.
The Inca did the unthinkable, and you were released to
travel south with the Spanish party.

All this follows you too as you flee into the desert,
moving up the dry coast in the sparkle of water, amidst the
damp weight of ocean winds. You and your followers
walk for hours holding a mouthful of precious liquid like
a magic stone, smooth and cool on your tongues. How
did you know where to go? It wasn't so hard, really; you
could read the maps painstakingly etched into mountain

walls, the old routes were plain to see, those who had gone before guiding you now.

And then one night, when you're all so exhausted you fall asleep long before dawn, sinking hungry and almost feverish into a rough woollen envelope to smooth the gravelly earth below you and protect you from the icy sky arching above, you find yourself dreaming of the tinkling of water in the Acllawasi fountains from that same afternoon when Almagro first gazed into your eyes. You wake startled and frightened that you have conjured him up and the old danger is back. There's a harsh slap across your face, but confused and reeling to your feet you realize that it is water, open your eyes wide to see eddies and waves tear the blanket around you and pull it off into the swirling darkness. There are shouts from the men and screams from the handful of women. You stand to find the water has reached your knees, would bowl you over, but the Incan officer you will only ever address as the Captain wraps his arms around your waist and pulls you to safety in a world where water has suddenly replaced dry land, is digging and carving and reshaping everything.

At first you all run witless and panicked before it, seeking a hillock, anywhere away from the water. Then as the sun rises slowly and warms and dries you, everyone falls into a deep sleep. As the waters recede, so too does the image of Diego de Almagro, turning from man to a shadow you hope will never flicker across your path again.

When you wake up, the desert has vanished. It can't have happened exactly like this, yet this is the way you will always remember it. First your eyes are closed, glowing with orange and pink. Then you feel something soft, light as a bird's wing brush your cheek. You open your eyes and all around you the white beaks of flowers are open like hungry fledglings gobbling up the light, bright red, pink, white and striped, small trumpets calling forth others. You rise slowly to your feet, your legs feeling spindly and unfolding like those of a newborn colt. The slopes around you are covered with fleshy green leaves bursting with sap. The purple cups of new blossoms have been raised as if to toast the sun, the cloudless sky, the gleaming path of a river that has appeared in the valley at your feet.

You stand up and walk, your clothes still damp from the sudden river of the night, but now you pass through the frilly cups of white flowers, the shivering mauve of others, the desert bushes bristling with yellow blossoms, sharp thorns. You lean down to inhale the fragrance of the blue sigh of the earth, your nose brushing a white heart pulsing with amber stamens, your fingers caressing the six long blue petals of a desert violet. They hug your hips, like someone who's been waiting, reach ghostly fingers up to brush your thighs.

All this is yours now, for a moment. Time has stopped. You gape at life's bright banquet of colours spread suddenly before you, an event that happens once in a lifetime. The sudden storm has even changed the course of rivers, turning their flow toward you as if you and you alone have been chosen to settle here, to bring a hybrid life to the abandoned desert. You can feel it in the cool breeze off the water caressing your face. Almagro has gone on to his own destiny and you are finally free to face your own. You feel the Captain come up behind you, but even as his fingers reach toward yours (he could turn you round, press his lips to yours, the silk of his muscles drape itself across your skin) other footsteps move in upon you, time starts to tick and flow once more. The foreign voices of this place ring out like chimes.

Diego de Almagro and his men ride across the Atacama, their horse's hooves rattling against stones rich in copper, gold and silver or, along the coast, muffled and struggling against sands composed of nitrates and other non-metallic minerals. They cross a landscape that will make some of the men who will follow them rich beyond their most ambitious dreams, or like a leech suck the liquid from their flesh, leaving them freeze-dried, reduced, a patch of calcium tracing a negative of life across a sheet composed of salt crystals. Farther south, in the Aconcagua Valley where Pedro de Valdivia will soon found Santiago, they pass through abundant agricultural land, but that is not what they are seeking.

By August, one year after leaving Cuzco, not so long after Ñusta's escape, Almagro bitterly concludes: *In the Northern part of the region under exploration, the Indians live together in villages of an extremely miserable sort. Toward the south, they are scattered through the countryside, living in caves and dressed in animal skins. These Indians are gross and ferocious, do not cultivate the land, eat roots and herbs and human flesh [sic] and resist all civilization . . . [We] dreamt of a country overflowing with precious metals and now we just want to get away, because the ground isn't paved with gold, as we were told.*[*]

Anxious to get back to Peru, where he's now convinced riches await him in the form of a new division of the land around Cuzco, Almagro gives the order to prepare the trip back home. He has spent his entire fortune. If he dies now,

---

[*] Diego Barros Arana

he will leave his son with only the empty name of a nobleman and none of the fortune that should go with it.
Nonetheless, before setting out across the desert he gathers
his men around him and tears up their IOUs, effectively
freeing them of 150,000 golden pesos' worth of debt. He
also gives them carte blanche to ransack the land and its
peoples in order to prepare for the difficult journey that lies
before them.

*It gives no small pain to reflect that although these Incas were
gentiles and idolatrous, they kept the order and governed so well
and conserved such enormous territories, while we the Christians
have destroyed so many reigns, because everywhere the Christians
passed, conquering and discovering, there's no other view but that
with fire we have passed, consuming everything.*[*]

Knowing they will never return, frustration burns like a
canker on their tongues and the Spaniards raze the countryside, stealing all the food they can carry, taking captives to
work as slaves, bearing their supplies on the long trip home.

The twentieth-century historian, Barros Arana, notes
that *Under the Inca, the valleys in which the Spaniards have
stayed these three months have reached a considerable degree of industrial prosperity. Their fields, crisscrossed by numerous irrigation
ditches and cultivated with great care, produce abundant crops of
corn. Modest homes, grouped together, could have become the origin of peoples destined to develop a much greater civilization. All
this was virtually destroyed and these poor Indians conserve the
saddest memories of these ill-fated guests.*

As they have done throughout their journey, the
Spaniards tie or chain their Indian slaves in groups of ten to
twelve, by the neck. If one dies, they simply cut off his

---

[*] Cieza de Léon (Barros Arana).

head and leave his body behind to mutely mark their passing, as they continue on their long journey back to Cuzco.
Unwilling to face the known hardships of the route
through the Andes, this time they struggle up the Atacama
itself, along what is known as the coastal route, their horses
and mules growing thinner, trailing behind them, then
dying, bleached bones gleaming like ivory in the wake of
the once-triumphant conquistadors, empty cages for the
footprints of their failure.

They ride, walk, stumble, toward a Cuzco where rebellion has finally sparked into conflagration. Besieged by
the warriors of Almagro's old friend Manco Capac, Cuzco
can barely maintain the lines of communication with
Lima, where another Pizarro brother struggles against a
similar uprising. Almagro's arrival could break the tie and
give the Spaniards control over Peru once again. But the
rivalry between the Spanish themselves will quickly explode into civil war between Almagro and the Pizarros. At
first Almagro will triumph, even sparing the lives of
Fernando and Gonzalo Pizarro. Then, during the Salinas
battle outside Cuzco on 6 April 1538, the Pizarros take
him prisoner. Three months later, he is put to death by a
Spanish executioner, their own version of the Sacrificer.
He is first garrotted, then publicly decapitated, and his
head is placed on display in a public square.

So ends the Spaniards' first incursion across the barrier
of the Atacama into the fertile valleys of what will one day
be cobbled together to form Chile.

Perched on its post, Almagro's severed head still looks
southward, yearning backward across time, blank eyes
meditating on the trail of blood, of dust and of rebellion. In
the end, this is all that is left of an estate that swelled from

nothing but a brutal swipe across the face to millions of pesos' worth of melted gold, then shrank again to the sharp edge of a sword.

Three years later, the only flowers still blooming are the bright heads of blood-red cups extended like a posy from the braided creepers that the people of this place call *lion's hand*, or *claw*. There was a child, born feet first, only to die. Ñusta, you refused to consider she might have been Almagro's, took comfort in the old Andean story of the Yactas. There had been lightning, yes, in the midst of the storm. It caught you lying with your legs parted to the night and made you pregnant. A bolt, a relative of Iyapu, the Thunder God, fathered your child. When she died you buried her with great ceremony, dedicating her to her father and adding him to your pantheon. This strengthened your hold upon your own people but also the Atacamenians who had accepted you to live in their oasis, had taught you their stoneless style of building, the way they tied the posts of cactus and the roofs of thatch together to shut out the sun.

After the child's birth-death had sanctified you once again, the Atacamenians took you along the endless watery tunnels where the light shivered and glowered on the rock faces as it wandered toward the fields, dripping tiny measured drops that sought out the seeds, making them burst and reach out until they broke through the cement-like soil and gave forth corn and later wheat, dozens of kinds of potatoes, the sweet fruit of the algarrobo, grapes eventually, brought by a lone Spanish traveller, fleeing from his own past and people. He married an Atacamenian woman and stayed, living amongst them. He alone was allowed, because he arrived before you and your small party of survivors. Now when you sit atop the low hill that hugs the town you gaze out on an island of green courtiers, their lacy garments ruffled by their swaying dance to the endless breeze off an ocean of rock. The tamarugo forest is flourishing and rich. It gives you trees for fire and houses, and basic tools to tend the fields.

You've spent hours up here on this hill, this gentle bump in the endless plain, days and months. During the long prison of your pregnancy, when the relentless weight of your belly pulled you ever closer to the ground, you spent much time, kneeling and praying. Mostly at night, when the Moon seems gentler. You can imagine the Moon doing without sacrifices, banning the Sacrificer even, sending him off to some place farther south to join Almagro. Each day the Spaniard's memory grows lighter and flimsier, a fear that can be faced, dealt with by the new woman you have become. Like the weaver you are by vocation and endless education, you have clipped the fabric of your beliefs, sewed, tied knots, added the wisdom of the Atacamenians. Above all, you worship the water that flowed from the hills on that singular night, the lying rivers that lasted just long enough to bring you to this place. The thunder too, of nature, not war, the link from heaven to earth. You've kept the Moon, although you're wary of the Sun, avoid his rays, build windowless houses to shut his power out.

Almagro himself came through here once, on his journey back to Cuzco, but you spotted the dust thrown up by his horses long before and planned accordingly. You said there would be a small advance party, and there was. You explained what must be done, and Atacamenians and Incans acted together. This knowledge of yours, of how the Spanish would arrive, what they would want and how to deal with them, both shocked and pleased the Atacamenians. You saved their lives, their freedom. For a while. By the time Almagro reached the oasis you and all its people had vanished. Almagro found only *many weapons and much clothing of Spaniards who had died. With many tears Almagro had them buried. . . It was a thing of great pity and compassion to hear the cruelties the Indians practised in the deaths they gave them, because their bodies were torn apart and their brains covered the walls. With the blood they had painted their wickedness, in such a way as to notify with clarity and certainty the capital animosity they felt toward the Christians.*

You rule, Ñusta, and the Incan Captain executes your orders. You have outlawed all sacrifice but one, condemned its worshippers to death. Any Spaniard who approaches the oasis across the frozen sea of your Norte Grande must pay for his sacrilege with his life.

Two hundred years from now at the crossroads far below, there will be a tavern, with a fierce barmaid who refuses to marry. She will wear your reputation and the new title, La Tirana, that has replaced your name. Because you have acquired quite a following, with your new hybrid beliefs and, above all, your thorough knowledge of the Spanish, the new scourge that hovers over this land, that has already begun to attack. The Atacamenians have accepted you and your followers, but above all, you, your leadership robed in the magical powers of the Sun/Moon/God/Goddess and the Thunderbolt's child you bore, evidence of your sacred nature in their language as well as your own, the rivers you drew to you, the new oasis you founded.

---

* Oviedo (Hidalgo's *Culturas*).

There are rules, strict and harsh. Above all, to be as ruthless with the Spanish as the Spanish have been with you. Not a single Spaniard must learn of your existence and survive. By now you have sent emissaries to the coast where they met the Chango, trading feathers, corn, the flesh of tame llamas and ocean fish, guano to fertilize the hard earth, shells to rattle with the spirits' breath or to glimmer like moonlight against a dark-skinned chest.

Slowly, like blind fingers, you have felt your way into the desert, have come to know well the different families of Aymaras and Atacamenians who move across it like the chasquis, spend the year moving between the four layers of the Atacama.

Some of your men have married. Some melted away with the caravans, their lithe backs erased by the odd mist of the desert, the camanchaca. But most, like the Captain, have stayed with their beautiful tyrant, the Incan priestess who can sing their world back into existence, even if it lasts no more than an evening.

All that you've lost, from their point of view, is your name. A worthless bauble now that the civilization that spawned it is fighting for its life, except that it does bind the Incans among your followers—helped along by your chastity. This is the unfortunate part of seeking both freedom and power. Something must always be sacrificed, if not human life, then a woman's sexuality may be substituted. Because the men have accepted your meddling with their beliefs, but only to a point. There are moments when you see the Captain observe you through half-shut eyes. Whether he wants to embrace or overthrow you is hard to tell, but your chastity is a major part of what holds him to his place, subordinate, below you. You grow almost tearful when you remember the desert's blooms, how they flowered so copiously, then died, and with them their promise of smooth skin pressing into and through yours, a yearning that now lies buried somewhere under the stony soil at your feet, like the wild seeds—not worthy of the precious water from the irrigation channels—that wait for rain. The seeds are patient, certain the Thunder God will send his warriors out to find them.

You, Ñusta, are not so sure. A human lifetime, after all, is much briefer than a seed's. So you stand watch on this hill, early in the morning, late at night, plated by the moon's silver light, an Incan priestess again, waiting for someone from beyond your own culture, a god perhaps, who might set free that part of you that remains in the thrall of the falling empire, even though its intricate clock-work is smashed, perhaps beyond repair.

When the captive's brought in, head bare, feet bare, and they throw him at all your feet in the centre of the circle, something stirs within you. He's your height, but his hair is as pale as the Moon's, his skin washed out as if he lived mostly at night. Beside him in the noonday sun you feel yourself swell like the powerful mainmast you have become, carrying the sails of your people. But something has eaten away the strength of that mast, the basic human longing to hold and kiss, to fall through someone else's flesh and come up gasping for air, to feel at once safe and infinitely endangered, not from outside but from within, threatened not by your weakness but by your own over-whelming strength.

When they release him he stands up slowly to his full height, not arrogant but not cowed either. When he sneaks a glimpse of you his eyes are dark blue as the night sky and the idea of his kinship with the Moon, the Goddess you've rescued and kept close by you for these few short years, excites you. You think you could convert him, perhaps use him in some way. For in spite of all your efforts at disguise, all your orders to sacrifice every Spaniard who sets foot in the oasis, the desert seems to beget Spaniards the way just a few brief years back it bloomed with the surprise of flowers. You sense that already a new incursion of the Spanish, this time led by Pedro de Valdivia, is clinking and creeping over the hot gravel toward you, bringing another cargo of headless bodies, leaking death across the desert. You think you may eventually have to negotiate with the Europeans. You remember Atahualpa's betrayal by his trusted interpreter, Felipillo, who used his position to lever himself up in the Spaniards' esteem, pretending to serve Atahualpa even as he plotted his demise.

This man could teach you more Spanish, out here where the desert is like a cage, instruct you in their ways and provide you with the tools you will need if you are to avoid following hopelessly in Atahualpa's footsteps. You discuss this with the council and eventually they agree, although the Captain argues long and hard against you. Perhaps he is really fearful that the man may escape and bring the Spanish soldiers back with him to the oasis, but you sense the undercurrents flowing beneath his words, jealousy perhaps, or fear that more violent change is again on its way.

When you talk together, words, arguments and gods' names fly like sparks, and that is exciting, but under the talk your very flesh, his and yours, is yearning toward each other, the pores open like mouths and cry out, your skin becomes transparent as a cloud, envelops the two of you. You are aware that the Captain is watching, you give peremptory orders, send him to San Pedro with a caravan to trade. This offends him, but you are the Tirana, the Woman Tyrant. He must obey your commands.

Together you and the captive walk among the tamarugo trees. Sometimes you argue so loudly the sparrows fly out of their nests in the billowy branches, your voices darting like the birds from tree to tree. This man is unlike any of the Spanish you met in Cuzco, the antithesis of Almagro. He speaks of a friar, Bartolomé de las Casas, of letters dispatched across oceans, impassioned petitions in the courts for strong laws to protect the natives of America, theses presented by the Roman Catholic priest and his supporters, arguing that the *Indians* are human beings not animals, countered by the conquistadors and their advocates. He tells you that you have his religion all wrong, that it is a gentle voice like the murmur of water in the vast reaches of the desert. That it abhors sacrifice and recognizes the soul gleaming in every human creature. He speaks of rights, rather than rites, and it takes you a long time to understand, hungry as you are for something to believe in beyond yourself.

His eyes, dark and blue, blaze at your tales of the journey across the Andes with Almagro, of the chains of headless bodies and frozen statues left to mark your route. *It doesn't have to be like that*, he says, over and over. *We can— we must—make it different.*

As you listen, you sort through your mind, pondering on how to bring these new truths home to your people. The Spanish are coming, you can see that now, one relentless wave after another, sweeping across oceans and over mountain ranges, pushing their way through jungles into the most intimate corners of this continent. You are trying to calculate how many will be like this man, who calls himself Almeida, and how many will be like Almagro (and how many will remain loyal to the Sacrificer, eager and willing to carry out his work).

When you tell him of your beliefs, of Tanta Carhua and how you almost followed in her steps, he is satisfyingly horrified and relieved in a private way. You can see and cheer yourself that he is glad you survived, not only in that gentle theoretical way he has, for example, when he begins a phrase with the words *in principle*, but also that he is deeply and intimately thrilled to have been able to meet you. Reluctantly, you must thank Almagro for saving your life, and your own ingenuity and courage for refusing to let him destroy it.

One day, worn out by all the heavy philosophizing, you begin to teach him the song Wawaki. I am the princess and you the prince, you tell him, as you try to wind his clumsy tongue around the Quechua. At the end of each line, you wag your finger at him, *No!* You tell him he must sing *No*, like this. And you demonstrate. Singing. Singeing him with your voice.

> *The princess:*
> If I am a star—*No!*
> Open your heart—*No!*
> And in the sun's fire—*No!*
> Half-close your eyes—*No!*

Then, painstakingly, line by line, you teach him the next verse, the prince's verse, his verse. He has a sweet musical tenor, sings like a boy, his voice soaring and gentle. He learns the music far sooner than the words, but eventually he gets them too. When he can sing it through without stuttering or laughing, you punctuate each new line that he learns with a whispered *Yes*.

The prince:
Only by moonlight—*Yes!*
You pretend to call me—*Yes!*
And when I approach—*Yes!*
You turn to snow—*Yes!*

The next day you sing him a new verse and he begins to translate it into Spanish, laughs as he figures out each new word or recognizes one that is already familiar. At the last line, a sudden silence freezes the air in the clearing where you sit. He looks away, out past the trees to the undulating lines of gravel and dust. (All forests are finite, but most allow at least the illusion that they go on forever.)

The princess:
If I pretend to call you—*No!*
Hurry to answer—*No!*
If I turn to snow—*No!*
Touch me with your fire—*No!*

Your lips move more slowly over the prince's next verse, emphasizing each new syllable, every word, so he can begin to understand it. He watches your lips shape the words, sees how your tongue adds or subtracts meaning with each new sound, how sometimes the words rattle or hum in your throat.

The prince:
When my fire burns you—*Yes!*

You spill into dew—*Yes!*
Are you illusion or wind—*Yes!*
Or simple folly?—*Yes!*

In the end it wasn't so hard for you to learn more Spanish. After all, you'd had some practice with Almagro and his men. You can even for moments be eloquent and fierce in the conquerors' language. But his tongue, as he feels his way through the Quechua song, trips and entangles itself in the unfamiliar murmur of a language fine and sweet as water. Sometimes you laughingly place your finger on his lips and have him watch and repeat after you as you sing. When you reach the last verse, however, he's become quite proficient. You don't have to explain the words. He knows what they mean. You pull him to you as you sing, seeing only his moonlit eyes but feeling his warmth envelop you, an animal version of the camanchaca. His tongue, his lips, as they move across yours, mutter a mixture of Quechua and Spanish as he moves them down over your breasts, pausing to taste the nipples, pausing to lick the salt all the way down to the meeting place between your legs, where a flaming arrowhead prepares to fly.

When you touch him into shape, you hear the water rustling again, not the tinkling of Acllawasi fountains now but the rush and tumble of the river that came to you one night, overflowing with honours and promises, many of which you won't live to see. You feel his flesh taut and pulsing like a wild animal, trembling with fear and anticipation in your hand. With your eyes closed what you see are the spikes of sharp yellow flowers shooting skyward like knife-edged flames. Then the pink petals of layered light, speckled with amber and gold, whirl between you like dancers' skirts, the cactus's dark pink bowls blooming and bursting with juice.

The ancient poetry floats among the tamarugo trees, seeps deep into the desert, long after you've stopped moving and lie still, wrapped in each other, full of wonder and light, tasting the fruit of the desert's promise made so many years ago, and now fulfilled.

You look at each other then, the dark and bright sides of the moon in an age where the Sun's supreme rule is giving way to the Son's. Either way there's no place for the pale delicacy of meeting, potential compromise. You are refugees in the tamarugo grove, which trembles lightly in the breeze. Life, you think, and try to feel relief, in the desert's mortal stillness.

You whisper the words in his ear, your lips like butterfly wings, tickling and tantalizing at the same time.

If you believe me dew (He holds your fingers to his
    lips, which shape *No!*
Bring your lips closer—*No!*
Even if it's folly—*No!*
Don't lose my trail—*No!*

It is folly. You know that as soon as the Captain returns and you can feel his eyes following every move you make, studying every gesture, every expression flitting across your face when your eyes meet Almeida's or avoid his. Punishment is coming, you should have known that, should have foreseen it, but now, as if to make up for your omission, you rail against it, shout your defiance at the council, the desert's fierce lovely Tyrant to the end. You try to shout them down, shout them back into submission, but you who taught them how to think can no longer dictate what they will think or how they will act in response to their terrible fearful thoughts.

Pedro de Valdivia has come and gone, there have been bloody skirmishes out in the desert. The Captain has returned with news of San Pedro de Atacama hung with the heads of rebel chiefs, the severed tongues of those who dared to argue or speak their own language, the women dragged off as a new kind of tithe for the Spaniards' use. Slavery in the great silver mines of Potosi is just around the corner and the whole desert tenses for the blow. Your magic is not working and now you have moved into the Spaniards' camp, offered him the chastity of an Incan priestess. You have called a meeting into existence, invited a new race to come into being. You defend yourself, argue that there are other kinds of Spanish people, try to tell them of Las Casas, his battle before the Spanish king, in name of America's indigenous people.

They reject this name, the whole idea, this new continent artificially produced from what can only be their collective defeat. For the first time they sense that this is what lies ahead, that the administration that served them so well in the old wars for conquest will not be enough, can never be enough (now).

They meet and deliberate and find this wrong, your actions so wrong. The Captain exhorts them, hammering home the accusations, their forced exile from Cuzco, their punishment for following a woman's word too closely. He stands before them, on legs carved by desert marches, his skin the colour of the rich soils of Tiwanaku's furrows, his voice thick with accents past. He demands that they pay for their crimes against the old religion. He argues that the only proper atonement is to resuscitate the old Incan law, the law of sacrifice. *She was born for this!* he argues. *This is her destiny and ours depends on hers!*

There's silence then, the deadly silence of a collective nod.

First they deal with the Captive, slitting his throat and letting the blood coagulate thick and red as a lion's claw on the dry gravel of the desert. Later, much later, late at night, his compatriot will steal into the glade in the forest where he lies, and give his remains as Christian a burial as he can manage, under a Christian cross.

Then they prepare the ceremonies, the songs, the dry aged chicha that will prepare their Huillac Ñusta, return her to her fate. She sits in her lodge plotting to avoid it.

7

THE EARTH'S
REFUSALS

➤

Pisagua and Pica/Matilla

On June 2, 1990, by the Grace of God, it was as if the nitrate-filled soil of the coast of Pisagua had decided, at last, to talk. Mumbling at first, but then with shattering cries.

— *Nelson Muñoz Morales*

15 July 1998

NIGHT BOILS UP out of the ocean, reaching dark fingers of mist inland toward the bare expanse of desert across which we are driving, Patricio, Camilo and I, having left the sparse trees, green spring and white marble tombs of Tiliviche behind us. We are thinking of spending the night there, but already our feet are dragging, even as the car plunges forward past the desert, toward the cliffs and the long, zigzagging descent into Pisagua.

On the road to Pisagua, a roadside shrine looks like a cross between a bus stop, a construction site and a doghouse elegantly marked by stones painted blue and white. The animita has taken up residence in this modest home, where someone has thoughtfully provided visitors with a white bench trimmed with yellow licence plates, squeezed under a narrow roof that seems to cast no shadow. The shrine itself is the typical shape of a child's drawing of a house, a wreath of pink paper flowers sitting on the roof. Beyond it, just rock and the brown crust of the desert, stretching in every direction as far as the eye can see.

On the road to Pisagua, in the midst of the desert, the Unita Hill version of the Sacrificer grins like a child's stick figure as he strides across the hillside, an axe swinging from his left hand, a severed head in his right.

On the road to Pisagua, silent crosses populate each empty nitrate office. The empty sea-chewed cradles of dead children. The emptied rectangles of graves along the cliff. Graves that yielded up their secrets. Graves that held none.

Pisagua was a major port during Chile's nitrate era, a century ago. Today, it is a tiny fishing cove. Among its other sterling characteristics, it is a natural prison, a human dot surrounded by thousands of miles of ocean on one side, hundreds of miles of desert on the other. Chile's rulers were quick to notice this.

During the 1940s, Chilean president Gabriel González Videla used Pisagua as a prison camp. There, under pressure from the U.S. he sent many of the communist supporters who had helped him to power, along with homosexuals, common prisoners of that time. According to Luis Muñoz Orellana, imprisoned there then, *For many years, the idea of making Pisagua a penal colony in which prisoners with long*

*sentences could remake their lives working in fishing-related activi-
ties was on the minds of many authorities.*

Many of the prisoners were journalists, their stay in Pisagua the price of trying to maintain a free press. At night, a
delegation of two or three prisoners would slip out of the
barracks and hide in the shadows outside the door of the
officers' cantina, where they would listen to the national
news, sponsored by Esmaltina toothpaste. They would
then glide back to their fellows, anxiously awaiting word
of what was happening in the country *outside*.

For a while, the prison was headed up by an army captain named Augusto Pinochet. He would later say that it
served him as a school in communism, teaching him that
the only way to deal with people of this political persuasion
was to eliminate them. In 1973, and again in the eighties,
he put it to use as a prison camp, shipping supporters of the
former government and some common delinquents
here—before *eliminating* them. Shades of Hitler's final solution, a bitter minor note that still echoes painfully along
these cliffs.

As we descend through the winding tendrils of the
camanchaca, Patricio grips the wheel, I clutch the car
door, my feet jammed to the floor where brakes would
have been appreciated. Out the passenger's window, I stare
down hundreds of metres of sheer rock toward a stony
ocean, the gulls splashing upward like spray, spying and
rushing toward us, then sailing away.

We are surrounded by the hollow sound of the wind
rattling around, death caught in a drum and banging away
with all its might, calling up life, learning to chase and imitate it, become it, the antara humming with pain, a holo-
caust of voices and souls borne on the mist, twisted by the

raging, ravaging wind, rising out of the pit at the edge between ocean and desert.

Pisagua. From the Quechua *pisi*, "little," *awa*, "warp." Or "little water," a hybrid of the Quechua and *agua*, water in Spanish. Try as I may, it still resounds in my ears as simply, Piss agua. To piss away precious water in the desert is like pissing blood.

Over the months, I have tried to dream Pisagua of the nitrate age back into existence, to cover the faded paint with bright colours, turn on the lights, bring the ships— hundreds of ships carrying bright silks, the polished ebony of fairy tales, wheat and water—back to float in the harbour like a flock of fat, satisfied geese. Piss. Agua. A major nitrate port, a battle site during the war of 1879, now barely a fishing cove, 167 souls flitting amongst the elegant old buildings. Their paint is peeling, their frames have settled into crooked humps and their old bones need shoring up, but they still lord it over the ragged children, their mothers in thin sweaters, the coarse-haired men.

The nitrate buildings include a prison, which now serves as a hotel. The Chilean authorities have declared many national monuments, a certificate that seems to guarantee they will not be touched, repaired or cared for, until they collapse back into dust. In the meantime, like dead insects, their carcasses shine on in the foggy sunset, even as they dry to carapace or are chipped away.

We stop to stretch our legs on the huge concrete dock that the ruined village stretches like a large rude toe into the sea. Patricio smokes a cigarette. Camilo and I watch two hopeful boys cast their lines amongst the oily waves and the bright yellow husks of fishing boats. A dead fish or two shine like desert silver on the slick surface below us.

And behind us, crushed against the cliff, three men drink beer under an improvised canopy. The fading light or their own history casts a gritty shadow across their faces. One of them is so huge his loose flesh cascades like a regal mantle down from his shoulders toward his shadow, flowing over the sides of the stool below him, his face rising above it like a weather balloon, reporting resentment.

The town, which looked almost whole, almost alive as we drove down the cliff toward it, now reveals the chipped cement and stained siding. The finely carved woodwork on balconies and posts has been further eaten away and hollowed out by the endless work of insect artisans. A tiny place, and yet we feel lost and trapped, the desert above the town collapsing toward us, the sea pounding at our backs.

Finally we ask the men about the prison camp—where was it? The emperor of flesh holds a thick knife to his lips between fingers as fleshy as drumsticks, chewing on something, even as he answers, *That was all a lie. Nothing has ever happened here. This is just a fishing village.* The Chileans' eternal order to deny, forget, pretend that nothing ever happened.

A companion, who sucks fervently on a bottle of beer, makes a vague gesture toward the town's north end, mumbles something about the cemetery.

We set out dubiously, sure by now that we do not want to spend the night, but anxious to capture something of a past that tore into our own present in June 1990, a past, we are all too sure, that will continue to blow like a sad mist into the twenty-first century.

We pass a monolith. It marks the day in October 1879 when the Chilean navy disembarked in Pisagua, on their way to defeat the Peruvian-Bolivian alliance in a place called Dolores (pain). It's the squareness of these monuments that always impresses me, their total disregard for the natural curves and cliffs that surround them, their total lack of reference to the thunder of surf on rocks, the smooth creeping veil of the camanchaca, the occasional cowed bush, a tiny green cloud floating just above the ground. This monument, like all those the military leaves behind, squats, a white cube in a square patch of sand marked by white stones or shells, its back to the sea, a small door gaping at a white cement post, in a similarly bordered square.

We wind onward up a cliff, which is that peculiar tawny brown of the desert. It's like the hair on an animal's flanks, fierce as a lion, still but warm, shifting slightly just when you think it might be dozing. We try to slip past without disturbing it, reduced to what we are, a naked, clawless species, our only defence an intelligence we seldom put to good use.

Almost thirty years before the three of us, the archaeologist Lautaro Nuñez (the head of the museum in San Pedro de Atacama) wandered here with a friend he called Pete. His voice still winds its way along these paths, haunting us as we stumble along seeking explanations for dimly sensed events. Unaware, we retrace his footsteps.

In 1971, Núñez and Pete started at the pier, as we do, and continued on foot through the town to the cemetery, and on to the old Spanish port, Pisagua Viejo. Nuñez's voice, his thoughts, speak across time from the northern city of Iquique in August 1990: *I was telling you that funeral rites involving the landscape, facing the absolute mystery of death, are an essential part of the human condition. . . You were fasci-*

nated that Pisagua seemed to be the Port of the Dead, inhabited by more mummies than living people in that bouquet of cemeteries that taught you the patience of initiates.

In Pisagua Viejo, Nuñez tells Pete about excavations that revealed a family from the Chinchorro culture, five thousand years old, including *a youth fractured in two because when they buried him they hit a rock. I don't think you understood.* They argue, because Pete does not believe his story of Max Uhle's discovery of a trophy skull wearing a turban amidst the neatly laid-out bodies, some with harpoons tied to their hands. Núñez continues, *What I was really trying to explain was how cemeteries, when added to one another, sum up the history of a culture, the way time passed through communities, each one different although all were lived in exactly the same environment.*

They stroll on to another cemetery, left like a footprint by another culture. There the dead, when Uhle found them, wore the finely woven shirts of Tiwanaku. The length of a living culture's reach expressed long after its death.

Pete misses the sight of a vandalized cemetery, some four hundred metres behind the ruined church, where the skeletons wear Andean ponchos. That was the last cemetery they passed by on their long stroll through Pisagua's history. They have no idea of the cemeteries soon to come. Nuñez writes, *We would both agree that as northerners we feel the dead are very close. . . We treat them casually because we live so close to them. We know they don't disappear like the rest of the world. They get thinner, dry out, dressed up as if expecting someone to arrive or something to happen. We share the same landscape in the desert's vastness. We're used to living with the certainty that there are more ruins and dead than cities and living people . . .*

For the people of Iquique, for our ancestors, dying is a ritual,
half sacred, half festive. A lot of pain, and something of entertain-
ment . . .

Patricio and I have come, bringing Camilo with us on
something of a pilgrimage, because we believe that memory is a ritual to be exercised and taught. Repeated too, as
in a prayer, poised on the tongue until all the meaning has
been sucked out, absorbed, turned into part of a new being
(body social and individual).

We have come because on 7 June 1990, twenty-one
perfectly preserved bodies were unearthed here, on the
edge of the cliff just outside the graveyard. Under the
watchful gaze of Nelson Muñoz, the Judge of the Pozo
Almonte district where Pisagua is located, the diggers
sweated in the relentless heat of the sun. This was not the
first time that judges and other dignitaries found themselves mopping their brows and broiling on this brittle
shelf, poised on the edge of the Pacific. Nor would it be
the last.

Seventeen years earlier, in September 1973, the ship
Maipo had moored off these same cliffs, in the nearby harbour, its hold bearing a cargo of three hundred prisoners
from Valparaíso.

When the ship started to move we thought we would all be
thrown overboard, remembers Hector Canales Morales, a
member of the Christian Democratic Party who was carried here in the dark and stink within the ship, along with
his workmates Juan Valencia, Juan Alarcón, Mario Morris
and Carlos Ponce.

Ashore in Pisagua, they were crowded into the old jail,
sometimes as many as fourteen to a tiny room. Recalls

Canales Morales, *Lieutenant Colonel Ramón Larraín** *was very cruel. He seemed to have an irrational hatred for all of us there. The torments we suffered caused several people go mad. The powerlessness, the desperation in that place were very great, because we could neither run nor ask for help.*

I remember that once a representative of the Red Cross visited, but the military shut up those of us who had been beaten the most and the wounded in the Pisagua theatre, so that the Red Cross representative wouldn't see us. The healthiest were forced to go to the beach so the inspector would think we were practically on holiday.

On 20 October another naval ship moored in the harbour, this time with a list of prisoners who were to be released. In spite of Larraín's bitter opposition, about one-third of the prisoners went free. But not all those who left the barracks ever returned to normal, civilian life.

I remember saying goodbye to Valencia, Canales, Morris and Alarcón, with whom I'd been friends at work for two years. They told me they knew they were going to be shot, because they'd already been warned. All of them appeared on the list of those shot in Pisagua except Ponce, but I think his body must be buried there among the graves, because he too was left behind, says Canales Morales.

Pete's younger brother, Hector Taberna, recalls the routine in Pisagua prison camp, after the 1973 military coup. Up for a five-minute breakfast—a cup of tea, a piece of bread—at 7:30 a.m., with lunch around 4:30 p.m., usually beans, garbanzos or lentils. The prisoners spent the rest of the day measuring cells with their feet, studying the walls, painted white, the bars, windows, doors all red, an

---

* Full name, Ramón Larraín Larraín. For the sake of clarity for English-language readers I've not used the second surname here.

infernal attempt at passing the time, as beaten, bruised and bloody, their *compañeros* came and went.

Many years later, Hector Taberna remembered, *It was on one of those dreadful days that the sound of machine gun fire, rifles and cannons woke everyone in their cells. We could hear their rattling from every corner. . . When it ended, Ramón Larraín, Commander of the Pisagua Concentration Camp arrived, wearing his campaign uniform complete with ceremonial knife, shouting: We had to do it! They paid no attention to the warning, sirs. They were shot to pieces. There in the sea, there are still some pieces. And if any of you try to run, you'll face the same punishment as those two fishermen who didn't obey the order to stop. This is a warning, sirs.*

On 20 September 1973, an official announcement in the press declared that six prisoners had been shot trying to escape from Pisagua. On 29 September, William Miller and Jorge Marón disappeared in Iquique. On one of his personal visits to the prisoners, Commander Larraín asked for six volunteers *to paint the front of the building*. All six ended up dead.

On 5 October 1973, Lieutenant Colonel Ramón Larraín, commander of the Pisagua concentration camp, appeared before the prisoners on the third-floor balcony. *I was watching, along with other prisoners, from the cages—that's what we called our cells—on the second floor. Another group was listening on the first floor. He said he no longer saw us as people, but rather as dogs, that he was disillusioned because six of our companions had tried to escape, but his valiant soldiers had stopped them, cutting their bodies in half with machine gun fire; their bodies were buried in the desert.*[*]

---

[*] Ex-prisoner (*La Epoca*, 10 June 1990)

On 11 October, a council of war sentenced five men to death. On 30 October, another council of war ended the lives of five prisoners. The deaths continued with or without the sanction of the war councils in January and February of 1974. On 15 January 1974, the army announced it had released six men accused of drug trafficking, but their families searched for them in vain. Sixteen years later, in June 1990, the bodies of five of the six would be found in the common grave in Pisagua.

On the Day of the Dead—1 November 1983, Angel Fernández, a Spanish priest, gathered with a handful of relatives and friends for a modest religious service. *We meet here this afternoon for something very important. We all know the dates and the details. Finally, after ten years, for the first time, we hold a religious ceremony for our companions.*

I have chosen the passion of Jesus Christ. . . After dinner, Jesus was taken prisoner in the garden of Gethsemane. The relatives, all those who are present here today, remember those who were shot in '73, remember in what circumstances, in what home, in what place they too were taken prisoner.

Afterward, Jesus was taken to high priests and later to Pilate. . . Let us remember how, once these companions were arrested, they were moved from one place to another, from one authority to another, and we know the precise names of those authorities, until they reached Pisagua.

After the derision, during which they showered Christ with insults, spit, blows, whipping, blasphemy and the crown of thorns, he was taken to Calvary, the place of execution.

At the other extreme of Chile, in Coyhaique, a region of volcanoes and almost endless rains and impenetrable forests, Francisco Iván Zamora stared at the television news in horror on that day in June 1990. As he watched the beautifully preserved bodies of Pisagua emerge from the earth, Zamora suffered a nervous breakdown.

A prison guard in Iquique at the time of the coup, Zamora had been moved to Pisagua and put in charge of the prison camp's statistics; he saw how army intelligence selected the prisoners to be executed, and he kept neat, careful records in army ledgers noting the names of those to be shot, although some deaths would never be admitted. Firing squads, fourteen men strong, carried out executions at dawn and after midnight.

In June 1990 Enrique Krauss, minister of the interior in the government that replaced the military regime, announced that General Pinochet, military president from 1973 until 1990, would not be removed as army commander-in-chief, and that the legality of his remaining would not be questioned. Nor would Krauss express an opinion on the ethics of those who ruled Chile while people were being shot in Pisagua.

In June 1990 the national press began to print the opinions and testimony of government spokespeople, the Roman Catholic Church, human rights lawyers, activists, witnesses who were frightened but determined to tell the truth, and their voices float off the pages, bitter, brittle as autumn leaves. President Patricio Aylwin committed himself to establishing the truth of what had happened in Pisagua. Fifteen of the bodies received full religious burial in Iquique, with the service taking place in the Cathedral, while scuba divers began to hunt for bodies at the bottom of the cliffs.

The whole country went into shock. Those who had always denied the reality of government-sanctioned kidnapping, torture and murder could no longer avoid the truth. Those who had been punished and ostracized for proclaiming the ugly truth were vindicated, and public recognition of the facts was accepted as a necessary step toward healing. Throughout Chile, clandestine graveyards began to open their dank mouths, releasing the bones and the stories of people slashed to death, pushed off cliffs or thrown into the rushing torrents of southern rivers. Lives abruptly cut short, doubly dead as their very existence was denied, smothered by complicity, and its bastard child, impunity.

Almost twenty years afterward, some families could finally lay the remains of their lost fathers and sons to rest. A coalition of human rights organizations and treatment centres for survivors declared that *For Chilean society, the findings in Pisagua have provided proof of a truth that has been denied and feared for many years. Faced with this, we professionals who work in mental health and human rights consider it necessary to collectively face the consequences of the trauma that has marked our society, because this is the way to begin to heal the damage done to direct victims and also the ethical, psychological and social damage afflicted on our society as a whole.*

For the relatives of those executed in Pisagua this has had an enormous impact, especially having to recognize the bodies of their loved ones. . . . Nonetheless, it is absolutely necessary for them to do this because they need to know what happened to their relatives. They need to bury their dead, not just any body. They need to hold a funeral for all the memories and the images of their family member, of the world of affection they built around him.

They also underlined that Chileans need to learn how to be shocked at atrocities all over again.

But General Carlos Forestier, Lieutenant Colonel Larraín's superior officer, has never faced charges for what happened in Pisagua. Neither has the lieutenant-colonel

who believed his charges were dogs, and acted accordingly.

Lautaro Nuñez returned to Pisagua on several occasions,
looking for the friend he'd nicknamed Pete, whose full
name was Fredy Taberna. He knows how Pete's life
ended. He has re-created it in his mind in every detail. He
speaks to Pete: *In the prison catacombs you said goodbye to your
brother. Then they took you and the others to the chapel. They
put you in the jeep, blindfolded. They let you out at the gate to
the cemetery. The chaplain took your arm and began his litany on
the walk to the centre of the cemetery, that same path that we took
in 1971 (who was the chaplain really praying for?).*

*Forgive me if I try to summarize what you could not see. Past
the pile of rocks at the back of the cemetery were the eight marks-
men. On your right, an officer with his arm up. On your left the
chaplain's litany. So they tied you to a post with the hill behind
you. In spite of all their torture you stood straight, very thin and
young, with that defiant chin even sharper due to the shaved beard
and the short hair. You were there as if nailed to a damp blue
coastal dawn. That sticky mist rubbed your blindfold. You sensed
then that something was happening to your left. The sound of the
prayers was moving slowly away. . . The officer dropped his arm.*

*Now you lie buried somewhere in Pisagua. Somewhere, laid
out between two cargo sacks, if you're complete, waiting for your
archaeologist friends to find you.*

What kind of pilgrimage is this? Our minds grope backwards, desperately missing the merciless pampa above,
while here below in the damp mouth of the sea our fingers
are chilled, our eyes confused. There, daylight still rules
over the plain. The sun admits no lies, nothing hides in the

shadows, no shadows are allowed, just the brilliant sky shining, sapphire-bright, the earth flat and hard as a tiger's eye.

We have found our way here almost against our will, reluctant, even afraid. To mark the memories that the army's monument has tried to suppress, to move the stone before the cave, to raise the lid. To remember, even where no animita has yet been built, just our thoughts, dull and persistent as a bass drum at three in the morning, the Andean wind howling its way through the Sacrificer's flutes, the dancers lining up in twos and threes, red circles pinned over their hearts, the soldiers firing twice a day, the radio announcer's voice, *shot while trying to escape*, the graves patiently drying, preserving, loyally holding their treasures, ready, as the desert always is, to give them back. They have been waiting, wait there still, eager to whisper their secrets into mourners' ears, to offer the comfort of a once-familiar face, dried and fragile as papyrus, a last grimace of fear written across it or the bright O of a mouth frozen in horror, in a shirt pocket a letter of love brittle as the dried petal of a forget-me-not.

We leave the car, to carry on by foot through a wrought iron gateway, rusted the colour of the desert. Here, on a sandy cliff that plunges like a suicide headfirst into the sea. Here, in the treeless desert where a forest of wooden crosses suddenly rises before us, salt-chewed and fragile. They govern this cliff, stretching as far as the eye can see, a capital city of the dead, those who flocked to the port, the nitrate offices with their dreams. Here are crude empty cradles reserved for children, an occasional elegant stone mausoleum crushed behind walls like the burly arms of bears. A rusted iron gate is marked by the Peruvian Beneficiencia, an iron cross still rising above the neat rows of niches.

I wondered where they had gone—the ghosts of the workers of the nitrate age, the survivors of massacres, grinding labour, poverty and instant wealth—wondered what happened to the uneasy peace that bound them to each other. Now I've found them, all buried in the cemetery of Pisagua. There is a cross for every one. Fragile as matchsticks, polished by the blowing sand, cross after cross insists that people lived here, that they were all once as tangible as Camilo, who is budding into adolescence with a gentle fuzz on his upper lip. His brown eyes are growing larger and more quiet, full of what he's seen, though as ever he's unwilling to comment. Real as Patricio, his whole life now reduced in the gathering dark to the orange tip of his cigarette, who was arrested, disappeared and rescued from the secret police in May 1991, a burning edge to their darkness, a light in mine. His rescue made Camilo and his brother Daniel possible after all. It made them necessary.

Real, here but gone, their bones have watched over bones and more bones, now the bones of our contemporaries, men who might have fathered Camilo's friends, had they survived. But Pete and his companions lie in unmarked graves.

These dead we must take into ourselves; they belong to us. The dead of our time, the victims of a generation's failures. They were wantonly sacrificed by the uniformed priests of oblivion who rose up and ruled civil society, waving their weapons like crosses and reserving the right to judge and to condemn. These too are sacrificial victims, not of the Incas or the Atacamenians, but of Chile today, the men who battled over copper, who raised their axes or guns or knives not for the common good, but to enrich the few who had come to take what they could find, the rapacious few who sacrificed the unarmed, the innocent, the naive.

On a narrow ridge between the sea and the cemetery, we stand for a long time in silence, staring at the rectangular pits in the desert, emptied of hopes, of bones, the odd shred of clothing. The judges have come, tears have coursed from the eyes of the relatives and the survivors, dried on their cheeks. Some have found comfort, but others only the prolongation of their search, down a gravel road through the desert that never ends.

I would have liked Pisagua never to have existed, or to be a place where I could still hear the strains of a Peruvian waltz drifting out of a window framed with lace, the air still scented with the French perfume of ladies and courtesans. I would have welcomed the illusion of an elegant gentleman folding me in his arms and swinging me out on a balcony to look at a black sea dotted with ships like stars. I could have wound my fingers through his hair and danced, I'm sure, but the pianos are closed or out of tune or rotten. There's nothing to see in Pisagua, just a memory to be revealed when the ocean winds shave off a layer of gravel to reveal the remains of a tattered shirt or the bare bone of a pointing finger.

Sometimes it seems that the desert is just a giant graveyard. We flee from Pisagua, climb the darkening cliffs, leave the place, old or new, dead or alive, behind us at the mercy of the pounding sea. Trapped in the damp heart of the camanchaca, our headlights like blunt fingertips fumble their way through a landscape we sense but cannot see. We reach the top of the cliff, then wind our way along the ravine of a dry river and back up into the desert. Finally the camanchaca releases its hold and we find ourselves flying again across the open: it extends like a woven tablecloth

before us, offering a grim silvery banquet, lit by a cande-
labra of stars that seem to fall in a gentle cascade all the way
to the tips of the distant mountains.

The next day we visit the Cerros Pintados, the Painted Hills,
miles of indigenous graffiti scrawled across a series of low hills
(well, compared to the Andes they're low) above abandoned
nitrate offices: llamas and caravans, figures leaping, dancing,
the delicate triangles of geometry, plans of the sky, maps of
the routes across the earth, all watched over by a forestry
service office, square and awkward as a forgotten lunch
box. It's like walking through the symbol-driven landscape
of an artist's mind, a great book flung down, left open for
all to read, whatever our language, whatever the strange
hieroglyphs of each time. Prostrate at the foot of these hills,
the desert has been blasted and raked through and combed
for nitrates. It rises like a wind-driven ocean, pounding away
at the base of the rare tamarugo trees, which stagger like desperate maidens, surf of stone and salt pounding at their ankles.

We explore the ruined walls of yet another abandoned
nitrate office, this one tucked into the base of the painted
hills, picking over the detritus of yet another attempt at
conquering the desert. When I raise my eyes, stretch my
gaze toward the distant horizons, I can see other offices
bobbing like ships on desert waves. This is a living museum and we are privileged to be here. Guideless, and with
no ready explanations, we dig deeper into our own minds,
listen to the voices of the past buzzing around us like radio
waves: signals received on the silent wire of a soul we no
longer acknowledge or really have a place for.

Chile is still in the thrall of gold fever, unable, even after
five hundred years, to shake off the cold sweats and compul-

sion that are its main symptoms: *I have come here to take gold and not to work the earth like a peasant*, as old Cortés said, when he arrived to take possession of his new lands at the dawn of the Conquest. The results of this approach have littered the desert with crumbling ruins we can't forget; visited once in a lifetime, they visit us forever after in our sleep. We build animitas of the mind, tend the green shoots of hope.

My eyes rake the irregular horizon. Somewhere on the long journey along these mountains, across this desert, Ñusta escaped. Somehow, someone placed her here at this juncture, the heroine of a story in which she founded a new town in the midst of the Pampa del Tamarugal. Like the trees themselves, she and her people put down roots, building their village on the road between Pozo Almonte and the oasis of Pica, a word that may be from the Quechua, could mean a flower, blooming in the sand. We are approaching her heartland but in some ways she seems more distant than ever. Like Alice in *Through the Looking-Glass*, we sense that the only way to reach that place is by going in the opposite direction, in every other direction. But at last we leave the dry gravel flanks of the Cerros Pintados behind us and turn our longing eyes toward the green orchards, the magical fruit of Pica and Matilla, known for their flavour, the rich wine of their juices, their caves' reflection undulating in the surface of a hidden pool, their duelling chapels.

Isaiah Bowman, the American geographer, is murmuring in my ear. He loves the Pica he discovered as the nineteenth became the twentieth century, and he can't resist taking my elbow now and guiding me through the oasis, an undercurrent of excitement pulsing in his voice.

He compares Pica's water tunnels to the *kanat* of Persia and the *kariz* of Turkestan, the *foggara* of the Algerian Sahara, the *retharas* of Morocco and the weep holes of California. Cut through soft sandstone, the galleries seldom require shoring up with timber. His voice, rough with excitement: *. . . fifteen main galleries, measuring a total of eight miles (12,980 metres), with the shortest being 100 metres long! Come along, come along!* he rushes us as we tear like the wind along the last stretch of molten highway. Ñusta's eyes glimmer in the dappled light of reflected water, follow our progress; a slight frown creases her forehead.

It's late in the day by the time we get there, the sun turning the adobe walls and the neighbours' skin to the warm gleam of beaten gold, light's last gift before dark. A tradesman from Iquique gives us a proud tour of his orchard, of grapefruit, lemons and a delicious orange whose juice flows down my chin, along my fingers, each tree rising out of sand, sparingly watered, the leaves brilliant and rich as the foliage of the rainforests far to our south. Three neighbours sitting on benches in the dirt road of the village of Matilla speak proudly of their battle against the snobs of Pica, against the desert, against Iquique's water diversion that condemns the oasis to death. They point to their church, they tell us we have to see *Golgotha*, and send us bemused to follow the path that begins at their fingertips, an unmapped route through their own peculiar version of history. Myth in the people's hands is turned upside down and opened like a cage.

Throughout the sixteenth century the Spanish settled only sporadically in the region of Tarapaca, including the Pica oasis. Fortune shone more brightly elsewhere in the south, especially in the fabulous mines of Potosi, in Bolivia. Toward the end of the century, however, the thirsty governor of Peru sent one Francisco Carabantes off to Spain to bring back the tender shoots that would make Pica and Matilla famous for their wine.

Earthquakes in 1768, 1868 and 1877 destroyed the villages, making it necessary to rebuild repeatedly. Toward the end of the eighteenth century, a plague devastated the already small population of the region. In 1809–1810, as most of Latin America began to rebel against European dominance, small-scale exploitation of nitrates began.

In 1827 the government of Peru hired an Englishman, William Bollaert, who explored the desert and its scarce oases on horseback. He describes Pica as a village of one-storey adobe houses with flat roofs. Streets of loose sand made walking such hard work that he rode his horse from one house to the next. Water from surface springs and underground channels or *cochas* provided sparse but sufficient nourishment to the vineyards, vegetable gardens and alfalfa fields, as well as the *grapes, used to make wine and* aguardiente, *figs, guavas, melons, chirimoyas, pears, peaches, membrillos, small sour lemons, pomegranates, prickly pears, dates, pacayes or pacaes (*Prosopis dulcis*), the highest tree in the country; the pepper . . . which the Peruvians use in most of their dishes. They also grow olives, cane for roofing, a little cotton, sweet potatoes . . . and other plants.*

Bollaert mentions Matilla's church, *built by an Indian architect.*

By 1857, the province of Tarapaca was divided into five districts, around the towns of Tarapaca, Camina, Iquique, Sibaya and Pica, which altogether included 29 towns, 10 *pagos*, 8 villages and a total population of some 19,000 people, 4,000 in Pica, making it larger than Iquique. The village of Tirana, named for the beautiful tyrant, Ñusta herself, had a meagre population of some 200 souls, with water supplied by wells sunk deep into the ground. Great scabs of salt covered the ground around the salt field of Pintados, near the geoglyphs we visited over a century later, vast expanses of desert sown with mirages—the Spanish describe visions of the ocean and vibrant forests thriving on the vacant earth.

In August 1879, smallpox attacked the towns, just months before the soldiers arrived to fight the nitrate war, placing Iquique in the Chileans' hands and breaking the oases' leadership for good. The old families, named Loayza, Morales, Baltierra, Zavala, Nuñez, Olazábal and Almonte, rebuilt.

With the Chileans' victory over Peru and Bolivia, the nitrate industry took off, devastating the trees of the tamarugo forest. Farmers peeled the salt crusts back from the fields and planted in the *canchones* (ditches) thus formed. But even the dedication of all the available land to the production of alfalfa wasn't enough to feed the 3,000 mules that were plying the desert, providing the main source of energy in the nitrate offices and carrying supplies from Bolivia and Northern Argentina to the settlements scattered around the Atacama. As the years advanced, the Peruvians who had owned the nitrate offices during the early years, many of whom lived in Pica and Matilla, yielded to the British and other foreigners, who had the money and the new industrial processes that would fuel the boom.

In June 1883, Ambrosio Valdés rode into town, proud as a puritan, to take charge of the ruined valleys and bring order to chaos. He was a great one for memos outlining plans to rebuild, his mouth pursed so tight his voice could hardly squeeze through his lips: The morality of these people *could not be more perverse. Drunkenness and orgies are constant. The total lack of control of their lowest passions has no limit. The religious celebrations have no other purpose than to lead to orgy. The character of these inhabitants is very detestable. . .* Small wonder that Valdés himself felt he was poorly received by the local population.

The social gatherings celebrated in the homes of what had been the Peruvian colony's local aristocracy were one man's meat, another's orgies. Valdés battled the Peruvians for eight months, struggling to end such perverse local practices as the men and women's habit of bathing together naked. The administrator who succeeded him at least managed to establish a modest school and postal service between the oasis and Pozo Almonte, and a system of public lighting. But over and over again, the towns fell into neglect and ruin. The nitrate fields went bust and former soldiers and workers roamed the desert like Almagro's men, pillaging anything they could find.

Every so often a flood like Ñusta's rushed down one of the narrow ravines that cut across the desert, destroying the carefully constructed irrigation channels, changing the course of rivers and springs, smashing the human landscape moulded from fragile clay.

On 18 January 1898, the Chilean senate transferred all the income of the oasis (from nearby nitrate offices) to the port of Iquique, because, it argued, Pica was investing its 130,000 pesos' worth of annual taxes in *disproportionate* salaries for its employees.

Today in Matilla, all that is left of the wine industry that thrived from the 1700s to 1912 is housed in a modest adobe building. The colonial-style press, the massive oaken vats and the other accoutrements of wine-making of the period are artfully placed around the dirt-floored room. For in 1912, Matilla and the oasis in general lost its last battle with Iquique, at least temporarily. The Chilean government expropriated the lands of small farmers located in the Quisma Valley, which supplied Matilla and where most of its grapevines were grown. Matilla fought back, refusing compensation, but the expropriation went ahead. Shortly thereafter, the Tarapaca Water Company (John North again) walked off with the water rights for the valley, piping the precious liquid down to Iquique where it sold at premium prices.

This was the Atacama's first battle in a war that rages silently across its surface to this day. Then, as now, foreign mining companies, supported by a national government that blindly equates development with growth, use the full force of centralist laws to impose their will over the rights of traditional farmers, many of them united in indigenous communities thousands of years old.

In the twentieth century, Bowman accurately predicted that although it was only fourteen miles from the Lagunas-Iquique railroad to Pica, the line would probably never be built, because the ore grades would not justify the expense. He added that *The traveler a century hence will still find certain groups unaffected, in the main, by the industrial development of the mines and the nitrate deposits of the desert of Tarapaca. The [seventeenth and eighteenth century] bells in the churches of Caspana, San Pedro de Atacama and Chiu Chiu . . . have served a line of people whose life has come down from earlier centuries almost as unchanged as the peals of the bells that have ushered out successive generations.*

Pica/Matilla is still stubbornly insisting on its right to exist, and now, at the turn of yet another century, in a time beginning to be plagued by climate change and global warming, when the Niño current has flipped us hopelessly from extreme flooding to overwhelming drought, I can't help wondering how much longer the water war between agriculture and mining will go on, and who or what will ultimately win. Perhaps time is gathering its strength, preparing itself (and us) for another pachikuti.

The Church in Matilla is dedicated to Saint Anthony, the patron saint of the lost. The parishioners, infused with their own rebellious spirit, have always celebrated their own rites of memory with the tools at hand. Beside the main altar, there's something peculiar about the model of the Last Supper. The figures are all life-sized and dressed in traditional biblical robes, but their faces are unexpectedly, vividly contemporary. Long-haired young men, some smiling, some foreign, some looking very Andean, sit at a table spread with fresh fruit of the area, rather than wine. They feast and lift their glasses in a bold toast, just a few feet from the altar.

But it's Matilla's garden on the hill that really astonishes all three of us. We're tired and inclined to skip the climb up the hill to yet another shrine, but the neighbours tell us we really have to see it, so up we traipse. Pato and Camilo admire the view while I wait patiently for a few minutes at a door into a low building at the top of the hill. A man stands guard, looking both proud and conspiratorial, which I find most peculiar.

As a couple of visitors leave, he ushers me in. I find myself standing on a small wooden balcony looking down into a room resembling a cave, at the effigy of a man strapped to a wooden table, surrounded by knives and whips, instruments for cutting and twisting and wrenching air from lungs, movement from limbs, screams from lips. As I back out, caught between confusion and shock, I read the lettering on a small plaque placed at eye level:

Don't be horrified at what they did to him,
but rather,
what they are doing to him now.

I find a bench conveniently placed a few feet away, and sit down, gazing out over the hills toward the ocean of the Atacama, dry as prehistoric bone. To my right, roses and geraniums release their perfumes in a small fenced plot, at the end of which stands an empty cross. Ah, yes. Golgotha. Even my biblical ignorance yields at last to some nugget of understanding lost at the bottom of my junk-filled memory. The place where Christ was crucified. The place of the skull, called *Golgotha*, from the Hebrew, *Calvary* from the Latin. A hill whose name derives from the shape of the skulls of those executed there.

Like the animitas, Matilla's garden of Golgotha is folk art, unedited, infused with the town's outrage. Their opinions never appear in the media. Instead, they bloom on signs posted among the flowers. *Golgotha, where we meet again* . . . I push open the gate and walk into the garden. On the cross another little sign whispers: *Look for me on the cross, and you won't find me. Look for me in your heart* . . .

The living man has opted for something else, abandoned his cross, leaving the trappings of godliness and death—his crown of thorns and a blood-stained cloth—behind. On my way out I encounter one last sign; large and roughly lettered, it reads in part:

If for you I'm still to be found on a cross
It's because your heart
is closed to me.

8

C O P P E R

M E N

Chuquicamata

In the end, gold mines impoverish those who own
them, silver preserves an equilibrium, and copper mines
enrich.

> – *South American proverb*

The alicanto bird lives on gold and silver. Its wings
shine in the dark, but it is so heavy it cannot fly. Those
who see an alicanto and decide to follow it will find a
fortune, but if it sees them, the bird will disappear.

> – *Oreste Plath*

c. A.D. 484

H E   W A S   A B O U T   five foot three inches tall, muscular
in build. Every day he rose early, put on a warm
woollen shirt and wrapped a heavy shawl around his
torso, then secured both in place with a sash woven of

white and blue threads. After twisting his hair into a series of neat braids, he went off to work, carrying his tools. These consisted of four or more hafted hammers, that is, sharpened rocks of the local diorite granite bound to short sticks by strands of rawhide from llamas and other Andean animals. He carried a hide bag and four baskets made of coiled grass, containing a collection of rocks and small pointed sticks of different sizes.

Before setting out, he tied twin strips of fur and woven wool around his ankles. Perhaps they were just ornaments, but it's more likely they were supposed to bring him luck, or protection when he was out there scraping away under the crust of the lonely desert.

Wherever he lived, it had to be near water. That meant that to reach his place of work, he must have hiked at least twelve miles, carrying food, fuel for a fire and water to set up camp for a few days, because there was none to be had where he was going. The winds there could reach 70 kilometres an hour, while daytime temperatures would rise to 65 degrees Fahrenheit in winter, 100 in summer, before plunging to well below freezing every night.

Work itself consisted of slipping himself like a human finger into a glove of rock, his arms and tools above his head like a diver, then pushing himself along a narrow horizontal shaft as he traced his objective through the rock. All day he would chip away at the atacamite ore, a native hydrous chloride of copper that bled from the cave walls, encrusting the veins of sulphide copper ores like dried tears. Perhaps he worked with a small group of friends or brothers, each one's body a thick muscular finger so that together they formed a couple of human hands. Perhaps he worked alone, dragging his bags of ore out of the tunnel, piling them high around its mouth.

He and his companions would have traded their raw copper nuggets with the families that ran the caravans across the desert, circling west to east, north along the Andes up to Titicaca, then back. The Tiwanaku empire was just coming to power when this miner lived and died. Perhaps the empire included copper as part of the tribute to be paid, backing up its harsh demands with the threat of military action or the Sacrificer himself. From Titicaca the gleaming metal would travel even farther north and west, toward the mosaic of cultures between the mountains and the coast and those squeezed between the desert and the Pacific Ocean.

Some of the native copper that he and generations of his fellows scratched so diligently from the rocky earth around Chuquicamata found its way into the objects discovered more than a thousand years later in the cemeteries of the Atacamenian villages of San Pedro de Atacama, about 100 kilometres to the east: the three bracelets and the breastplates found in Larrache and Sequitor, made around A.D. 500, the *rompecabezas* ("head-crushing") hammers from the seventh and eighth centuries, and the copper chisels used to carve memories out of the stony landscape.

Earrings encrusted with turquoise, worn and lost or carefully buried during the tenth century A.D. were found in Solor. There were also axes and knives for domestic use from the fifth to the tenth centuries, and bells cast between the eighth and twelfth centuries. In Sequitor a copper arrowhead, along with pins, needles, brooches and chisels from the fifteenth century, marked the beginning of the Christian era, on the South American continent. Around Coyo and Solor, crucibles and a chunk of melted copper also appeared, indicating where at least some of the copper ore had been worked, giving a heated, heavy birth to some of the marvels found scattered around the different villages.

How did they process the copper they scratched so painfully from the underbelly of the earth?

Garcilaso de la Vega, in his treatise on the origin of the Incan Kings of Peru, reported that the Indians *smelted by blowing through copper pipes, half an arm in length, more or less, depending on whether the smelter were large or small. They would cover one end of the pipe and leave a small hole out of which the air emerged compressed and stronger. They'd bring together eight, ten and twelve . . . and would go around the fire blowing through the pipes. They also knew how to make tongs to take the metal out of the fire . . .*

They also use small, portable ovens of mud to smelt silver and lead. . . In these cases, *they didn't smelt with bellows or even the copper pipes, but rather they let the natural wind do the smelting. . . At night they'd go up the hills and place themselves on the high or low slopes, depending on the way the wind was blowing, a little or a lot, to temper it in a more or less sheltered spot. It was beautiful indeed to see in those times, eight, ten, twelve, fifteen thousand little ovens burning on those hills and heights.*

Mining and metalwork using gold, silver and copper had developed in the Central Andean area about a thousand years earlier, around 700 B.C., and from there spread northward, reaching Mesoamerica about A.D. 1000. Diego de Almagro himself sent Captain Gómez de Alvarado with a group of miners to look for mineral deposits and *they found mines and ravines and ore as well worked as if the Spanish themselves had worked them.*[*]

---

[*] Oviedo (Vicuña Mackenna).

For the peoples of the Andes copper was everything that iron was to ancient Europe, and perhaps more. They used the *anta*, as they called it, for fishhooks, knives, adzes, carpentry tools, needles, pins, brooches, mirrors, the keys to everyday survival. Copper was also used to make the shallow dishes that held hallucinogenic dusts during sacred ceremonies.

Throughout Peru, Colombia and Ecuador, *tumbaga*, a gold-copper alloy, was widely used, as was bronze, an alloy discovered around A.D. 1000. Artisans knew the secret of blending copper and tin to mould chisels so hard they could use them to cut through granite and basalt, even turquoise and emeralds. *That wise man Humboldt took one of the chisels found in a silver mine near Cuzco to Europe where they found it contained 96 parts copper and four parts tin, that is, a bronze alloy, the like of which has not been seen again,* Vicuña Mackenna notes. And Gutiérrez too reports that Diego de Almagro, on his way back to Peru in 1536, stopped at Chiu Chiu, where he was able to refit his horses with copper horse-shoes at a nearby Incan smelter that produced *a combination of copper and tin whose secret has been lost.**

The jewellery was exquisite, cast into intricate designs representing the Sun God and other deities, engraved or embossed to express the shifting views of the universe and humanity's place within it, the moments of pachikuti, the story of humanity's beginning. Masks with turquoise eyes and other features formed by inlaid shells were common, as were necklaces mixing the different elements from the four layers of the Andes, shells from the coast, the polished turquoise, pink and brown of desert and mountain stones,

---

* Gutiérrez (Chuquicamata Tierras Rojas).

the iridescent feathers of Amazonian birds. The piercing eyes of the Sacrificer often glared out of ceremonial pieces, turquoise chips, hard and sharp.

Fernández de Oviedo reported that before it passed into history and was forgotten, he had to record how *the Indians know full well how to gild the pieces and things they model from copper and gold. And they have so much delicacy and excellence in this, and give such a bright shine to that which they gild, that it looks as good as twenty-three-carat gold or more. . . They do this with certain herbs and it is such a great secret that any silversmith of Europe or elsewhere, who knew how to use it, would be a very rich man.*

This miner, with his windblown braids and rough woollen clothes, may have been among the first of the artists who for generations sketched their stories on the cave walls of the Atacama, or scratched their ideas under the glaring light reflected off the hills. During his people's ceremonies he may have coaxed shrill cries from the antara or drawn forth the deep voice of the skin drum called the *bombo*.

We would never have suspected his existence at all though, never have been able to deduce from his clothes the presence of llama herds and probably some agriculture nearby (men or women dedicated to spinning fine wool and weaving heavy garments, able to withstand the sharp extremes of heat and cold) if it had not happened that one day, the narrow gap in the ground where he worked collapsed. The movement of the rock was slight; it broke few of his bones, but its weight forced the blood into his hands and feet. The pressure on his ribs and lungs made breathing impossible.

From the moment Diego de Almagro set foot in the great wastes of the Atacama in the early days of 1536, the search for minerals was on. But the Spanish conquistadors, spoiled by the wealth of gold and silver already refined by the Inca, did not expect to labour over their findings. *Why pursue trade when the ultimate object in view could be had directly, in exchange for a few sword strokes, a transaction quite in accord with the past eight centuries of Spanish history?* asks Otis Young, in the broad accents of a modern-day American scholar. He adds that *As the Age of the Explorers gave way to the Age of the Conquistadors, gold by the ton flowed east to Spain, upsetting alike the diplomacy and the economy of Europe . . . the booty of Mexico and Peru was the sum of centuries of patient, grain-by-grain accumulation, and when it was gone there was not a great deal more to be had immediately. Scores, perhaps, of lesser Conquistadors attempted to duplicate the feats of Cortés and Pizarro, but failed in their objective, for it did not exist.*

The precious metals, already refined and worked and there for the taking, may not have lasted, but the mentality did and does.

As in the rest of America, the Spanish in Peru divided the newly discovered Chile into *encomiendas*, large tracts of land, which it promptly bestowed upon its loyal servants. Some settled the land, working the indigenous peoples who were part and parcel of the agreement. But many tired of the conflicts and the hard work and moved on to conquer new horizons. It was only when gold or silver was discovered that the Spanish were sure to play out their role, assuming control and working their native labourers to death to extract all the wealth they could from the raw desert—as they did in the legendary mines of Potosi in Bolivia, and Huantajaya in Chile.

It is ironic that this great country, so fertile in ores and metals, became the tomb of the hopes of the first conquistadors. Upperclass Chileans have an accent thick as clotted cream, and I imagine Alexander Sutulov, the Chilean mining historian, talks like that—as if he had a huge chunk of that cream in the back of his throat and was speaking through it.

The rich surface ores of silver and gold were quickly exhausted, and the kind of mining shifted away from the simpler techniques dependent on cheap, unskilled labour and toward underground mining, which was more dangerous, requiring more skilled workers along with more sophisticated technology.

To develop these mines the Spanish relied heavily on a 1556 textbook by Georgius Agricola, *De re metallica*, which Otis Young calls *the first and greatest of mining textbooks*. Young also notes that wood, water and iron were crucial to European mining of the period, and with all three scarce in its new colonies in Mexico and the Andes, the Spanish used stone instead, and leather binding in place of bolts, employing local tradespeople to build arches and masonry to brace the walls and ceilings of their underground galleries.

The silver ore would be chipped or blasted out, then gathered into baskets weighing around 100 kilograms, which porters slung on their backs, suspended on a rope that wound around their foreheads. They would then walk, sometimes for miles, up the notched logs that were the mine's version of a staircase, using a candle perched on a large stick to light the way.

As with bailing (the use of pails on long hoists turned by horse-windlasses to literally bail water out of the mines)— Young's voice again—*the method appears almost neolithic but it was effective, required little capital, and was quite flexible in use: the more profitable ore there was to raise, the more* tenateros *[porters] were employed, without need for much, if any, additional capital expenditure.*

For want of water, the Chilean wheel, *one or two great stone disks set to revolve upon a common wooden axle, with their edges running in a circular masonry trough*, was used to crush the ore, an operation done with water power in Europe. In Spain's American mines, workers filled the trough with ore and horses turned the axle to crush it down. The wheel was originally adapted from a Mediterranean device used to crush olives. A heavy wooden arm with huge blocks of stone hanging from it would rotate around a circular room, finely pulverizing the ore.

Finally, a process invented by a merchant named Bartolomé de Medina in 1555 was used to chemically reduce the ore. In this process, the finely crushed ore was spread around a patio and workers sprinkled salt, mercury and copper over it. Horses then trampled and crushed the mixture for days on end until the mercury was consumed and a paste rich in silver produced.

But by the 1700s, ore grades began to drop and it became harder to recover enough ore to keep a mine really profitable, especially with the Spanish crown controlling a monopoly on salt and mercury and exacting its *royal fifth* in tax on all silver produced. In Mexico, at least, this first led to the creation of a university course for the training of mining engineers, but war between Spain and France in Europe encouraged rebellion in the colonies and the decades of struggle for independence left little in the way of resources or attention to improving the mines. The result, then as now, was that mining technology fell behind the demands of the ores that were left to extract and eventually governments like that of Porfirio Díaz in Mexico resorted to asking foreign mining companies to come in and help modernize the old mines.

Disease and forced labour in the mines and on the Spaniards' encomiendas decimated the population, destroying the fine balance that once existed between the environment and the people's needs. In 1552, two decades after the conquest of the southern Andes began, Cristóbal de Molina observed that *the drop in the number of Natives since the Spanish reached this land is so great that without there being noteworthy mortality rates if not from war and outstanding work, many regions that had 5,000 or 6,000 Indians when the land was first shared out now have barely two hundred and the valleys and lands where they lived are empty of men and full of the herds and ranches of the Spanish, which has given rise to the argument that the Spanish in this land are generally more friendly toward raising cattle than human beings . . .* *

Molina also describes the extraordinary innovations used to create the *fertile and abundant* gardens and valleys of the north, with their large buildings and wealth of gold, silver, textiles and animals, even in the absence of water, including a technique used along the coast in which seeds of corn were planted inside small sardine-like fish. This provided a fine crop three or four times a year.

For the first three hundred years of the Conquest, the Atacama was administered from Lima, Peru, then split between Bolivia and Peru as these countries emerged. At the beginning of the nineteenth century Chile was still a tight little green ball curled up in the fertile central valley, surrounded by the Andes to the east and the Pacific to the west, and bordered on the south by the Tolten River. To the north lay the bare waste of the Atacama, with its poorly defined borders.

---

* de Molina (Hidalgo's *Culturas*).

In 1870, Chilean prospectors found the legendary silver mine of Caracoles, then in Bolivian territory, which went on to produce some 855,000 kilos of silver, worth US$207 million in 1975 dollars. Copper mining came to the fore in the nineteenth century and for a while Chile even led the world in production, but its epoch of glory was still to come.

In 1899, as the nitrate industry dipped and soared, the in the desert. The Restauradora mine, near a place called Chuquicamata, was simply a cluster of huts surrounded by a stone wall, in the middle of the Atacama, twelve miles from the Calama oasis and water. The hardy group of men who worked there used a container and a single pulley hoist; some of them stayed above ground to lower it into a shaft, others, deep in the earth, loaded it with atacamite-containing ore that they chipped from the walls below using tools and techniques not all that different from those used for thousands of years by the indigenous people of the Atacama. They shovelled their bucket-loads against a screen to separate out the ore from the gravel, then used an anvil and a small forge with bellows to further process the metal.

When the mine had started nobody knew, but its importance to the Chilean economy had shot up and down like mercury in a barometer, marking fine weather and fierce economic storms. Between 1707 and 1729, ships carrying wheat to the northern port of La Caldera developed the habit of trading it for copper, which they used as ballast as they continued their journey down the coast. In 1747, Fernando de Aguirre (a descendent of Francisco de Aguirre, who had travelled to Chile with Pedro de Valdivia almost two hundred years earlier) shipped out the first load of copper bars. Others soon followed his example, among them the Portuguese Almeida, one of whose

ancestors may have entwined his life with that of Huillac
Ñusta.

For the first hundred years or more of Chile's existence,
copper was considered of so little importance that when it
was needed for cannon, for example, officers would send
their minions up into the hills to gather it, as if they were
gathering wood or brush for brooms. Chile's sole export of
the time, writes Benjamin Vicuña Mackenna, was *a bit of tal-
low for the public and private lighting of opulent Lima* and a bit of
dried horsemeat for the African slaves there. In a curious foot-
note to history, Mackenna adds that most of the bullets that
the Chilean rebels fired against the Spanish during their wars
for independence were made of *indigenous Chilean copper.*

*Throughout the Colony, gold was the metal that placed Chile
among the world's largest producers. Independence . . . meant an
end to the gold, but soon the charm of silver came to the fore, dominating the national landscape for several decades, particularly
when it came to mining,* observes Sutulov.

Circa 1832, Carlos Santiago Lambert found a way to
process the sulphide ores whose leakage had created the
native copper mined by the Andeans. Lambert set up a
Swansea-style furnace in 1831 which he managed to keep
secret until 1841 when disgruntled workers fled his mine,
spreading the news of his discovery. Copycat production
methods at other mines promptly doubled, then tripled
production.

But the discovery had already made Lambert an even
wealthier man.* It also solved a major problem facing Chile's

---

* In 1825, Lambert loaned the Chileans 120,000 pesos to finance their
efforts to dislodge the Spanish from the southern islands of Chiloe,
their last stronghold in the country.

copper industry, because his process introduced a profitable treatment for sulphide ores, just as the Atacama's rich oxide ores were beginning to run out.

José Tomás Urmeneta was already a wealthy landowner when the mining bug bit him. Raised by an uncle who died poor (*sure proof of his honesty*, comments the dry voice of Vicuña Mackenna), Urmeneta studied in Providence, industrial capital of Rhode Island, where *the snow leaves the ground for four months of the year only, and from the hearts [of its people] never.*

A modest package of sewing needles from the workshops of Rhode Island, sold for five hundred pesos' profit, not only paid for Urmeneta's passage home but also marked his beginnings as a successful businessman. After roaming the world and living off the proceeds of imports he brought back with him to Chile, Urmeneta tired of commerce and moved north, where he took charge of an abandoned mine belonging to his brother-in-law, and began to work it. Hardly had he blasted away his first chunk of mountain when, in 1842, he discovered a pocket rich in ore. He spent the next year exporting it to England, thus earning the fabulous sum of 200,000 pesos and a passion for mining that would drive him for the rest of his life.

Not content with this success, Urmeneta decided the pocket was really part of an insanely rich vein, and he spent the next fourteen years trying to find the rest of it, sinking his fortune into the rocks and dust of his attempts. Perched haphazardly on an ass's rump, he roamed the desiccated slopes until many were convinced he had gone mad.

But some time in November of 1849 or 1850, his luck broke. Near the seaside resort of Tongoy on the Pacific coast, Vicuña Mackenna tells us *the happy and stubborn industrialist, son and grandson of Celts hardened by work and faith, found himself the richest man in South America, owner of a royal vein of purplish bronze, 70 per cent pure and two yards in diameter.* He began to drill its shafts and galleries, and enthusiastically spent seven hundred thousand pesos to have a railway built from the town of Tongoy all the way to the mouth of his mine.

Urmeneta spread his wealth around, supporting schools and firefighters, and contributing to both the Capuchin nuns and the Masonic lodges, which were then challenging the Catholic Church's hold on Chile. He died in 1878, his health having begun to decline *from the day that prosperity first gathered him to her affectionate but treacherous breast*, as old Vicuña Mackenna puts it.

The discovery of the Tamaya mine with its massive reserves (for a while it was responsible for a quarter of all Chilean copper production, turning out the purest bars available anywhere before electro-refining came in during the twentieth century) boosting copper production significantly. In 1831, with Faraday's discovery of the induction of electric currents, it began to take off. But it was the invention of the telegraph that caused demand to rage like a fever.[*]

---

[*] In fact, world demand for copper grew from 44,000 metric tons (mt) in 1840 (when it was invented), to average 100,000 mt during the 1860s and, with the discovery of the telephone (1875) and the lightbulb (1879), hit 125,000 mt per year throughout the 1870s. Demand pushed the price to its highest level, perhaps ever, between 90 cents and US$1.50 per pound (1975 currency). (In contrast, as of February 1999, the price of copper had plunged to less than 65 cents per pound on the London Metals Exchange, probably its lowest level in history.) Copper was also used in sheets for ship building, and in the form of tubes and boilers for steam-driven vehicles and motors. (Sutulov).

Chile, however, could not keep pace. As world demand rose, consumption devoured its high-grade copper reserves. Where before it had been possible to find ore containing 10 per cent or even 15 per cent copper, by the end of the nineteenth century grades had plunged to between 2.5 and 3 per cent copper. This required concentration of the ore before smelting and refining it, a technology that Chile did not have.

Says Sutulov, *The unequivocal message is that every mineral and every metal has its hour; its relative value and importance change not only due to the relationship between supply and demand, but also as a function of its industrial uses and humanity's immediate need for it.*

Of the 748 mines in existence at the close of the nineteenth century, only fifty had any kind of mechanization, all very rudimentary, in spite of the fact that many mines plunged as far as 1,500 metres down into the earth. In 1899, the Restauradora, with its muscle-driven pulley system, was one of the few survivors. It was here, sometime in October 1899, that one of the miners working underground must have choked back a shout and squirmed his way backward out of the tunnel and up the shaft to his fellows, mumbling incoherently of something—or someone—lying down below in the gallery he had been exploring.

That bundle of cloth and dried flesh turned out to be a perfectly preserved body.

When he and his companions ventured back down the shaft, they discovered a man, lying on his side as if asleep. And when they dragged him back out into the sunlight for the first time in over a thousand years, they noticed the greenish fingers, curved as if they still held tools—

hammers shaped using rocks from the desert above. His feet were as casually crossed as if he'd been caught sharing a glass of wine in one of Monet's picnics.

His multiple braids led them at first to assume he was a woman. In fact, an early newspaper headline (doubling his age) trumpeted: *Aged 3000, But She Has Traces of Beauty.*

He had been perfectly preserved—in 1923 an X-ray revealed few broken bones, no cuts or scratches. His skin had dried rapidly, maintaining much of its natural shape and tension. Only one unheard-of change had occurred. Over the approximately 1,400 years that he had lain under the earth, copper had seeped into the natural white wool of his shirt and cloak, tingeing them green. The man's skin, too, had sipped of the metal hidden in the ore. After examining the miner's body in 1921, Louis Sullivan, a physical anthropologist, concluded: *The mummy presented by Mr. Morgan is infiltrated with copper and the body is preserved in great detail. Even the contours of the muscles remain. It is evident that the individual was a well-developed adult man in the prime of life . . .*

The copper miner had become the Copper Man.

1912 – Guggenheim and Sons

In the early 1900s Chile's rich copper reserves began to attract the attention of foreign, especially American, interests. Entrepreneurs like William Braden were visiting to take a closer look. In Maine in 1904, Braden pulled together an initial investment of US$4 million and set up the Braden Copper Company to administer the El Teniente deposit, located about 100 kilometres south of Santiago (it is still in operation today). In his constant search for financiers, he contacted the Guggenheims, and on 11 January 1912 the Chile Exploration Company (Chilex) was set up to run Chuquicamata.

At the time, most of the readily available higher-grade ores had already been skimmed off, but the demand for copper was on the rise and engineers were sweating over their research, looking for ways to recover the metal from the low-grade sulphide deposits of porphyry copper that were left.

During the twenties, among the problems for workers in Chuquicamata, according to Santiago Machiavello, were *The poisonous vapours and smoke of the plants and the resulting asphyxia, the excessive weight of bars and rods of copper, that is the cause of thousands of hernias, the work of children along with the degeneration of the race, the danger of the powder plants, the right to association as the worker's means to ensure he is respected as a human being, respect for the right to rest on Sundays, as per the November 17, 1917 law, the effectiveness of Welfare Departments, the implementation of free hospitals in the plants, that not only look after accidents on the job but also take care of all workers and their families whose health is affected by causes beyond their control, strict suppression of alcoholism, as a way to regenerate our people and to reduce accidents, the neutralization of poisonous gases that return to the rivers after being used in industrial processes, the abolition of all privileges enjoyed by people of the same nationality as the company and many others . . .*

Eulogio Gutiérrez, who had worked as a copper inspector at Chuqui's smelter, adds that infant mortality rates were *terrifying* and painted the picture of a kind of Lourdes

---

* Santiago Machiavello Varas (Gutiérrez).

Grotto in reverse, churning out handicapped people and invalids *by the hundreds.*

Men from more than twenty different countries from around the world had somehow touched down in the oasis of Calama, to find work in the pit. Through Gutiérrez's eyes I see the men, *deserters from some ship, survivors of some catastrophe or another* . . . as they stride out over the desert horizon with the rolling gait of a sailor, to stand dwarfed before the massive gates of Chuquicamata, a duffel bag over their shoulders, still stinking of the tar, a smelly old pipe squeezed between their teeth.

Chilex ran its own supply stores for the workers, but also allowed pedlars onto the premises, provided that they paid the company a tax. Wages ran about seven pesos per day, while in 1920 the daily costs of basic survival items were:

firewood	1 peso
meat	2 pesos
beans	0.6 pesos
potatoes	0.8 pesos
bread	1 peso
sugar	1.2 pesos
noodles	0.4 pesos
onions	0.2 pesos
lard	0.4 pesos
tea	0.4 pesos
squash	0.4 pesos
TOTAL	8.4 pesos

The powder storage rooms were dangerously close to the workers' living quarters, Gutiérrez complained, and accidents were commonplace. In one work area a stretcher waited, strategically placed, with a sign warning *I am the bed of the careless man . . . used more than necessary. . .* A crude drawing showed the stretcher standing on two handles, with eyes, mouth and nose, and a bloodstain shaped like the outline of a hand.

Gutiérrez complained that the Americans working at the plant, even the less skilled ones, received far better wages. *The Directors of Chilex are, like us, Americans of European origin and therefore should not classify the Chilean as a "black man" as opposed to the "Yankee" or white man from the United States.*

Like the nitrate offices that dotted the desert around it, Chuquicamata spawned a strong union movement that faced violent repression when it declared its support for the labour efforts seething around it, both in the desert and beyond. In December 1919, Chuqui's workers marched in support of Antofagasta's railway workers, then on strike, only to find themselves plunged into a state of emergency, 600 of the camp's workers under arrest. From then on, observes Janet Finn in her book *Tracing the Veins*, the company used time-honoured techniques to keep the workers down and break the union, including spies, blacklists, timely pay-offs to local and national politicians. *The history is one of a compromised democracy, in which the Chilean government contested and acquiesced to the demands of a powerful corporation that was often backed by U.S. government policy and politics,* Finn observes.

The chains binding Chilean copper to U.S. interests tightened during the Depression, when the U.S. placed a high tariff on copper imports to help stimulate recovery at home. This pushed unemployment in Chilean mines to 66 per cent during the early thirties. Ten years later, as the end of World War II brought yet another downturn in copper prices, Chuqui's miners again went on strike, only to face government intervention and the arrest of their leaders. During the late 1940s opposition newspapers were shut down and repression increased.

Union leaders were arrested and a lot of them were sent to Pisagua for one or two years, one woman told Finn. *When the men were sent to Pisagua, the women and children were put out of their houses in Chuqui, because [the houses] belonged to the company. My comadre, she was from Coquimbo. Her husband was sent to Pisagua and she and her children were sent to Punta Arenas. I don't know how, maybe by train. They had to make their way back to Coquimbo by boat while her husband was imprisoned in Pisagua.*

During another strike, in 1953, fear of Pisagua still haunted the workers and especially their families: *I was so scared because I was . . . afraid my husband had been arrested, or sent to Pisagua or some other place, or even worse, I was afraid he'd been shot.*

In 1966, Chuquicamata mine was on strike again, in solidarity with workers at other foreign-owned copper mines, Kennecott's El Teniente and Anaconda's El Salvador. Organizers were arrested and Salvador Allende, then a senator and soon to become president, was banned from the premises of Chuquicamata. Finn quotes a strike leader who recalled the military taking over the town in an attempt to break the strike, facing down two thousand marchers, *with lots of violence and arrests. But they kept going in spite of the violence.* When the strike continued at the Salvador mine, *government troops opened fire on a large group of miners and their families outside the union hall . . . killing seven [five men and two women] and injuring dozens.*

The Vietnam War was then at its height, and copper was essential to the U.S. arsenal. Anaconda's property at Butte, Montana, was on strike for nine months, which *affected tens of thousands of workers nationwide*. . . But the strike was useful to the mine owners, keeping the company's profits rolling in at just the right amount, with no unfortunate build-up in stocks to push prices downward.

1998 – Chuquicamata

Driving through the desert junkyards outside Calama amidst the acrid smell of burning garbage, it's not hard to imagine that one is driving through a kind of underworld where lost souls or, in this case, poor souls, are punished for their lack of initiative and commitment to the predominant system. To the north, across the flat stones of the Atacama rise low hills like the triangular vertebrae of some prehistoric creature. In the hollows, spirals of dust fling themselves from one cliff to the next, or whirl upward, small tornadoes thrusting themselves against the bare slopes, then collapsing as new torrents of dust—the wind made visible—gather and rush again toward oblivion. Huge chimney stacks vomit towers of steamy gases into the air until it looks as if the hills were labouring to give birth to the wind, the clouds, the earth itself, all starting as dust. I've shot through the black depths of the desert night as if through space, and noticed how the lights of Chuquicamata hang above it, shining like diamonds or the origin of stars.

Closer up, though, it's clear that today, Chuquicamata is an industrial city in decline. Once the world's largest open-pit copper mine, at some eighty years old (or more, depending on how you count) it is also perhaps the oldest, in a world where copper mines have an expected life span of thirty years. A paved ribbon of asphalt sixteen kilometres long cuts across the desert from the oasis to the fortress-like mine where it sprawls in the foothills above the squashed oasis of Calama. A town, complete with a hospital, a cemetery and several supermarkets, huddles between the massive hole that is the main pit and the smaller one called Mina Sur. A huge torta of waste material from the mine, very similar to those left behind by the nitrate offices, lies beside the pits.

Every day, usually around 5:00 p.m., the earth is shaken by a violent blast, a man-made quake designed to rip huge chunks of ore loose from the sides of the pit. Every year, the pit sinks deeper and deeper into the earth, ruthlessly raising costs (the gas, the oil, the maintenance) even as the richer ores grow scarcer and harder to find.

Trucks the size of two-storey houses, each wheel taller than a man, drive round and round the edges of the pit as if in some insane children's game, rumbling to the bottom then groaning and screeching their way up the spiral to where, amidst the thunder of falling chunks of mountain and the squealing of machinery, they dump their loads—150,000 tons of ore a day—into the primary crushing plant. There it is reduced to a large gravelly river, piled onto a conveyor belt and stored in the silos that in turn feed the concentrator plants.

Next, the gravel is poured into spinning cylinders where it's mixed with water and crushed to a sandy paste, which flows into the flotation cells where more water and chemicals are added, air is injected and the whole mixture is shaken like a giant chemical cocktail. Particles of copper cling to bubbles of air and form a thick spume on the surface of the liquid, called collective concentrate. From the 1.1 per cent grade of the copper ore, the concentration of copper has now risen to 32 per cent, along with 1 per cent molybdenum ("moly"), gold, silver and other minerals.

The water is squeezed out of the mess and recycled, while the waste tailings are moved out to a storage dam in the desert. In the meantime, the oily liquid with its dark rainbow-streaked bubbles and their cargo of minerals is run through another plant. There the moly is extracted and the concentrate is passed through drying fields, then moved into the smelter where copper blister, 99.98 per cent pure, is produced. After further purification in a warehouse that I remember as the size of a football field, with an atmosphere worthy of the movie *Alien* (the floor covered with quietly bubbling tanks like giant incubators, all religiously watched over by anxious caretakers), the final product emerges: great plates about a metre square of almost pure copper, ready for shipping to markets around the world.

The main processes of smelting and refining haven't changed significantly since 1900. Newer mines, like Escondida, Chuquicamata's dashing competitor to the south, rely more on the heapleaching technology: the gravel is drenched with a constant spray of sulphuric acid and other chemicals that wash the copper out of the rock and collect it for solvent extraction and electro-winning. Heapleaching is incredibly cheap, compared to the old concentrator-smelting-refining process—about half a cent per pound, compared to over eighty cents. But to date it can only be used on oxide ores, although there is some experimentation with sulphides.

I spent a day visiting every corner of Chuquicamata, talking to the managers of the different production units and even driving far into the hills to take a look at their experimental sulphide leaching tank. I passed brilliant turquoise pools glistening in the sun, inviting the swimmer in me to dive in. But for all the tempting beauty of their "waters," these are toxic chemicals, mostly acid. In the rooms that govern each plant, each step in the process, men and the rare woman sit like astronauts at their controls, in round or square chambers, lined with panels that blink with green, red and other coloured lights. Television screens often cover most of the walls around them, like windows opening onto a myriad of planets. Technological discoveries are keeping Chuquicamata alive.

Each time it has been about to yield to exhaustion, some new invention sweeps in like a super hero to save it, permitting further exploitation of ores with ever decreasing grades. It's even become possible to recover copper from some of the piles of tailings left behind by older operations.

The old mine still spews tons of sulphuric acid and arsenic into the air and has been blamed for serious leaks of pollutants into the nearby river. It has also robbed nearby towns, thousands of years old, of their precious water, reduced them to empty terraces, a handful of adobe boxes with locked doors virtually all year round. If I retreat from the hills of Chuquicamata and take the highway east toward San Pedro and the Andes, I can turn off and, slanting slightly northward, pass through the towns of Chiu Chiu, Lasana, Ayquina, Turi and Toconce. Their names suggest the kind of universe that science fiction is made of, suggest that the past can be touched. The great cities of the

Atacama, reduced to villages, still cling to its surface, barely surviving.

Chiu Chiu (its name like a bird's cry, plaintive and shrill) was once a paired city with San Pedro. Its name, Atacama La Chica (Little Atacama) to San Pedro's Atacama El Grande (Big Atacama), reflects not the rich suburbs and poor slums these terms might suggest in a modern city, but the dual nature of every Andean and desert town, each place, each street, each leader a mirror reflection of another. Out to the east of Chiu Chiu, the Incan highway stretches, like the memory of an embrace, to hold four more cities balanced on its arm, before disappearing over the Andes. I follow it now, trace the fading petroglyphs on the stones along the road to Lasana, pause where the road opens out into a narrow valley green with flowing grass, the dense hope of crops and a silver streak of water.

Lasana. A low hill rises out of the centre of a narrow valley. A handful of houses seem to have been scattered like seeds around it: an adobe school house, dusty playing fields. I stop the car and get out, walk up the hill to the ruins of the old stone fort, the Pukara de Lasana. Crisscrossed by staircases and honeycombed with cubby-holes and narrow alleys, it stands roofless and open to the elements—and the public. There are no guards to ensure that its visitors treat it with the respect it deserves.

Many visitors have in fact walked away with a piece of the Pukara, but there's still enough left to fill me with awe and longing. I hear Grete Mostny's voice joining the others that whisper along its empty hallways: *The dead were buried in the houses themselves, in graves dug in the floors of the rooms and often lined with stones or slabs. In some cases, when the precipice itself formed one of the walls, they would open a kind of grotto to place the dead person there, covering it up afterwards with a pile of stones or wall of slabs.* Thus the house served also as a place of burial and worship, a kind of family temple where the most essential rites were performed.

And like the Pukara of Quitor near San Pedro, this one denotes a time when the peaceful settlements of the desert oases found themselves under siege, whether from the Incas or from quarrels among themselves. The size of the Pukara and the quality of the surrounding agricultural land indicates that about eight hundred people could once have lived or found refuge here. I can't help feeling how welcoming this fort would have looked to Huillac Ñusta, if she had passed it on her journey with Diego Almagro. But then the fierce resistance of the Atacamenians would have struck, the battles that sparked and bled all the way along their path through the desert. I wander along the narrow rocky alleyways that once served as ordered streets, see a small plaza that formed the centre of the fort, the chief's house to its left, the remains of a two-storey building at the top of the last alley.

Everything is so raw, so abandoned, enhancing the sense that the people who lived here have all just stepped out, will be back any second now, Ñusta walking unattended among them, a ghost, inspiring no awe, her destiny dealt with, her long hair floating free, her clothes as ragged and untended as any hippie's.

Curiously, several of the windows form the shape of small, distinct crosses. Others are square, the doorways rectangles, an indication they are not of Incan design. Sometime during the ninth century A.D., the Atacamenian culture began to assume a recognizable shape, pushing its way northward around the twelfth, toward the Nazca valley and the culture that produced the extraordinary geoglyphs known as the Nazca lines. The Nazca people belonged to the Chincha Confederation and demonstrated, according to Roberto Montandon, who studied the Pukara, *an artistic sense and a perfection that would be hard to match*, in both their ceramics and their weaving. They also used adobe in their buildings, although it doesn't seem to have reached the Atacama until three centuries later, when Incan colonists created two-storey houses in the Pukara of Turi and the town of Zapar, as well as the modest house in San Pedro de Atacama's central square.

But stone was the medium of choice for the great cultures of the Andes, the massive mountain ranges reduced to puzzle pieces then reshaped by human hands to create the massive temples, hill-sized pyramids and finely wrought sculptures of Tiwanaku. Infused with religious meaning, the power of ritual was expressed in the longevity of rock. The Incas also turned it to their purposes, developing the characteristic trapezoidal shape of their doorways and the massive foundations used first for their own palaces and temples, later for the Spaniards' mansions and cathedrals.

But long before the first contact with the Chincha or the arrival of the Incan colonists, the Atacamenians also developed their own expression in stone. Theirs was a simpler vision, focused more on practical use than decoration. The building of the Pukara marked the evolution of their society from peaceful agricultural villages scattered throughout the desert to a time when restless feet and the excitement of travel brought either invaders from abroad or conflicts within their own confederation.

Standing at the edge of the fort, looking out on the neatly tended fields that surround it, I can feel Ñusta's sharp stab of sadness at the sight of the fort today. So much effort, so much of the artisans' skill, so much pride fallen into disrepair.

I drive farther into the desert, fighting the sense that the car—hurtling forward at 100 kilometres per hour is barely advancing through a landscape of pink granite, the bright chips of mica sparkling as if the landscape were a black diamond. As I approach Turi, flocks of llamas and sheep break the flat monotony of the plain, grazing on the plumed grasses around the *bofedales*, narrow channels of water that cut through the gravel. I pass a few long rectangular houses made of large stones. As always the sense of human habitation, but as always no one is visible. An old truck is parked by a one-room adobe house with a thatched roof, but no figure coming out to see who's driving around the desert.

Guessing, I turn off on a track that leads north toward a dark ridge of mountains, stop the car and wander for a while around the fallen rocks, the remains of what was once the Atacamenians' largest walled settlement, the Pukara of Turi. The museum of Calama displays a proud photo of the fort, seen from above and looking almost intact. From ground level I see mostly fallen walls and rocks, a jumble of lines and space, where walls and windows, roads and roofs have yielded not to the weight of the landscape, but rather to that human need to reuse, recycle, re-create. This is the largest of the desert's ruins, a footprint of memory 240 by 160 metres, roughly rectangular in shape, all that remains of one of the great cities of the Atacama. The surviving edges of a wall about three metres high still hugs the town protectively. Outside, to the north, the Incan highway runs by, on its way from the Andes to Chuquicamata, then the coast.

The people who lived in Turi used clay pitchers and pots to prepare their food, stone shovels and copper chisels to work their jewellery and build their rectangular houses. Wooden posts, now gone, once held up the thatched roofs. The few openings in the protective wall whisper of fear, eyes straining against the dark, any sharp noise outside tearing sleep into insomnia.

Someone at some point discovered adobe and brought it back, using it to build several of the houses. Among them is the House of the Inca, a two-storey building standing on a large, lonely plaza on the city's northern edge, just off the Incan highroad. Its back is turned to the rest of the city, its walls twice as thick as theirs (1.6 metres), and both house and square are accessible only from the road.

. . . *It seems the invaders weren't too convinced of the good will and peaceful spirit of their subjects* . . . , Mostny observes. The Incan inhabitants gazed out at the city or the hills through a few very small windows. They were unwanted, never really safe.

Out of sight, the city's people carried out their daily routines, pouring metal into stone, grinding grain, the echoes vibrating eerily through the wall as they echo now through centuries. My ears reach out to capture them, fill with the drumming of the wind.

Large fenced-in spaces speak of corrals, used when some threat forced people and animals into town. So shepherds came to shelter here, to trade their wares, to offer fresh meat to the city people during feast days and celebrations.

But the city's main activity was probably processing the raw ore torn from the earth by miners like the Copper Man. The central street, side streets and passageways of Turi are strewn with mortars, large stones almost a metre long, half as wide and a quarter as high. Many contain rows of dents, like little cups. Whoever worked these mortars dropped the cylindrical stones that served as their pestles nearby, and the ground is peppered with a fine gravel rich in copper silicate.

In the northeast corner of what was once the bustling city of Turi stands a peculiar circle of igloo-like stone structures joined by a wall, a single bracelet that may once have served as a ceremonial burial area. These, and the pillaged graves scattered across the low hills beyond the highway, are the city's only circular structures. While the hillside graves were little more than piles of stones, here the hands that laid on the layers of rocks did so with extraordinary care, gently caulking the seams with grout.

But perhaps they're ovens and the most skilled inhabitants of Turi melted the ore down here, guiding the course of bright streams of molten copper the way their gods watched over the watercourses.

The Incan highroad here is 4.5 metres wide. Stones were cleared off and lined up on each side to mark the separation between mere desert and a road that came from somewhere and was on its way to somewhere else. Along this road, leather sandals and the soles of bare feet, burnt and hard, tried to walk away the silence. The air, clear as glass, reveals it running eastward all the way to San Pedro de Atacama, then south through Peine and down to Copiapo on the Pacific coast. It fills me with an odd feeling, the way wind fills a billowing sail—the sense that I've wandered through the old wardrobe and back into Narnia, only to discover the ruins of Cair Paravel, the corpse of the children's empire, waiting for their return to restore it to life.

A light breeze saunters along it now, bringing echoes of Cuzco's main square where it all began, nine hundred leagues to the north, and the places where it split in two (the coastal and the mountain route) only to meet again here in the Atacama. Every four leagues, travellers could rely on *sumptuous houses that they called tambos, where there was food and clothing* and every half league, there were *posts for sending messages and orders from hand to hand.*

In contrast, the main road to which I return now is barely a trail through the desert. I follow it east toward the mountains and Toconce, stopping briefly to drive through Ayquina, a thriving town by Atacamenian standards. The narrow road that winds through it is crowded with stone and adobe houses, sharp rectangular blocks sprouting from the desert, but it is virtually empty. In recent years the empty town has doubled and tripled in size, new houses reflecting the growing importance of the village's patron saint, the hundreds who gather annually for the local festival of remorse and renewal. For all the movement of the desert's peoples to the cities, the call of their beliefs draws them back for the annual feast in ever larger numbers. These visitors pay a fee and build their shoe-box shelter to the requirements of the local council. They come, build, dance and leave, more of them with every passing year.

Onward, and now the road begins to wind upward toward Toconce, and I lean forward into the windshield, following the narrow road that spirals up and around hills, then down into adjacent valleys. Only the enormous candelabras of the cacti (*Echinopsis atacamensis*) betray the presence of water somewhere deep within the rock.

As I approach Toconce the landscape shifts, the plunging canyons suggesting narrow mountain torrents and deep bubbling gorges. The town itself is a child's toy, a green tri-angle of fields and flowers, lined by the coloured boxes of one-room adobe houses, many with traditional thatched roofs, topped with white crosses.

The village and the church float on adjacent hillsides, island peaks emerging from a rippling sea of dust, neatly ordered terraces lapping at their edges when the wind ruf-fles their alfalfa and wheat. Like the survivor of a ship-wreck, the church looks out over a narrow gorge at the cliff opposite, which begs for a waterfall, but is stained and dry. Past the church, rows of parched terraces like reefs echo the green ones behind me. They recall a time when Toconce was a prosperous town on a major highroad, messengers flashing along it like electronic beams, not this sleepy inward-looking village. Even Bowman, his critical voice always at my shoulder, notes *If the few people now liv-ing in many a valley were to set about making terraces as extensive as those lying about them, they could not do it in a lifetime.*

I spend a couple of hours wandering around Toconce, admiring the neat squares of the houses, the wild and domestic flowers that nod in the breeze. Once I think I hear the voices of a man and a woman talking. Once I turn suddenly and realize there's a man below me, digging something out of a dry ditch.

But he doesn't answer my greeting and I'm left with the sense of a town populated more by spirits than living beings.

In the nineteenth century, Iquique fired the first volley in the water war when it lobbied Santiago and won the right to use the waters of Pica and Matilla, whisking it off in pipelines to the coast, where it gave the port plenty to drink, carried off its sewage and supported the industrial processes that gave it life. By the twentieth century, Pica and Matilla had been reduced to shadows of their once prosperous selves and the scenario for the war was shifting from the coastal area to the interior of the desert. The casualties were the towns I'm now driving through, in the upper reaches of the Loa River: Toconce, Ayquina, Turi and Caspana. The water that nourished the crops on mountain terraces, crops that once fed a sizeable population, was tamed and piped to Chuquicamata and eventually the other mines that would inhabit the desert. Gutiérrez describes how in 1911 *600 men worked almost a year and a half to lay the pipe to bring the water from Toconce to the Chuquicamata plant, which is 2,940 metres above sea level. The pipe is eight inches in diameter and ten kilometres in length.*

In 1923, the Guggenheims sold the Chile Exploration Company and with it Chuquicamata to the Anaconda Copper Company, which would administer the mine until 1971. But copper, like nitrates before it, had become the great source of Chile's wealth, and politicians both right and left were becoming increasingly itchy at the fact that it was entirely foreign-owned and foreign-controlled. U.S. control of the copper industry and, specifically, its price-fixing policies, robbed the country of some US$500–US$800 million[*] worth of income during World War II and another US$300 million in the fifties, during the Korean War.

Chileanization, by which part of the copper industry was to return to Chilean and governmental hands, began

---

[*] Sutulov calculates that during WWII thanks to the U.S. fixing the price of copper at 12 cents per pound in August 1941, Chile lost over US$1.1 billion and in taxes US$800 million, while companies continued to receive 25.8 per cent profits.

in 1966, when Congress passed a law to turn the U.S. copper companies operating in Chile into *mixed* companies,
51 per cent owned by the Chilean state. The next year, El
Teniente was the first to undergo the process, followed
by Chuquicamata and the smaller mines of Salvador and
Andina (which was not yet in operation). But many
Chileans considered that the partial nationalization of the
country's greatest wealth just wasn't enough.*

These and other sweeping changes were extremely
threatening to the country's once all-powerful elite, whose
wealth was based primarily on the large chunks of the
Chilean landscape they controlled. The old landowners'
political control—they either told their farm workers who
to vote for or simply filled out the ballots for them—had
been swept away by political reforms that guaranteed a
secret ballot. On 4 September 1970, Chileans elected the
world's first socialist president, Dr. Salvador Allende, at the
head of a coalition that included the Socialist, Communist
and smaller Christian Left parties. With 1,075,616 votes,
compared to his rival with 1,036,278, Allende won, just
barely, and his election required ratification in Congress.
The U.S. teamed up with powerful members of Chile's
elite, including, among others, Agustín Edwards who owned
(and still owns to this day) the daily newspaper, *El Mercurio*.

---

* The Chileanization plan, which required a US$500 million invest-
ment, coincided with a peak in copper prices, producing US$564
million, that is, paying for itself, during the six-year term of the Frei
government, with average annual taxes received by the government
and average annual profits for the companies rising from US$88 mil-
lion (1959–1964) to US$167 million (1965–1970), in the case of taxes,
and US$45 million (1959–1964) to US$94 million (1965–1970), in the
case of profits. (Sutulov).

Together they began to pressure the armed forces to step in and seize power. On 22 October, a pro-coup group within the army kidnapped their pro-democracy commander-in-chief—and killed him. Congress ratified Allende's election, but the attempts to overthrow him continued.

There was, however, considerable consensus about copper. In July 1971, Congress nationalized Chile's main copper mines and holdings by changing Article 10 of the constitution and adding a temporary provision stating that *in the interests of the nation and the State's sovereign and inalienable right to freely dispose of its wealth and natural resources, we nationalize and declare that the foreign companies that constitute the large-scale copper mining industry, including Compañía Minera Andina, hereby become part of the full and exclusive domain of the Nation.* Thus the Copper Corporation of Chile (CODELCO), the world's largest, was born.

Two years later, at least partially in response to U.S. pressure to regain their hold on Chile's copper, the military seized power in a coup. Democracy was over, at least for the next seventeen years. Brutal repression, torture, the disappearance of political prisoners, among them many of those who had attempted to run Chuquicamata during the Allende government, turned fresh air to fear, corroding social discourse and virtually freezing the country's social progress.

Sutulov, a true representative of conservative Chile, notes merely that *on September 11, . . . order was once again established and a period of reconstruction of the country began. The mining industry regained its former vigour and immediately demonstrated its ability to produce efficiently.*

The military government began negotiations to compensate Anaconda and the other companies affected by nationalization, but any effort to restore the mines to their

original owners was blocked by powerful forces within the
military government itself, which refused to hand the nation's main source of wealth, and therefore development,
back to the foreign companies that the whole country had
resented for decades.

In June 1999, Patricio, Camilo, Danny and I spiral our way
over the mountains into Andacollo, a small town lost like a
single star in the Andes mountains. Religious fervour is all
around us, thick as the chill acidic air. Night has fallen by
the time we arrive, and we find ourselves descending into
a pit staked out by the industrial lights of mines, which
have crowded in upon the town. The weekend mass is
blaring from the loudspeakers of the local cathedral. The
town's total population is about 12,000, but Andacollo is a
major religious centre, its Virgin ruling the town with the
iron fist (or at least lungs) of the priests. The only radio station will play religious masses the entire weekend we are
here, and on this first evening of our visit, the voices of
priests reciting prayers and liturgies are carried everywhere
by a massive PA system strung throughout the entire town.
     At first I am entranced. I stop in at the *Little Cathedral* to
see the mass. It is an impressive sight, the altar dominated
by a figure of the Virgin in a shiny white gown, flanked by
white porcelain vases exploding with red gladioli or white
lilies, which hover like alien spaceships high above the
head of a priest clad in red satin. He is welcoming visitors
who have taken advantage of the weekend to come to the
Andacollo sanctuary and he is celebrating peace, *which is the
fruit of justice and the possibility for healthy community relation-
ships, where we understand each other in spite of the differences
we always have.* He makes no direct reference to General

Pinochet, Chile's former dictator, yet the speech seems to be all about him, how he took power and held to it for so long, and how many Chileans still think of him as a hero and a saviour—though at this moment he is under arrest in London for his role in the forced disappearance of political prisoners, one of the hallmarks of his regime.

The next day we drive out to the Chepequilla area to visit with Mirta Vicentelo, vice-president of the local neighbourhood association, the Junta de Vecinos number 12. Her small, impoverished community has been fighting the incursions of a copper mine, Minera Carmen de Andacollo, owned and run by the Canadian firm Aur Resources. Aur runs the Louvicourt mine in Quebec and is exploring for gold and base metals on its forty properties in Flin Flon, Manitoba, fifty-two properties in Val d'Or, Quebec, and six in Reno, Nevada.

The company's 1998 annual report states in crisp, business-like accents that *Aur has established itself as a low-cost mine developer and operator experienced in both underground and open pit mining. Acquisitions, exploration discoveries and the development and efficient operation of new profitable mines are the cornerstones of the Company's strategy for long-term growth.*

In 1996, after completing an environmental impact assessment as required by Chilean law, and having received approval from the regional environmental commission to continue, Aur started up production at Carmen de Andacollo, producing 47.1 million pounds in 1998.

In their public pronouncements at least, the large foreign mining companies that began to flock to Chile in the early nineties, as the Pinochet regime ended and elected government took over Chile once again, were remarkably sensitive to social and environmental issues. They'd been burned once in the early seventies, when strong feeling against foreign ownership led to a unanimous vote for nationalization in Chile's national Congress, and burned again by environmental movements in the seventies and eighties in North America.

Placer Dome Latin America (PDLA), for example, has its head office in Santiago. Along with the usual experts in explorations, mine operations and sales, the company also has a director of sustainable development, Rick Killim. When it started up its Mantos de Oro gold mine in the early nineties, PDLA openly said that one reason it had been attracted to Chile was the end of the military regime and the return of an elected government to power. In a country where major business leaders were still widely proclaiming that only General Pinochet could guarantee stability for business, the foreign companies' support for democracy was a welcome contrast.

But *when it comes to a negative public image, mining ranks right up there with tobacco*, says Killim, and so, for the past decade, foreign mining companies in Latin America have tried to respond intelligently to environmental concerns. *We don't want gold rings to go the way of fur coats*, Killim adds.

As the twentieth century ends, Chile is producing 40 per cent of the world's copper. Almost half of foreign investment is in mining, while 40 per cent of Chile's export income still comes from copper. Many companies have chosen to use Chile as their base for exploring mining in Peru, Bolivia, Venezuela and Argentina.

Placer Dome published its first *Sustainability Report* in 1999. More than a list of efforts or results, it also identified some unsolved problems. The company began to look for an independent environmental auditor to review their record, much as chartered accountants check financial statements. Killim says the report and the action it led to are signs of the changing times. *Mining is long-term and these days you need a "social licence" to operate, as well as the official permits. If you don't get on board, you'll go out of business.*

Mining's main impacts on the environment include toxic smelter emissions, conflicts over scarce water resources, and closure issues, particularly the problem of abandoned tailings dams. Mining the Atacama, where natural levels of arsenic are particularly high, is a special headache. Small-scale miners who operate with little education, precarious financing and no training also do considerable environmental damage. If you care about the Atacama, where do you put goal posts? No environmental damage whatsoever? And then what do you do about the country's dependence on the hard cash that mining brings in to finance education, health, and social services such as lunches for thousands of schoolchildren every day?

Under Chile's 1993 environmental law, all new mining projects must go through Environmental Impact Assessment. However, César Padilla, who monitors issues involving mining and the environment for the Latin American Observatory of Environmental Conflicts, is still concerned. The Observatory has been advising Mirta Vicentelo's community group since 1997. *With few resources for enforcement, and faced with other areas where the aggression against the environment is much more obvious, the Chilean government tends to demand little and to leave a lot of the enforcement to companies themselves,* Padilla says. *This makes it difficult to form a picture of the real situation.*

Nobody is quite sure what to do with the millions of tons of tailings. Many were simply dumped into seemingly dry watersheds and left behind after mines closed. *In Chile's Fifth Region alone*, says Gustavo Lagos, the mining engineer in charge of the Catholic University's Mining Centre, in the past thirty years, *there have been eighteen reported collapses of tailing dams resulting from earthquakes. Every one of these collapses has resulted in damage, of differing magnitude, to the local population and the environment.*

Juana Galaz, a mining engineer who was Coeur D'Alene's environmental manager until recently and also headed the National Mining Society's environmental commission, was working as an independent environmental consultant when we spoke in June 1999. She had pioneered more environmentally aware mine closures in the region, modelling these efforts on experiences in Canada and the United States. According to her, *The key problem is that mines close down at times of economic crisis when prices are low. That means that you have to put aside the funds and take measures well in advance.*

Everyone agrees that the new closure regulation is necessary. But there is no agreement on how to handle the financial guarantee that companies should put up long before closure, especially now, when world copper prices are the lowest this century.

> *The rain is falling on my town,*
> *my lover is weeping*
> *beyond the mountain . . .*

While Danny plays with the family dog, Mirta's father takes Patricio and me on a tour of their once blooming orchards, a mainstay in the family economy that went completely awry after the mine arrived on the scene.

We've always had pollution problems because of mining—for hundreds of years, he says. *But the problems here in Chepequilla only began when the company started up. In three years, it has done more damage than ninety years of regular mining.*

As we turn mottled yellow sprigs of parsley over in our hands (*The earth is killing the plants*) he paints a picture of life in Andacollo before the mining companies arrived. It was up and down—you'd earn well for maybe three or four months, but that would be enough to carry you over the hard times. *We used to pan for gold, or you'd find gold just fifteen or twenty centimetres under the surface. That's what Andacollo's always been like.* But little by little, the large mining companies began to buy up the rights to explore and mine the area's resources, leaving the small-scale miners with slim pickings indeed.

As we walk under avocado, orange, apple, fig and peach trees whose upper branches all look as if they've been singed, he tells us that the two mining companies employ perhaps two hundred local people, where once *99 per cent of the men worked in small-scale mining.*

In a corner of the family garden, rabbits chew on lettuce leaves. *They've had a lot of conjunctivitis, skin allergies and the like*, Mirta's father says, but the only remedy is to move away from Chepequilla. *It's the same with all the neighbours. We see the damage to the trees, our houses, but we don't know what's it's doing to us.*

18 June 1912

Thirteen years after the discovery of the Copper Man, one Edward Jackson sits at a desk in Santiago and writes a letter to an associate, F.D. Aller. Perhaps a file folder lies open on his desk as he prepares to answer Aller's questions. He picks up a photograph taken just after the discovery of the Copper Man, gazing for a long time at the face of the men portrayed therein. In the picture, the mummy's new owners stand on the hillside where he was found, the miners themselves seven shadowy figures behind them. It is not clear what the miners are wearing. The men in the foreground, however, are dressed in starched shirts with rounded collars like crescent moons, smart hats and city suits. They stand like conquerors, their leather shoes poised in victory amidst the dust.

One of the men owns the mine where the Copper Man was found. His name is William Matthews. Another may be a Frenchman called Pidot, who was renting the mine at the time, although he is not mentioned by name and the photograph may be nothing but a ploy by Matthews to demonstrate his ownership of the mummy.

Jackson's pen scratches across the clean white sheet of paper, tracing a history of the disputes about the ownership of the Copper Man, disputes that began in the moment of his discovery in the mine, and have never stopped. Jackson himself was excited by the prospects for the find and immediately upon hearing of the discovery, he offered 500 Chilean pesos to buy it. But the miner who received his offer refused, because he thought that like everything else he dragged from the mine, the mummy rightfully belonged to his employer, M. Pidot. The pen traces the name of another man from the photograph, Norman Walker, who offered to pay 2,000 Chilean pesos, but was also refused because Matthews, the owner of the mine, was bitterly disputing the right of Pidot, who only rented it, to the Copper Man's remains.

Jackson writes, *Pidot argued [that the mummy] was ore as it assayed something less than 1 per cent of copper and Mr. Matthews argued he had only rented the mine and not the miners.*

A year after the discovery, Jackson bought the mummy outright, for 1,000 pesos, through José Toyos, his representative in the town of Ovalle. However, a condition of the transaction was that Jackson had to pay Toyos an additional 500 pesos, and that the two men would each hold a half share.

I paid him 500 pesos and when I received it in Antofagasta it was already minus a toe which I think someone cut off in Chuquicamata for a keepsake, Jackson writes. It is a rare warm afternoon. His wife and children must surely be outside seated on white wicker chairs around a glass table, sipping cool drinks or squirting each other with a hose. *I exhibited it in my house and when a Mr. Pérez de Arce offered to take it down to Valparaiso to exhibit it, giving me half of the profits, I accepted. It was exhibited in Valparaiso and Santiago and then I began to get offers. As I never saw any of the profits I decided to sell it through my brother John Stewart Jackson, who eventually did so to two gentlemen . . . for 15,000 pesos, this sum to be paid 5,000 in cash and 10,000 pesos in three months.*

The "two gentlemen," Torres and Tornero, took the mummy on tour in the U.S., where it was featured at the Buffalo Exhibition. But *they had some trouble with it in the custom house. They always asked too much for it and so could not get rid of it, and as they prolonged their stay in the States they gradually got into debt and at last the mummy was embargoed by creditors in the house Hemenway & Co., New York.*

The two entrepreneurs later managed to return to Chile, their fares paid by the Chilean consul. But in the meantime, Mr. Jackson writes, he was most unhappy, as he'd received (and duly shared with his partner, Toyos) only the first 5,000 of his 15,000 pesos. When one Raimundo Docekal of Antofagasta travelled to the States, Jackson gave him power of attorney and $500 in U.S. gold to go toward the mummy's recovery.

Docekal, alas, was shipwrecked in the Straits of Magellan. Nonetheless, by some miracle he eventually reached New York, from which city, Jackson says, he sent me *several encouraging letters . . . but when he began to ask for more money, I refused. . . He then made some sort of an arrangement with the creditor, cancelled the 10,000 pesos still owing me and sold it in New York and never sent me a cent. I looked for him when I was in New York*, Jackson adds, *but found it rather too big a place to find him.*

Where exactly the body went after the Buffalo Exhibition remains unclear, but in 1905, J.P. Morgan donated it to the American Museum of Natural History, where it presumably remains. The stone spades and hammers, the hide bag, the coiled baskets and other objects found with the miner's body had already been sold to the U.S. National Museum in Washington, D.C., for $100. They proved difficult to recover, but by 1912 the museums were able to carry out an exchange that reunited the Copper Man with his tools.

In 1953 Junius Bird, an American anthropologist who did some of the earliest field work in Latin America, and a geologist, Charles Milton, examined the body. Bird's article on the Copper Man contains some stunning photographs, particularly of the miner's hands extended in working position as they were at the time of death. In that photograph, the finely muscled right hand reaches out, palm open, suggesting tenderness or a generous gift, while the left hand curls protectively below it at wrist level, one disharmonic finger curled hook-like above it.

By now, perhaps, Jackson is tipping himself back in his chair and staring blindly at a wall. The afternoon begins to sink under the weight of evening, the scent of jasmine wafting into his room as he finally leans forward, picks up his pen, dips it in ink and writes his last thoughts in the letter. The whole transaction brought in some $2,500 and cost $2,300, earning him *only $200 . . . I came to the conclusion*, he reflects at last, *that it is a sin to deal in dead men's bodies, and shall not do so again.* He puts down his pen, thinks a moment, then picks it up again.

Mummies, he adds, *went up terribly in the market after our find.*

9

T H E

D A N C E

➤

La Tirana

Since we've seen each other, a game goes on.
Secretly I move, and you respond.
You're winning. You think it's funny.

But look up from the board now, look how
I've brought in furniture to this invisible place,
so we can live here.

    – Jalal al-Din Muhammad Rumi, Persian poet (1207–1273)

Midnight, 16 July 1998
La Tirana, Tarapaca region, Chile

IN SOME WAYS she is the original wedding doll, with
the white veils foaming down over her long black
hair, the grave, almost sleepy face. She looks gently
downward, a sign of either eternal humility or permanent

superiority. She is La Tirana, and she has been placed on the dais high above the rest of us, from which vantage point she has a great view of the square and possibly human frailty as well. There is a blankness to her eyes though, as if she were drugged or self-engrossed. Whatever the reason, she seems barely aware of what is going on around her. Maybe she is simply somewhere else, this shell presented here merely to fool us. Sometimes she wears satin robes of rich cream or pastel blue, or pink bubbling with white lace. Sometimes she wears a crown, but more often just a veil. Usually she holds a small barefoot child in her arms. He too looks down, with a little more curiosity perhaps, his arms open as if to receive or give an embrace.

On this cool summer evening in La Tirana, on the road between Pica and Iquique, the desert smokes around us with thousands of fires, as if we had arrived late to a devastated battlefield. The smell of charred flesh is that of roast animals, however, the quintessential Chilean barbecue, the desanctified ritual of the sacrifice carried on in its mixed modern-Andean incarnation. And much of the smoke is car exhaust, dust and dregs from the long lines of cars that sparkle like strings of glass beads along the roads reaching out into the desert to the north and south of the village; they crawl at last into the small town where they dance the slow waltz involved in cruising for a parking place, the same the world over.

Patricio and I left Danny behind but brought Camilo because we wanted him to see the living reality that could seem so dry and distant from a Santiago school. We walk past the low adobe dwellings of the modest town, but we can barely see them for the crowds, many of them tourists like us, dressed in ordinary city clothes. As we approach

the main square, which spreads like a concrete football
field before the old church, we see more and more girls,
boys, women, men, all dressed up in shiny costumes that
gleam under the powerful spotlights that shine down from
above. Excited voices crackle around us like the bonfires.
The spotlights blaze into the dolls' faces. Adults crowd
around them, actors murmuring excitedly in the wings,
anxious, half breathing, half holding their breath. The air is
saturated with the amplified voices of the priests, who
stand regally on a large dais in front of the church, droning
steadily through the ritual phrases. They are as dull and
monotonous as the costumes and whispering below are
charged and electric.

Like an argument, the priests with their amplifiers
impose their mass, the ritual raising and lowering of the
chalice, the steady, insistent talking, talking, talking is like
someone scolding or trying to dominate a meeting, ignoring all the other voices. They speak for their God, the One
God, and a male god at that, but the dancers love the wedding doll, the woman who holds the priests' god, a small
helpless child, in her arms, who loves and suckles him and,
perhaps, on occasion gives him a slap or speaks to him
sternly, because for her he is simply a small child that above
all needs to be taught. Patricio, Camilo and I, Christian
only by culture, not conviction, stir restlessly. We came to
see the dancers, not the priests, and we find their insistent
lecturing an irritation.

Whether pagan or Christian, the rites go on, and tens of
thousands of the people who have made their lives in the
desert are here to see that they do. The priests resist, their
words pelting the ear. But the eye rules supreme: we
watch the men in the crowd whispering anxiously, flirting

teens giggling, anxious mothers tweaking and retying ribbons and shoelaces and clasps. A young girl tosses a river of coloured ribbons over one shoulder, pretends not to see the men hopping or shifting from one foot to another, their sidelong gazes.

The church itself looks more like the castle from a fairy tale, blazing with Chilean flags, a huge dome flanked by a guardian turret on each side. From afar, the whole structure of crinkled tin looks light and airy. Around the church, the central square is a pointillist print of white shirts, a garden of satin flowers gleaming and swaying in the breeze, of bright costumes topped by the dark O's of tens of thousands of heads.

The Pacific Ocean gently laps the cliffs to the west, and the Andes rise regally to the east, invisible under a mantle of darkness, but sensed, the limits to a world we have only begun to explore or know. What we see on this cool night in the middle of winter, out here surrounded by the Atacama, is what could be an enormous church picnic of sorts, with folk-dancing and gossiping, feasting and flirting. We sense their seriousness: the dancers refuse to perform for others' entertainment, refuse to be treated as just another folk group. They dance for La Tirana or they dance not at all. But their dancing is just the most vivid, visual expression of their ceremony. Everything has its place, every movement its meaning.

This is a universe, in and of itself. The tight little groups of dancers, each forming its own solar system, cluster around a banner and the doll enthroned above us on a regal litter, equipped with poles for parading her around the town, like the Incan princess she once aspired to be. Patricio, Camilo and I move easily between the clusters of nervous, proud dancers. Everyone is growing impatient with the droning of the priests when, well after the appointed hour of midnight, they finally fall silent. Smoking flares sear the sky, gunpowder chokes the air, a trumpet sounds, a drum. Voices like satin ribbons braid a song and the dancing explodes around us.

Each company, twenty or more men or women, sometimes mixed, line up face to face and whirl, leap, stamp, hop, crouch, stretch to the rhythm of their own drums—marching drums, steel drums, the deep bass of the Andean bombo, the shrill exuberant shout of trumpets and trombones, often decorated with the yellow, green and red pompons of the llama herds high up in the Andes above us. The sikus, pan pipes, are here and the antara played by the dancing, hopping, whirling dancers, the music flung out from the writhing bits of iridescent arms and skirts and shirts like drops of sweat or fragments of coloured glass.

Part epiphany, part cartoon, there's a lot of Hollywood in the costumes of the crowd: the fringed jackets of Redskins, the silk kerchiefs of Gypsies and dark-skinned Ali Babas, the high boots of the Cossacks, Bullfighters, Sailors, Spaniards and Cowboys; there are Bears and Apaches and Queens with crowns. Over the decades these new characters have joined the traditional Owls, Shepherdesses, Dark Skins, Llama Tenders, Devils and other dancers.

Somewhere in the midst of this I suppose is Huillac Ñusta, but I cannot find her. This is what remains of her on earth, the finely dressed dolls, the impassioned dancers with their fancy dress embracing all the colour and kitsch of fairy tales, the magical reign of the church, the chanting priests, now silenced to make way for the fire and smoke and frenzy that whirl around us.

And then when I least expect it I feel her come up behind me, her breath, impatient in my ear, a voice that can turn firecrackers to stars.

Let me tell you how it was—not how it *really* was, because I cannot tell you that, but how it was and is for me.

The age of the soft shining metals, gold, silver, copper, and their gods of Sun and Moon, our goddess of the earth, the Pachamama, was being sliced into tiny pieces by a sword of iron, a metal we'd never heard of. Our laws crushed under boots that marched forever toward the progress of the few at the expense of the many; the festivals where worshippers danced and whirled like dervishes, vibrating like the Andean wind in the throat of their instruments, attacked as pagan debauchery by the new moral authorities.

So I devised a plan. Let me say, confess, that I was dead by then, but the Christian God too did most of his work post-mortem. Why should I let death stop *me*? I sat crouched on the mountain peak, directing heaven's rains to earth and my people's pleas to the gods who still dared to haunt the heavens. When none answered I began to think up the answers for myself.

Between them, the Andes and the Atacama embraced miles in every direction, as they always have, from ocean to Amazonian jungle, from rubble and desert all the way up the purple slopes. It was I who ruled that the antaras of the Andes should blow their wild music and volcanic winds through the Roman Church. But for that there had to be a story, a foundation of words on which the structure of a myth could be erected. For hundreds of years, I whispered it into the dreams of travellers and workers, the

women who wove from dawn to dusk, the men who
guided their livestock up and down the rocky staircase of
the Andes, leaving narrow lines of hoofprints across their
high plateaux.

Then, at the end of the nineteenth century, I moved
the pen of a Peruvian historian, Cuneo Vidal, and he
began to weave the ribbons of words, song and movement
together so they would last. For the first time he turned
my story into those words you people lay out across your
endless pages, starting with our departure from Cuzco,
complete with ten thousand Indians, and twelve *willcas*,
captains.

Okay, sure, he changed a lot of the story around. This
was a collaborative effort after all. But there are parts I really
like, for instance that section, you know the one, where he
says that *under a layer of apparent submissiveness* our hearts *beat
with an urge to hatred and vengeance*. And I like the fact that he
remembered my name and used it. It made me feel real
again. He muttered it under his breath as he wrote . . .

*For four years, surrounded by her brave followers, Huillac Ñusta
lived free of the ominous foreigner's repression. For four years, the
fierce and wild forest was the last fortress of a persecuted race and
the final sanctuary of a forbidden faith. It was their rule to put to
death all Spaniards and all baptized Indians who fell into their
hands.*

*Huillac Ñusta was feared for a hundred leagues in every direc-
tion. The Spaniards called her—and by a tradition that has never
died she's still called—the Beautiful Tyrant of the Tamarugo.*

*One day, her warriors brought a Spaniard to see her, captured
in the tamarugo forest. When she interrogated him, he said his
name was Vasco de Almeida, and that he belonged to a group of*

miners from the neighbouring port of Arica that had come to find the legendary Mine of the Sun.

The Council of Ancients met and ruled that he must be put to death with no further delay . . .

Huillac's heart had never doubted or hesitated for a moment before, steeped in the passion of hatred and thirst for vengeance, but even so, her entire being trembled as she heard the sentence, as harsh as it was inevitable. An unknown instinct for pity bubbled up from the deepest chamber of her heart, where her own roots clung to the past, the initial shoot of her rancour.

Just one glance from the noble prisoner was enough to produce this enormous metamorphosis in her.

At that precise moment, his youth, his noble bearing, his stoic disregard for death, all caused Huillac to love the man whose life had been placed in her hands, the hands of a warrior and a priest. Even so, the four moons prescribed by the ancients went by, and soon the Spaniard had only a few days left to live.

And occasionally they spoke of his beliefs.

The prisoner spoke of his own religion. He spoke of one all-powerful God, creator of Heaven and Earth, and of how he lives and breathes in the endless expanse of the Universe. He spoke of Mary. He spoke at last, and it was then that the Indian princess drank in his words with the greatest eagerness, of the comforting notion of immortality, and by virtue of the same, of the survival of soul over body, reserved for those who in this sad life suffered from hunger and thirst for justice, love, happiness.

"So, if I were Christian and died in your faith," Huillac asked the Spaniard, "I would be reborn in the future life and my soul would live united with yours, forever and ever?"

"That is so, my love," Almeida answered.

"Are you sure, my darling?"

"My religion, which is the source of all truth, teaches me this."

"Then baptize me, Spaniard. I want to be Christian! I want to be yours in body and soul, in this earthly life and eternity!"

"God has illuminated your understanding. God has called at the doors of your heart. If today I adore you as a pagan, there will be no affection in the world equal to mine when you become a Christian tomorrow."

"Tomorrow at break of day," Almeida added, in solemn tones, *"you will be my sister and wife in Jesus Christ."*

The sun shone over the lofty profile of the Andes. Tall and straight as she was, and calm as anyone whose actions are the result of a solid resolution, she walked with her beloved to the fountain in one of the clearings, where she knelt on the ground and crossed her arms over her breast, in an attitude of humble waiting.

Almeida took some water from the fountain, poured it over the head of his beloved neophyte, and pronounced the sacramental words: *"I baptize you in the name of the Father, the Son and the Holy Ghost . . ."*

He didn't finish. A cloud of arrows expelled from the surrounding forest fell on them both. One, well aimed, pierced his heart, and he collapsed like a young sapling struck down by a lightning bolt.

Huillac, fatally wounded, called her willcas, her priests, her ancients and her people to her, and fighting the pain of her coming death, spoke thus: *"I die resigned . . .*

"I die happy, sure as I am as a believer in Jesus Christ that my immortal soul will rise to the highest heavens and contemplate the face of its Creator, at the foot of whose throne my beloved husband already waits, thanks to you.

"If, with my love and my conversion to the faith of the enemies of our forefathers I have hurt your beliefs and caused harm to

our nation's cause, please grant me your mercy and your forgive-
ness. I am resigned to pay with my life for what you consider my
error. . . But if you want the last princess in the line of your Incas
and the last priestess of your religion to die in peace, then promise
you will bury my body beside my spouse's, and raise above our
tomb a cross, the Christian's cross."

When, sometime between 1536 and 1540, Friar Anthony
Rendón Sarmiento, priest in the Royal and Military Order
of Our Lady of Mercy Redeemer of Captives, first evangelizer of
Tarapaca, contributed to the Tamarugo destroying the idols of the
gentiles and raising the standard of faith in Christ, he discovered,
not without extraordinary amazement, a cross placed on a recently
covered tomb.

The apostolic gentleman saw in this a sign from Heaven and
he decided to raise on the spot marked by that holy symbol a
church, the same one that to this day bears its original name, Our
Lady of Carmen of the Tyrant, halfway along the road from the
nitrate region to the town of Pica.

It was hard to die. I'd spent the better of my life preparing
for the sacrifice, one way or another, but when the moment came, I confess, it was not easy. Once the council
had made the decision, they were gentle and honoured
me. They fed me well, although I was not hungry and
more inclined to fast. They were set in their resolve. But
let me tell you, I could have changed their minds. In the
end, I didn't try. As they prepared the special alcohol, the
ears of corn, cast the small silver figures that would accompany me forever, I sat in my lodge and wove as I had not
done for years.

The girl helped me, bringing the finest llama's wool,
dipping it into the colour of Almeida's flesh, young and

healthy, produced by the onion, or the bright purple of the distant mountains, the amber of desert flowers, those same blooms that welcomed my reign, my desperate escape into freedom. I will never forget, never regret what we did, all those acts bitter and bloody or bright with the seeds we planted and the corn that captured the sun's essence for us to eat and be strong, the juices of the algarrobo delighting my tongue and sweetening everything I saw.

As my hands wove, so did my mind reach out to the four skeins of the desert and the Andes, our four-storey world with its ribbons of colour, the very ribbons of our existence stretching east to west, cutting deep ravines lined with modest green across the long north-south axis that lies between Cuzco and the Mapuches' land far to the south; the fine stitches of the endless caravans of llamas and mules criss-crossing the desert from coast to mountain peaks, braiding together the four ribbons of life that en-sured survival above the hot abyss of the desert.

The blue ribbon is the generous coast, where fish, shellfish and birds thrive. Where no human settlement was possible, the Chango lived in their canoes, trading their surplus, their dried fish nourishing, their polished shells decorating the shrines of the high Andes all the way to Titicaca and beyond into the Amazon.

The green ribbon is the forests. In the mountains' gen-erous lap they harbour my beloved tamarugo trees, which like the water-loving willow sink their roots deep into the barren desert, find liquid drops of mercy hundreds of feet down. They still brood over the plains, like giant, absent-minded birds. For me, the tamarugo forest whispers of tenderness, that single moment when our flesh drew to-gether and two alien peoples for a moment touched.

The yellow ribbon is—you might think it's the sun, but it's really much closer than that—the foothills, shot through with mauve streamers of light, pale shoots, the baby teeth of new corn, pretty and spoilt on the mountains' knee, nourished by shy rivers, poking silver noses among the bofedales, the channels that spread like hairs or nerves, making life shiver all along their edges.

And the deep purple and deep white ribbons are the altiplano, the fourth storey, the roof of the world, where I am now. My eyes follow the shepherds who come to pasture their llamas in the spring. From this place come dried meat, wool, leather, textiles, quinua, the Andean rice, herbs, salt, animal fat. Each stone the shepherds throw onto the eternal *apachetas* is another letter in my name, which breathes among the peaks forever.

When the winds cool and rain begins to freeze, the shepherds herd their produce-laden animals down toward the farms of the oases below, helping to harvest potatoes, garlic, corn and other crops, picking the fruits of algarrobo and other trees, trading their way all the distance to the coast, then moving backward across the desert and back up into the foothills, carrying the creeping warmth of changing seasons, news and food, riches and rituals, change caught and controlled in tradition's ceramic jar.

But I also watched as the land of the four-storeys began to break down, as the mines chewed up the men from the villages and destroyed the women who followed them down to the offices. With each crash they were spat out, and they drifted like spirits to the coast and the illusion of a job. In the places they abandoned the untended land lay fallow, drifted back to desert on dry winds. Debts, lost land, forced work and money pulled people off land we never lived on year-round to begin with. The Spanish noted their absence and declared the lands *empty* and subject to expropriation.

At first, I meant to argue with the council, to convince them that they needed me to serve and guide them through the decades of occupation to come. But they wouldn't listen, and when I cast my mind into the future, seeking out arguments, I fell silent. For the first fifty years, the Spanish would make few forays into our oasis.

Only after that would my people need me. Without the sacrifice I would be long gone by then.

Thus, as I wove, I watched how in the years to come the lands of my lovely Pica would be among the first to be given away under the Spaniards' system of encomiendas, allotments. On 22 January 1540, even as I sat weaving my last fine cloth, Francisco Pizarro sliced up the land around the oasis and granted it, and all its native inhabitants, to one Lucas Martínez Begazo. Later, the land and all its inhabitants—my people, who followed the star of Yacana in search of the two llamas who would give birth to a new nation—were bequeathed to Andrés Jiménez, followed by Martín Pérez de Lezcano.

In February 1557, Juan de Castro officially took possession of the oasis of Pica, in a ceremony attended by many of the original inhabitants of the oasis, including their *cacique*, leader, Ynatue. I watched, angry and helpless, my twitching hands leaving great knots in the work that I would later lose precious hours unweaving. Juan de Castro took Ynatue by the hand and removed his cape, draped it around his own shoulders, and thus took over my oasis.

Juan de Castro, however, was far from pleased with the lands that he'd been granted. Two years later he traded his rights for land elsewhere, and Lucas Martínez, an old man who fought on Francisco Pizarro's side against Almagro, took over the encomienda. I hated Almagro, but I hate his enemy more: in 1554 he joined Gonzalo Pizarro's rebel forces and rose up against a Spanish governor who tried to eliminate the encomienda, the system that turned us into slaves. The rebels lost, but what did that matter to the Spanish? The next year they took possession of their lands, just the same.

For most of the nineteenth century the earth, the Pachamama, will be my ally, as we struggle to throw off the Spaniards' attempts at conquest. Pachamama will rumble and heave, sending earthquakes to destroy the churches, hoping they won't be rebuilt. But *Pica was still in ruins as of 1884 and it seems that the only person who'd fixed some of the damage was a Spaniard named José Durán who, with little means, [became known as] "the builder of all the churches in these places."* They cling stubbornly to their faith, the poor Spaniards who follow the conquistadors.

Smallpox, war, all the devastation we could wreak was not enough. Even as my hands move through the warp, my skin soft and blooming under the lanolin, I can see more Spaniards coming down from the mountains, or descending from ships moored off the coast, the endless trains of mules drawing them ever closer to the desert's green heart.

But I don't give in. Even though I can see that a Spaniard will one day fling our cloth around his shoulders, and by this gesture claim my heritage away, I am already weaving another. I have begun to see how people who win may lose more than they think. So I weave and plot how we can win by losing. This is not my choice, but it's all that's left to me and I will not accept defeat. Ever.

And there will be rebellions. I prick my fingers and let the blood flow, burning like thunderbolts, to ignite, deepen and strengthen the dye. Hope holds my breath for a century, as I think that perhaps here I will find an argument to convince my people to let me live on, to guide and lead them as only I can do.

High up in the Andes, between 1736 and 1750, the first major rebellion, an attempt to restore Tawantinsuyu, our empire, will shake Oruro for thirteen years, as people rise up to protest the high taxes and the religious services imposed by the conquerors.

Barely thirty years later, José Gabriel Amaru and Tupaj Katari will lead another rebellion, just a protest at first, against corruption. I whisper in their dreams at night, send them nightmares of the lithe monkeys of the Amazon beheaded by iron swords, betrayed. *The Spanish will refuse to negotiate*, I warn them, sending messages in the entrails of the fetal llamas that they sacrifice, my cries twisting like volcanic smoke, until it collapses on the peaks. When the messenger comes with their dismissal, the rebel leaders declare their right to self-government, decree their separation from colonial rule, and disobey. They are crushed, but once again, between 1809 and 1825, as the Spaniards' descendants born in Peru rebel against Madrid, native armies besiege La Paz. They fight the Spanish and their local descendants, both at once where necessary.

But this too will fail to restore my rule. For a while I feel the tendrils of despair sucking my strength, bringing me so low I can barely rise from my bed each morning.

My cloth is long and wide; it threatens to reach the door and spill outside, as I cannot. Time is running short.

One morning I woke up singing. A bright dream casted its light around me all morning and every colour gleamed as gently as the water reflected on the walls of the underground channels that nourished my oasis. What do you know of love if you've never seen the way the green leaves bloom and giggle in the midst of that vast waste? Never tasted the pungent juice of a lemon from Pica running down his fingers, piercing your tongue?

What do you know of freedom, if you've never noticed how water can find a passage down from the high peaks of the Andes, along the steep ravines, moving underground, dripping and flowing, gently, surely, secretly, all the way to the Pacific? How the Loa twists like a whip or the puma's tail, elusive, stubborn, a narrow chain of silver joining shoreline to peak?

As the fine cloth piled up at my feet, I got my first clue of what I should do when I looked ahead to February 1583. This is what I saw in my dream. High up in the Andes in the village of Copacabana, a Spanish governor named Santiago Churutupa is willing to compromise to achieve conversion (a rare echo of Almeida, whose blood was still lying dull and red like a withered flower on the hard earth outside). He orders that the image of the Virgin of Copacabana be carried out to the shore of Lake Titicaca and venerated there.

Through his memories I relive the Incan festivals celebrated with dance, seeing again the high priests carrying the long line of effigies of Incan kings and queens over their heads in feather-lined litters, marching them from one religious site to another, blessing and begging, negotiating a new year's riches by offering part of the old year's wealth, seeking as always to balance what must be taken by something that can be given.

Now the marchers carry the effigy of this Virgin Woman, and I catch a glimpse of myself in her. They heft her high on their shoulders and pause at each of the sacred sites, invoke the old gods' intercession before the great creator Viracocha, and this lady's intercession before the great god of conquest. He has punished them so cruelly with fevers, blood, loss.

The dancers with their precious cargo reach the lake just before dawn, shooting fireworks skyward with their infinite prayers, their letters to the dead lighting the path of the sun's arrival.

Ten years earlier, in the silver-drunk city of Potosi, the Spanish governors organized a similar procession with thirty altars, half for the Spanish to celebrate the mysteries of the new testament, the other half for the Indians who dedicated them to the Virgin, the Pachamama. In the procession, fifteen companies of native dancers, two hundred dressed as Incan authorities, marched and whirled through my memories of what's to come, wearing the costumes and customs of every native group. Fifty Spaniards dressed for the Spanish court follow, carrying Santiago on high, St. James, their patron saint of battle, followed by soldiers, flags and pennants. These, in turn, gave way to two thousand miners and in the centre of it all a float with the silver virgin of Potosi, the goddess of wealth and ambition who works her spell throughout the city. Fireworks and plays celebrated the history of the Incas for days, then end in a bullfight, Spanish games, a masquerade.

In the years to come, on the first Sunday of each festival, a group of dancers called the Incas, armed with bows,
lances, arrows and slingshots, will lead the parade, dancing
to the rhythm of drums, the massive flutes and pipes of the
Andes and the Amazon. In 1834 the priest Michel D'Orbigny will describe dancers in strange and exotic costumes
raising a pole and braiding sixteen coloured ribbons
around it with their movements.

He sketches the Moxos people, tells how their priests
would fast to achieve the strength of the tiger. Their tense
ceremonies once included human sacrifices and their
dancers wear the feather headdresses of Owls. They are
fierce people, who will spend whole days learning the
rituals of the new gods at the church, but in an instant's
rebellion execute the priests.

D'Orbigny speaks of one dancer who swept open a
black velvet cape to reveal a great golden sun tied to his
breast. And the Jesuits met with the most stubborn resistance when they tried to convert the rebellious Chiriguana
people whose territory stretches from Bolivia, through
Brazil and into northern Paraguay. In the nineteenth century they declared a leader, Tumpaichy, to be the real Virgin Mary, María Chesús (Mary Jesus), and used the cross
only to defend their villagers from the foreigner's disease.
Miracles were nothing to them, since their own priests
were adept at them.

You, with that strange watery name you carry everywhere throughout this desert, should understand this: I
study the Loa for days on end, the lying rivers, the notes of
the antara bleating like a lost kid in a frozen pass. And then
I lift my eyes and follow yours from one book to another,
those things you call calendars. You are urban people, your

cities no longer fed by our great highways among the fields, you follow the written word unquestioningly. For you, time, a year, the calendar that measures both, is a neatly printed page to be torn out and tossed away, an endless progression of pages toward the end of one paper year, the beginning of another. You forget the origins of this ordering, that it is a circle, the endless cycle of the seasons, crucial to crops and livestock. Survival, the reason we invented time. It is too easy to lie to you.

Finally, as I finished hemming the garment they would soon wrap me in, I knew that I had devised a way to subvert the seasons, to wind our beliefs through the future the way the Loa steals its way through the apparently empty desert.

Scratch this in among the shapes in your notebook. My town, the town of La Tirana, is located *halfway along the road from the nitrate region to the town of Pica*. It stands—write this down—*almost literally at the crossroads between the old colonial oasis that had struggled along for over a century and the new industrial reality that swept the desert coast in the 1700s*.

All the corn, the gold, people's lives, poured out through this hole in what was the perfect circle of our system, and turned into a line, a shining strand, pulling us to extinction. Struggling to pay debts, taxes, the villagers found themselves forced to survive on one storey alone. They watched their men and women move off down the valleys and out of the mountains, but the cycle of movement and trade and enrichment ended in the long fruitless wait for their return. It was as if the wind and the rain had died, down by the ocean.

Individual beliefs survived in solitary splendour, like the lonely pillars left by shattered temples.

The priests burned whole towns because the people worshipped idols and had never gone to confession. That's when I taught them to use *Christian camouflage*.

The Spanish authorities blamed the ruination of the Indians on the priests who created a series of drunken festivals for the patron saints of small towns. But to me those priests were like the incarnation of Almeida. I would stroke their soft flesh at night, whisper the sweet truths of the dance through the hairs on their chest, kiss the gentle smiles that stole across their lips. And while they were sleeping I made the dancing bloom in people's minds like those strange wild flowers, in places where they never should have existed.

All those people whose minds held millennia of cultivation and the canchones and camellones of Tiwanaku just walked down off the mountains and into the desert. They went to work in the nitrate camps, or wandered on down to the coast, lured to the slums by the richest of illusions. They called us *a burden on the Chilean economy*. What would you have done?

By now, you know that the first official mention of the Well of Our Lady of Carmen of La Tirana comes in the baptismal record of a Spanish child born there and registered in the parish of Pica in 1780. Among the sparse trees, settlement sprouted and the area's only chapel was built. By 1791 a large complex of storage and sleeping areas had grown up around the well, surrounded by grazing animals. The Spaniards and their African slaves often had to fight off thieves. The Africans too were invited to my dance.

Just to the north the tamarugo trees still formed a dense forest, moping about in their droopy fashion, like aged dancers in long dresses, still trying to squeeze a sense of grace and lightness from weary limbs and wasting muscles, depressed, or perhaps anxious about the sterility that surrounded, was pressing in upon them.

By the end of the eighteenth century, families, slaves and servants clustered around the wells, dedicated mostly to mining and basic farming. Occasionally flash floods would destroy the fields or create new ones, where the salt could be scraped off the surface and alfalfa, lettuce, onions or potatoes would cover a *canchon* with their green stems, watered by an apparent miracle. *The earth would germinate in a surrealistic way: with no rivers, no rain, no fog . . . just the underground charity of the Pachamama*, as my scholar, Lautaro Nuñez will one day put it.

The great Earth Mother of the Andes was both a woman and a *virgin*. She needed no man to carry out her tasks of generating life, whether human, animal or plant.

Up in the mountains the dancers remained pure and faithful to the past, but I threw my lot in with the nitrate miners and the tough wives who managed their paycheques and the camps—they were so full of illusions when they arrived, so quick to see visions when they drank, so enraged at work and delighted with the burning lights and lines of their theatre! And they fought back, were careless at their losing, lost, and in their outrage, protested for a hundred years. Still protest. This, then, is winning while losing. This is the way the world gets changed in the end, by these uncommon common people, the ones who have to forge their puny efforts into some kind of power, reinvent the wheel every time they try to stand up on their own two feet. We keep our eyes fixed on the huge horizon, alert to the possibility of a major quake. And yet all the while, resistance is stealing its sticky tendrils through our lives, clinging to defeat, pushing against it in order to rise above it.

Now you stand in my square, before my church, and have trouble recognizing me. In some ways I don't blame you. In some ways, I do. Let's go for a walk through the ruins of the old church. Here's where I learned to legalize the marriages, baptize the children of Peruvians, Chileans and Bolivians.

How do you think I felt as I watched the miners cut down the tamarugo forest and drain the water from the wells, the two- or three-tiered towers of their colonial-style churches standing like lighthouses above a flat sea of rock? Believers registered the miracles, and my punishments, and I urged them to sort out their beliefs for themselves. I blinded a man who failed to keep a promise to me, returning his sight once a year, just long enough for him to participate in my festival.

I have a rival in my church, where two figures vie for absolute power before the altar. One comes, as my followers say, from *the legend about the Indian woman*, while the second image is modelled from stone and *comes from Italy*. Even here in my sanctuary I am never totally in charge. This bothers me, but I won't give up. The women of Bolivia bring me pearls, while fishing people from the coast lay a large silver albacore at my feet. My female servants dress and groom me, performing those small intimate tasks that I once performed for my Coya. Once a year, just as we did five hundred years ago, the men gently lift me onto the dais and carry me in triumph around my square. The Chinas (that's from Quechua, my tongue, and it means maids and servants), literally dance attendance on me.

I have welcomed them all now for five hundred years, the Morenos, the dark-skinned people from Africa, the Diablos, devils, with their elaborate masks from the Bolivian highlands. You can't imagine how exciting it has been to watch them come. From the nitrate offices of Buen Retiro, Carmen Bajo, Camina and Campamento Libertad, the Collaguayas, wearing white shirts with little bags of old coins pinned to them, carrying a parasol in one hand and a spindle in the other. From Alto de San Antonio, the Collaguas, in their short pants under a poncho flecked with gold and an odd high hat. From Angel and Josefina the Llameras and the Cambas respectively, and the Lichiguayos with their gigantic pan flutes. They would gather at the crossroads in Pozo Almonte and I would follow the dense, dusty cloud of their progress as they walked by foot or by cart, setting off firecrackers, throwing out confetti, leaving small offerings of fruit, candles or gifts, as they greeted, danced and played their musical way along the avenue to La Tirana. Me.

With the dawn of the twentieth century came the first companies of Chinos from the sanctuary of Andacollo, carrying Chilean flags, wearing the three-cornered hat and white cape of the Spanish, but dancing to the tambourines and whistles of those they still call *Indians*. In 1907, workers formed a company of Chinos in Paposo. In 1908, in the nitrate office of Carmen Bajo. With the crisis of 1940, Iquique too acquired its own companies of Chinos, as unemployed workers flocked to the city. They never forgot me and I learned, little by little, to watch over them.

Bonfires, fireworks, altars, an arch of triumph, pennants representing each company of dancers, rituals sacred and profane. Today, the Diablos from the high Andes still dance

transformed into pumas by their masks, echoing the symbols on Tiwanaku's Gate of the Sun. The Morenos are still
here, dressed now in long satin pants and capes, wearing
something like a crown on their heads. The Chunchos,
too, from the jungle, who came with Bolivian immigrants.

At the moment when pachikuti struck and the coin of
my time flipped toward yours, Poma de Ayala described
their dancing: *All these songs are accompanied by a flute they call
the pipo and to this music they dance, holding each other's hands,
in a circle. . . The other dances include the one called Varmi Auca,
Woman Warrior, where the men dress in women's clothes, carrying
their arrows, and sing to the sound of their drums. . .* They dance
here still. For me. The mirrors embroidered into the
Chunchos' hats still reflect wealth, draw luck.

The shepherdesses and the memory of shepherdesses
are here too, in the Cuyacas—urban women who remember the powerful rural societies of the past, dressing in styl-
ized costumes that incorporate indigenous elements. They
come and dance before me, they braid the ribbons of the
harsh, rich colours of the landscape still, the weavers of
the Acllawasi freed to roam the hills and weave the landscape around their pole. The Pastoras and Llameras are
similar, but they still live in rural Aymara communities.
Well into the 1980s these women would dress for me at
Easter, rebirth in Autumn.

The Chinos too, in their traditional brown with their
Chilean flags. You write: *They are the sole group allowed to
dance in the church during the festivities,* but the truth is they
must dance their respects to me, the Chilean dancers. If
they don't, I won't emerge from the sanctuary.

Throughout the 1930s, as the nitrate offices boiled over
with workers and their families from all over Chile and

indeed the world, the traditional Andean symbols weren't enough to express the resulting soup of beliefs and needs and meanings. Oh my friend with your strange name, you wouldn't believe how I laughed when in 1930, Manuel Mercado, who had been a leading Chuncho dancer, left his company and founded the first Redskins company of dancers. Straight from Hollywood, rather than the Andes, this narrow view of native American Indians was frozen for decades in the costumes and steps of his dance for me. Their lances, gestures, rhythms and eyes viewed in the new movie theatres burned themselves into his brain and he adopted them as his symbol. I was taken aback at first but then I realized they were constantly battling against the Europeans, winning, by losing. Soon new companies sprang up, Dakotas, Sioux, Beavers, Blue Feathers, Red Feathers. I gave them my blessing. City companies, elegantly dressed, became known as the Pitucos (Snobs), while others wore the lonely face of the Argentine cowboy, the Gauchos, and still others the Mapuches and the Araucanos.

They transgress when they do this, wallow in transgression, risk the dangerous shards of broken rules. Perhaps your first reaction when you saw them was to wonder if they were racist. But the fact remains, my victory, they're proud they're "Indian." They flaunt it.

Always the underdogs, they dance their way to religious ecstasy and transformation, disguised as bird or beast or the exotic peoples of another continent, rebellious spirits all.

Juan van Kessel's voice aches with recognition. *The dance . . . is much more than "folklore," . . . more than art and sport, is play and prayer, aggression and humility, veneration and offence; it is fantasy and reality, but more than anything else, Andean dance*

*is the maximum expression of Andean social reality. The dance
incarnates the most sacred of religious, cultural and social values
they share and defend as if it were their second language, but an exclusive and secret language that [they] seem to appreciate, practice
and defend more than their own native tongue.*

Let me tell you that losing is like dying from a long,
slow disease. Whether you fight or accept it makes no difference, so how do you go on from day to day, wrest small,
significant victories from your defeat that will matter
more—and forever?

That's why it occurred to me to teach them the dance.

We dance for water, for relief, but above all, we dance
for the joy of it, so there will be joy, always, wherever people are condemned to lose. This way they will always
know, always be prepared, for when the time comes for
celebration.

Unlike the sacred dances that still go on in sanctuaries in
Peru and Bolivia, my dancers don't represent the turbulent
soul of rural villages. Their names reflect their struggle for
legitimacy, the need for legal status in an urban, hostile
world. I come from the city, and even five centuries later
my heart still lingers there.

They can never forget to mention their Chilean identity in this uneasy, cobbled-together nation. After the 1879
war, the Chilean authorities moved the date for my dancers
to the official Day of the Army, 15 July. In 1900 the government closed the Andean sanctuary of Las Peñas and
banned all dancing, costumes, ceremonies and indigenous
languages, branding them primitive and uncultured.

For fifty years, the media treated us as primitive and
ridiculous, while union leaders attacked the Church and

the clergy for their anti-worker conservatism. They also criticized the alcoholism and prostitution that accompanied many of the religious festivals, although they were careful to tolerate the religious convictions of the miners themselves.

My cult embarrassed the Church hierarchy and they banned dancing inside the church. In the 1960s, my dancers organized in their own defence. The bishops, pressured by dropping numbers of the faithful, began to speak of our *somewhat simple and childish faith* as fertile ground for developing mature, adult beliefs.

Isaiah Bowman, this man who travels at your elbow, recalls that every town had its own patron saint, before whom the people danced. While visiting my beloved Pica, he watched a procession arrive with their patron saint on a litter, from the neighbouring village of Macaya, *a copper-producing town of 600 inhabitants, sixty miles northeast. . . She came asking for alms, for it had proved a hard year at Macaya, and an appeal was thus made to the generosity of the inhabitants of Pica. Their patron saint was carried out to meet the visiting saint, and with fife and drum the united procession returned to the village, parading the streets to the church of San Andres.* They needed me . . .

He notes that the spirit of the old prayers for abundant rivers and a rich harvest breathed through the new devotions. The rites of the Christian religion were but new forms for the melancholy chants of the ancient Quechua or Aymara tribes, new settings for the old and simple prayers of the folk about the border of the Puna de Atacama.

In 1968, a new voice joined the choir of arguments about us, suggesting that *For the Church, it is no compromise to receive these cultural expressions in the heart of its community, but rather its own nature brings it to accept and even to stimulate this cultural diversification as a sign of its universality.* This attitude contrasts sharply with a regional newspaper, the Antofagasta *Mercurio*, which on 25 June 1968 published a banner headline announcing that *While the Americans Are Exploring the Moon, We're Still Tormented by the Strident Boom-Boom [of native drums].*

The dancers' rituals revealed *an unfortunate foreign influence* (from Peru and Bolivia). Chileans were *modern*, while Peruvians and Bolivians were trapped in the primitive, indigenous past. Still the dancers grew and thrived, they organized like unions, their numbers swelling from 5,000 in 1953 to over 12,500 thirty years later.

I sent my first groups of pilgrims off to Tocopilla, a small port on the Pacific coast between Iquique and Antofagasta, in 1949, when migrant workers move there from Iquique. In 1964, the troupes organized a federation, just like the region's unions.

In July 1965, the associations of dancers united to form the Federation of Religious Dances of Our Lady of Carmen of La Tirana. The new group turned its leaders into national spokespeople, making it easier for them to battle with Church and media alike for our survival.

Juan van Kessel notes that the minutes of the federation's meetings tell the story of *a long series of negotiations and conflicts with City and Regional authorities, the Chamber of Commerce, the Police and the Armed Forces . . . of efforts to get official permissions, of negotiations with bishops and priests to be admitted "with full equality of rights."*

Throughout the sixties, when massive rallies were heralding the major political changes introduced by the governments of Christian Democrats and later the Popular

Unity, the dance companies held their own festivals in
Antofagasta, Tocopilla, Arica and Chuquicamata. With
the support, at last, of the Church hierarchy, they also survived the military regime, although the 1973 military coup
brings death to fifteen of my dancers, and many more face
exile. The others take refuge in the apolitical, religious
nature of their activity and within three months of the
coup have resumed their meetings and their organization.
We are used to repression. The price of the church's protection, however, was its growing influence on the dance
companies.

My leaders defend me though. They complained to
Juan van Kessel *that the Church placed too much emphasis on
Jesus Christ and not his mother. They give preference to the mass
and we're practically losing the indigenous part of the festival, the
traditional part. For example, they do mass: we can't dance. We
can't make our entrance, we can't do our farewell, that is, everything that is the most important about this. . . The festival is for
Mary. The people of the Tirana belong to the Tirana to the death
and they will always defend the Virgin. This is what the priests
won't accept. Now they say: Mary doesn't come first. Mary's after
Jesus. . . And that's what people won't accept.*

When the Pope came to Chile in April 1987, the bishops of the Norte Grande expected my dancers to go to
Antofagasta and perform before him—at their own expense. This was too much—all their fund-raising goes to
ensuring they dance for me. When the bishops protested,
my leaders asked, *Why should La Tirana have to go to see the
Pope? Why isn't he coming to pay his respects to La Tirana?*

I saw you in the museum in Iquique. Cuneo Vidal was
growing out of date. And there you were, wandering

among the glass cages holding the shattered fragments of my past, unable to put them together. It is a past you and I have come to share. I turn my back on the future still, my eyes bright and staring out of my cage, at you. You felt it, I could tell. The way you stood there transfixed, drank us in with those eyes of sky.

I watched you scribbling, the way you copied the words off the white card that labels us. Now, listen to Grete Mostny. I would whisper in her ear too—I'd wait until she dozed off while sitting in one of our graveyards. *Human sacrifices, as supreme sacrifices, were relatively rare . . .*

The Mapuches, the one nation we Incas never conquered, say that *we die three times: the first in our flesh; the second in the hearts of those who survive us; and the third time in their memories.* This is what I managed to subvert. I learned a lot from Almeida's stories of Jesus Christ.

Death is a kind of amplifier, picking up a message and broadcasting it down through time.

In the end, when I left my home and turned again to the mountains I focused on the joy of walking again. I had thought that leaving the oasis would be almost unbearable, would make me cry out in pain, but when I turned my back on the tamarugo forest I turned my back on Almeida dead and walked to meet him where he might live again. As my legs carried me back toward the mountains, those peaks I'd hiked across just a few years before, it all lay clear and sharply etched before me: where I was going, and why.

Almost five hundred years later, as you stood gazing at me in the museum of Iquique, you noted the finely woven red cape that I wear, tied with a burgundy sash, the bracelets of silver and gold. You made a rough sketch of the fine-painted ceramic dish that lies beside me, along with a wooden spoon and the remnants of a small bag embroidered with bright emerald feathers from the Amazon. My girl lies at my feet. I cradle her head in my lap.

Our skin, you added, is fine and pale as paper. Our eyes are closed. Bows and arrows lie nearby as if we might need protection, as does the head of a sacrificed dog, wearing a crown of harpoon tips. You admired the artistry of a beautifully woven bag, covered with diamond shapes in yellow and red thread, streaked with turquoise. You noted how it seems to wait patiently to be picked up again; you wrote, *The position of the woman and the girl in the Iquique museum suggests both affection and relaxation. The girl leans back into the woman who leans back into what would originally have been the mountainside. Their legs are neatly crossed under their cloaks, which are warmly wrapped around them.*

With no one and nowhere to return to, we turned back to a landscape composed of our gods, the huacas that could be rivers or ridges, peaks or an extraordinary rock in a ravine (*Turn back with us . . .*). We retraced the footsteps of our victorious army until we reached the closest point to the sky (*Follow the echoes of our chants*). But even as we retraced the past we changed it, our footsteps faltering, my eyes pained but clear, writing with our paths across the desert and back up into the high peaks of the Andes, that one day, one day, this would all be different. Then they laid me down (*Lie with me for a moment, here*). They gave us chicha to drink and I pulled the girl toward me for what I thought would be one last embrace. They tried to imitate the old ceremonies, but without me to lead them they had to improvise.

At the last minute they included the girl in their package to the gods (*We can hold her between us*). Perhaps they were worried she might try to carry on my memory. We both did anyway (*Join us*), dreaming the future into being during the long sleep of our death. They offered the Sun and Moon. I accepted (*Accept them with me*). And let us go on to meet.

They buried me where Earth meets Sky.

They placed me where the strains of their music would always drift, the vivid purples, reds and yellows of their costumes flicker like sparks or drops of water, the vibrant gesture of their dance meet the trembling of volcanoes. I fell asleep praying, pray still; pray with me . . .

Carry me, Father Condor,
guide me, Brother Hawk.
Tell my darling mother:
Five days have gone by
in which I neither ate nor drank.
Lord, note-taker and accomplice
Chasqui, carrier of messages:
I beg you to carry
my words and my heart
to my beloved father,
please tell my mother!

After the dancing ends, Patricio, Camilo and I return to our rented car, a small bubble of metal and glass scuttling across darkness itself. We retrace the road between La Tirana and Pozo Almonte and take the turn-off back to Iquique at Humberstone. I sense, as I have sensed driving highways elsewhere in the fog, the sharp points of trees aimed like lances at the sky alongside us. But they are not there.

Bowman, at my elbow, insists there is no truth to the stories of algarrobo forests buried under the Atacama due to catastrophic climate change. Yet I can't shake the unconscious sense of trees, just as I can't forget the rhythm of the drums. A jungle swallows up any human path almost at once, but in the desert a trail remains forever.

Across those trails of rock and time, the dancers have come, keep coming, on foot, by bus, by truck and train, bringing with them technologies for irrigation and building, knowledge of where to find water in the desert's arid depths, their own views of the universe and their place, our place, within it. The Conquest, electricity, our own ignorance, have yet to stop them.

As I grapple with my southerner's instinct for trees, so Ñusta's dancers struggle with her legacy, organizing in their own way to dance and worship the female deity that Christianity offered them, that they imprinted over their own heartfelt image of the Pachamama. They rise like yeast through the society that has attempted to crush them. They have joined and fought with the workers of the nitrate offices, the copper unions, the workers in the ports and on the railways.

But they have continued to build their identity around the slender, pliant column of their own beliefs, winding their coloured ribbons and reinventing the intricate ecology of their landscape as they dance, braiding their history into their present, weaving their future and tying its knots with the vivid threads of their past, the cherished flags of the great empires of the Andes.

10

ENCHANTED
VALLEY /
ROCKY CREEK

The Desert Creeps Southward

I've asked no one
who I am,
If I'm made of rock
or of snow,
with no shadow
and no tears.

– *Traditional Quechua poem*

June 1999

W E ARE PAINTING OUR HOUSE. I have one last trip
to make. One last month to finish this book. A
last month to learn to let it go. Everything is in
boxes, as if we were moving away. Patricio and I have practically divorced (*You have no colour sense!—You're completely*

colour-blind!—The only colour you *like is* pink!—*You have a sick feminist paranoia of pink!—Well, let's just paint everything white then.—No way! How about the same colour as last time?— It turns my stomach!*). In the end, pale yellow mostly.

But then the bright dark blue we chose for contrast turned out to be a deep nocturnal purple. Turned out, meaning, after we had painted several ceilings, a wall in my office, the trim in the children's room and the bathroom. Patricio is nervous. The kids aren't sure they like it. I turn back, over and over again, to a blanket I bought on my first visit to San Pedro de Atacama. A blanket woven from llama wool soaked in the brilliant, extravagant colours of the desert. The colours all the rule books (are there really rule books, or is it just the oral tradition that preserves and enforces all these terrible rules?) say should never appear in the same room, never mind the same bizarre fabric. The fluorescent pinks and impossible purples. The same yellows and reds and oranges that we saw over and over again as we travelled the desert. The fresh greens of young spikes of grass as they poke their noses out of the cool protective earth to sniff the relentless heat, the infinite blue air, the shining fragrance of the sun for the first, often fatal time.

Like those odd, clashing colours, the fabric of this book where I have camped out for so long has sown together the Quechua poems, Atacamenian voices, the whirling dancers of Aymara ancestry, the rough or elegant words of the Spanish priests—Father Le Paige, Juan van Kessel, the Chileans and foreigners who tried to capture a fragment of their soul and somehow rescue them, my own *gringa* eyes—after twenty years, those old Canadian convictions seem stronger than ever.

One long weekend in June, my income tax refund burning a hole in my pocket, I pull together four of our five-member family and we set out for the north, one last time. We are heading for the gateway to the desert, the area where it first closes the arid jaws of its strength on the soft green land that composes Chile's fertile central valley. That, perhaps above all, is the great oddity of travel in our time. We no longer have to do things in order. Airplanes permit us to jump around, start in the middle and explore northward or southward or simply go around in circles, as I did around San Pedro. While Huillac Ñusta and Diego de Almagro, and all those who followed, had to pay the high price of travel across the mountains, then the Puna, then face the Atacama desert itself before they could finally rest and restore themselves in the green oases of Pica or Copiapo farther south, I have explored the desert piece by piece, fitting together each section like a puzzle or, perhaps more lastingly, like the delicately stitched squares of her quilt.

Searching for some last message from Huillac Ñusta, I find a poem/prayer from the sixties, a cry of pain that cuts sharply into the vibrant joy of songs from before the Conquest, her prayer, which still tempts the pagan in me back into the fold (*May the joy in your eyes / come with the dawn . . . your infinite will / be all that flowers*).

Dios Santo
Holy God, holy, holy:
The poisonous snake, the snake with no poison, adore you,
The fish play like light in the river,
The worm crawls along calmly,
The hummingbird trembles and burns,

The frozen pampa's straw cries out,
Holy God, holy, holy;
They come for you.

This is a much more frightening view of the universe and our place in it than the words that first drew me toward Huillac Ñusta. The puritans have reached America and made it theirs. Where do we go to next?

When after a long drive, zig-zagging across the countryside, we finally stop and get out of the car to stretch our legs, we have reached a place called El Valle del Encanto (Enchanted Valley), otherwise known as the Quebrada Las Penas (Rocky Creek). Like light itself, the plaintive strains of Ñusta's songs sift the landscape, illuminating the figures scratched, carved and painted into the rocks along the creek thousands of years ago.

This area is just 50,000 to 100,000 years old, a mere babe in geological terms. It has none of the overpowering magnificence of the Andes' great stony heights soaring between Chile and the rest of the continent. Yet there's something about this gentle low valley, the way the massive slabs of rock lie tossed about, as if a giant teenager had come this way, got fed up and dumped them, leaving them strewn about like discarded clothes.

Danny, at seven, runs free, happy to be out of the car, happy to go hurtling through pepper trees and low shrubs, clambering over rocks, running his fingers through the deep hollows carved like earthenware cups into the rocks, especially down by the river. Cups for mixing the paints they used to etch their visions into the rocks or their own faces? Cups for pounding the grain? Cups for the blood of sacrifice?

Camilo, at fifteen, is more dignified. He maintains an adolescent distance, roughly shadowing Patricio and me as we wander along the paths. Unlike Danny, we resist the temptation to explore the delicate etchings in the rocks with our fingers, contenting ourselves with running our eyes over the enormous rockfaces that lie scattered around us like paintings in an abandoned art gallery. Everywhere we look they take us by surprise, the square, owl-eyed faces under their enormous crescent headdresses, the stick figures running or walking, surrounded by smaller two- and four-legged creatures. Sometimes rays radiate out from their heads like suns. One looks strikingly similar to the figure we saw on the Unita Hill outside Iquique, an arm raised in greeting, the other sagging under the weight of a heavy object whose contours have been obscured by time. One life-sized figure about five feet high looks like nothing so much as a pot-bellied cook on a hot day, the balloon of his chef's hat echoed by the enormous round-ness of his belly.

When this narrow ravine was first rediscovered in 1949, archaeologists initially thought the extraordinary drawings and paintings covering many of the rockfaces were the work of the Incas, but excavations in 1964 revealed that two separate prehistoric cultures had used the valley. The first, from the Archaic to Paleo-Indian period, were hunters and gatherers who passed through the valley, using it as a stopping place as they moved eastward from the Pacific Ocean, crossing the desert toward the Andes some 8,000 years B.C. They left arrowheads, stone tools, a wide variety of seashells and the burial site of a single figure, who was found curled up as if in sleep, still holding several knives of sharpened mussel shells in his right hand.

A second period of human settlement reached this gentle valley some time between A.D. 95 and 240, when the El Molle culture, hunter-gatherers that now had domesticated herds of llamas and alpacas, and were beginning to use agriculture, settled in the valley. But apparently none of them ever settled here permanently. Nor does it seem to have been the main highway between the coast and the Andes. It may have been an alternative route or, more likely, given the extraordinary display of prehistoric drawings that lie scattered on rockfaces and the low cliffs of the ravine, some kind of special gathering place for the peoples that roamed and were in the process of settling this difficult region.

Grete Mostny, with Hans Niemeyer, another archaeologist, whispers in my ear (What will I do without her? How go back to life outside this world, this book?), *This is an art form that began with hunting parties and was carried on in later periods by the farming-ceramic-based cultures. They used every possible style, from naturalism to abstraction, combining from the start both extremes in the same picture, as pictograms or ideograms. The same breadth is clear in their treatment of themes: the juxtaposition of animals, signs and hands, the exuberance of the scenes depicting hunting, warfare, pasturing, religious ceremonies or the walls of symbols. Due to our lack of knowledge of the cultural context, today it is inexplicable and incomprehensible. This rupestrian art—like all art—is a medium of communication between the artist and her/his society, a society to which we do not belong.*

Almost 80 per cent of the figures standing, hunting, fighting, dancing across these rocks are human, ranging from the simplest stick figure to heavily adorned faces with masks or tiaras. Styles and techniques criss-cross the rock walls that stretch like interconnected chambers along the ravine, blending together, arguing, complementing, contrasting with each other, a silent cacophony of world views that we can't decipher, can only attempt to feel. Oddly enough, while the first two periods of human settlement in this part of the desert clearly identified with this place, there is no sign that the Diaguitas, who followed them elsewhere, ever settled or placed a foot here. What would have kept them away?

For all our digging, our measurements, our accumulation of scientific knowledge, the insistence on proof, objectivity, it is always the mystery that draws us to places like this valley, hidden in the desert's folds, partway between Ovalle and La Serena, 440 kilometres north of Santiago. A child stands by a river and can't resist the temptation to pick up a rock and throw it in. An adolescent feels the weight of a sharp stone on her palm and starts to scrape and scratch a story into the blank rock, leaving the footprints of her ideas to be polished by the wind, gradually sanded down until only the vaguest memory of her passing remains.

We seek shelter, we build, we travel as endlessly now as ever, using all the advances our machines have brought, the wonders and terrors of technology, to retrace the narrow paths through desert ravines, the sweeping highways perfected by the Incas. We fly, we ride, we walk, but we always search. Danny is shouting with glee. Camilo lounges languidly against one of the enormous rocks. I squat finally to run my fingers over the smooth hollows of the cups cut into stone beside the river. One rock has forty-four of these rounded holes like little cups marking its surface, in no apparent order or design.

As night falls we slow and stop, reduced to stillness here in the abandoned galleries of their thoughts, the river muttering softly under its breath, the rocks around us heaving a last dark sigh as they turn to silhouettes against a sky that passes through every possible shade of purple and pink, orange and red, until it's turned as dark and fathomless as the ocean. This is where the heartless Atacama spreads northward, drier and drier until life is an ever-shrinking drop of water, evaporates, is gone. This is where the Atacama begins to sift its way gently, silently, mercilessly southward, a border it doesn't cross but rather pushes relentlessly toward us. We can spend hours watching, and never see it.

> You will be my sweet deception,
> I will be your dark shadow . . .

I am not telling this journey in order, for some reason cannot tell it in order, because the order we saw it in had little to do with the meaning we found there. But I can say that we began in the country's urban, smog-choked centre, Santiago, drove north along the Pan-American Highway, along the coast, noting the occasional eruption of rock and the way the sun seemed to be strung like a medallion between them, lying on the throat of a flesh-coloured sky that was gradually blotted out by thick brushstrokes of purple, navy, black, the work of a despairing artist who can't stand the sight of his own efforts at day's end.

We reached the beach resort of Tongoy where we spent the night, then carried on to the legendary Elqui Valley. There the landscape, neatly criss-crossed by vineyard wands supporting the grapes used in wine and pisco (brandy), seemed to have been stitched together by genteel ladies a century before. We stopped in Vicuna to visit the museum of Gabriela Mistral, the first woman and the first Latin American to win the Nobel Prize for poetry (1945).

I should have liked the Elqui River valley more, still feel guilty for not being more impressed. A massive dam was going in about halfway along, and the narrow highway was often lined with poor housing developments, squatting amidst the fertile fields like trailer camps without the wheels. We spent the night at the end of the valley in the town of Pisco, then took a quick detour to see the hippie-inspired marvels of Cachiguaz. As a veteran of Vallican and other such havens settled by American draft dodgers, and a wide range of communal experiments by Canadians seeking to build a better world in the interior of British Columbia, I found Cachiguaz more like a pale imitation than the genuine expression of someone's collective attempt at soul or at least community. Perhaps I'm just getting jaded in my old age, or looking for the right past in the wrong place.

All along our journey, signs proclaim, *Let's Stop the Desert's Advance*, announcing intentions rather than towns. We see no trees, just scruffy shrubs like dried heather amidst the outcroppings of rock, which formed striking silhouettes against the drowning orange of the sun.

We rush southward, then out toward the coast to catch Fray Jorge park before it closes, a delicate place wrapped in the tissue paper of endless regulations, all aiming to protect what remains of a treasure already plundered, the barn door locked now that half the horses have been stolen. We are in the midst of the Niña phase of the cycle touched off by the Niño current, which has caused devastating hurricanes and natural disasters throughout most of the world. In Chile in the past few years it has dragged us from the most extreme and lengthy drought in the country's history, through flash floods (in the winter of '98), followed by even more arid extremes this year, which led to constant power failures and rationing of electricity for several hours a day, throughout most of the country.

But there is something of poetic justice to the Niño, the current named for the Christ Child (because it usually appears around Christmastime in the south). I can't separate the image of the strange seething phenomenon that warms the surface currents, winding like a bright snake through the Pacific, from the desert that seems to lie so passively alongside it. Even to my modern mind (or perhaps there has been some meeting between Huillac Ñusta and me, some transmutation that I was not completely aware of) there is something of the clashing and mating of gods amidst the roar of thunder and lightning's quick bright hiss from heaven to hell in the Boy's relationship with the desert that stretches its length beside him, dry and sharp as a blade. The Boy who, like Woolf's Orlando, between one generation, one cycle, and the next slips out of the man's body and into the Girl's, La Niña, his mirror reflection, who brings frigid temperatures and has taunted us with insufficient rain this winter.

Whatever, I am perversely grateful to the Girl-Boy. Every five to ten years, their cycle brings torrential rains to Chile's Fourth Region, the semi-desert that announces the bare expanse of the Atacama, between the cities of La Serena and Copiapo. Seeds stored amid the arid gravel of its surface soak up the long-awaited moisture and Chile's northern desert briefly blazes with the silken colours of wildflowers. For a few months, earth normally packed and hard as cement briefly blooms with the brilliant ochre, crimson, teal and mauve of its patient, persistent flowers.

Thanks to the 200-mile limit, at some points, Chile, this sliver of a country, is actually more water than earth, more liquid than solid. And yet, according to the Corporacion Nacional Forestal (CONAF), 62 per cent of the country's land currently suffers from serious degradation due to desertification, with the desert advancing southward at a rate of one-third of a kilometre per year.

Alarmed by what desertification could do to the country's resource-based economy and a national territory that is just slightly larger than Texas, CONAF and some non-governmental organizations have begun innovative projects to study and recover affected areas before it is too late. But underlying the issue, in a country that frequently suffers from severe and lengthy droughts, is the whole question of how the country administers its water, an increasingly scarce resource. While some experts argue that the current market-oriented policies are the best solution, international experts and local non-governmental organizations warn that Chile could be headed for disaster. With the country's legislation on everything from pension plans to water rights serving as a model for Latin America, Chile could take part of the continent with it.

Before heading north, I spoke to Samuel Francke, who holds a doctorate in soil science, and is chief of CONAF's National Water Basin Management office. An expert in desertification, he paints a sobering picture of Chile today, the territory first patched together by the Incan empire, then the upstart Chileans a century ago.

The Atacama occupies about a third of the country's mainland territory. Forty-seven million hectares, almost two-thirds of the national territory, are affected by serious to very serious (34 per cent), moderate (44 per cent) or slight (22 per cent) desertification, meaning that these soils have lost 40 to 100 per cent of their soil depth, among other indicators used to evaluate erosion.

Trained in Germany, Francke recommends reforestation as the main tool for turning the situation around, particularly in rainy southern Chile, where wide-scale slash-burning to clear land for farming destroyed the original forests and left the soil exposed and vulnerable to erosion. However, he warns that the forestry industry practice of burning after harvesting pine plantations, for example, can be extremely counterproductive. The use of heavy machinery and prolonged exposure of soil after harvesting (often six to nine months) can also help undo the good that pine plantations have done during the twenty to twenty-five years they take to grow in this country.

A few months later, across town, at the bustling offices of a moderate non-government organization, the Committee for Defence of Flora and Fauna (CODEFF), I spoke to Miguel Torrico, a forestry engineer. He pulled some graphs from a file that showed how Chile's rainfall has steadily decreased for the past century. In the nineties, it has come perilously close to the bottom of the graph, even for normally rainy regions like the south.

What we don't know, he says, *is whether this is part of a longer, one-hundred-year cycle and we could now see a recovery. What is clear is that drought is a permanent part of Chile's reality, but the government has yet to face it, whether we're talking about its energy policy, agriculture, the environment, desertification or water.*

Drought, a virtual constant in Chile's northern desert from the First to the Fourth Region, has crept southward over the past four years and with it the desert itself.

We used to talk about desertification in the oases and the Fourth Region only, says Torrico. *But now it's all through the country*. Francke likens it to soil cancer. In April 1999 the capital city, Santiago, with a population of five million people, faced power shutdowns as part of rationing when electrical supply failed to keep up with demand, due to water shortages at hydro-power generating stations.

Flowers blossoming on the raw dust of the desert are an extraordinary sight, but even more amazing is the water-loving forest tucked away on a narrow strip of northern Chile's Pacific coast. Fray Jorge National Park flourishes all year round, offering much of the vegetation to be found in Chile's temperate rainforests a thousand kilometres away in the stormy south. In the park, Andean flickers (a salt-and-pepper-coloured woodpecker), gouge their meals from the bark of southern water-loving trees like the *canelo* (named for cinnamon because of its fragrant bark). The green-backed firecrown, a hummingbird, vibrates among *arrayan*, *olivillo* and *petrillo* trees that are far more typical in the rich, jungle-like forests of southern peaks around the city of Valdivia.

The forest itself was discovered in the early 1600s, about a lifetime after Huillac Ñusta and her people escaped from Diego de Almagro. Benedictine monks, building a cathedral in La Serena, a major city one hundred kilometres to the north, ran out of wood. One Friar George (Fray Jorge) set out to find more and eventually stumbled across the forest that has born his name ever since.

In the centuries that followed, settlers burned most of the area's scarce forests as firewood or as part of efforts to eliminate the pumas, wildcats and eagles that attacked their herds of cattle and goats. In 1941, concerned that the extraordinary forest had shrunk from an estimated 400,000 to 200,000 hectares and was continuing to disappear, Chilean authorities declared the area a national park.

At first we are disappointed by what we find after the long drive toward the coast. A dull sun shines on the tourist facilities where we stop, so I can go to the bathroom. A sleek young fox follows me, almost within touching distance, almost to the door. Often, alongside the road, we see the plains stretching away on either side, covered with clusters of an aloe-like succulent called the *Chagual chico* or *Puya venusta*, red speckled heads floating a metre or two above the green leaves. We see three more foxes on the road up into the coastal foothills where we expect to find the forest. And we pass grove after grove of cactus splashed with the red petals of their blooms. They look as if they've been wounded, then clumsily bandaged, and the blood is seeping through, as they march, hunched over, the war-weary veterans of the botanical equivalent of World War I.

When we finally reach the forest, we find ourselves clutched in the damp clammy fist of the camanchaca. Danny, indignant, refuses to get out of the car. Patricio, Cam and I make a quick foray along what turns out to be a very short visitors' path. The forest ranger who accompanies us can't tell us much about what we're seeing. This is a far cry from the thick jungle-like temperate rainforests of the south, where we spend most of our free time. And yet.

The next day, however, I leave my family behind and return to the park, this time accompanied by Saul Molina, a forestry engineer who currently spends most of his waking hours studying it.

Although Fray Jorge's wooded area is technically classified as a rainforest, *It's really a forest of mist*, says Molina. He is part of a team of academics and forestry engineers who are working on an ambitious project to prevent further desertification of the park and reforest with the unusual species native to it.

He points out that of the 1,200 to 1,500 millimetres of water that a forest like this one requires every year, less than 10 per cent actually falls in the form of rainfall in Fray Jorge, with trees and shrubs harvesting the rest from the camanchaca, the heavy fog that blows off the ocean most mornings only to travel across the desert and drop the precious rain it carries on the Andes, as it rises over them on the way to Argentina.

There are a lot of signs that the park is seriously deteriorating, Rodrigo Hernández, another forestry engineer, told me earlier in the day. And here the miracle begins, because for a change, people here have organized to try and rescue the park—starting with knowing it better. He is working with CONAF, in charge of the multi-disciplinary team of academics working to save Fray Jorge's forest. *There are a lot of pathogenics—bacteria, fungi, parasites, insects—attacking the trees. We find a lot of clearings where the trees have fallen but there's no regeneration.*

Many have studied individual aspects of the bizarre forest that lives on ocean mist surrounded by the world's driest desert. But no one until now had tried to combine study with practical experimentation to heal its ills. Hernández and the team of forestry, botanical and other experts working on the project hope that their studies will not only save Fray Jorge's forest from succumbing to desertification, but will also serve as a model for others' efforts elsewhere in a world where global warming has suddenly become a major threat.

Hernández is convinced that the results will make the enormous effort and expense worthwhile, but there is also an ethical edge to his efforts. *What's happening to Fray Jorge isn't the result of a natural process. The park has suffered most of this damage at the hands of mankind and I think we have an ethical obligation to try to repair it.* He is also convinced that the park is a biological treasure chest, packed with genetic and other information about the history of this part of the world. Perhaps most important, in an era of growing concern about the wide-ranging impact of global warming, Hernández is convinced that these *studies of what happened here and what is coming with climatic change will have enormous importance, not just in Chile but internationally.*

The ambitious four-year, US$800,000 project, 56 per cent financed by the regional government and 44 per cent by CONAF, combines several areas of study: available water and how to increase it, the soil-nutrient cycle, the presence of fungi and bacteria, artificial regeneration of tree species, baseline, including existing species and a detailed map of the area. The group is halfway through the project's second year.

Molina takes me to see the project's working areas and other facilities. In the greenhouse, seedlings no higher than my fingers huddle in a space a couple of metres square. They are fragile reminders of how little is known about most of the tree species that are native—and unique—to Chile, Fray Jorge's among them.

Outside, we visit the sunny slopes that cling to the cliffs hundreds of metres above the ocean. Molina describes how the forest grows, pointing out the thickets of trees that move down the steep slopes that look out over the Pacific, thirsty for mist. Test areas that we visit are demonstrating that an aggressive creeper called *yelmo* is choking all new tree and shrub growth other than its own, he tells me, pointing to thick tents formed by the fleshy leaves of the vine, which block out all sunlight and cover entire chunks of territory, swarming over the drooping trees until they die. In the sudden warmth of clearings behind the chilly tree thickets, the skeletons of dead trees lie dry as tinder, no sign of new growth among them. On these cliffs, warmth and exposure make life difficult, regeneration impossible, because there's no way to reap the rain.

Beyond them, in some of the clearings left by the dying forest, large black screens drink in 100 to 200 litres of mist every couple of days, filling tanks that will be used to water the slopes once Molina and his colleagues plant them with seedlings later in the year.

Unlike the scientists of CONAF and the northern universities, which are using their own studies and experiments to beat back the effects of desertification in the park, the non-governmental organization, CODEFF, has applied a different strategy to fighting desertification, by fighting poverty itself.

In December 1998, CODEFF completed the last leg of a five-year project funded by a US$300,000 grant from the European Community. The NGO's team focused primarily on working with people, all in the Fourth Region, where the park is also located. They started their five-year project by asking everyone from the regional governor (a presidential appointee) on down to teachers and schoolchildren what they knew about desertification in the region where they lived.

We found that political leaders were totally unaware of the issue, Miguel Torrico says, *in spite of the fact that they lived*

*in an area that was very threatened by it. School children knew
all the stops on the Santiago subway, and they were studying
English, but they didn't know anything about the desert around
them.*

Above all, the initial survey found that the poverty of
marginal farmers was a major contributing factor. *If you've
got the resources, you can bring in the water,* says Torrico. *But
someone who's poor will cut down a tree because he's desperate for
firewood, or his goats will eat whatever grass there is.*

To raise awareness, project leaders started by holding a
series of seminars for journalists, community leaders, and
farmers, and distributing some 4,000 specially designed
colouring books to the region's schoolchildren. But they
went one step further, helping 105 poor goat-herding
families to build cement tanks to store their meagre water
supply and build drip irrigation systems to help them grow
crops, primarily for their own use. Funding also went to
buy seeds and build fences to keep goats away from some
kinds of vegetation. They also offered courses in basic agricultural and animal husbandry techniques.

The result: *Things really changed for the people we worked
with.* Torrico pulls out pictures of the cement tanks being
built in the amidst of sand and dust. Others, already full of
water, are surrounded by lush green vegetation and the
occasional row of trees.

With roughly one-third of the country already covered
by the world's driest desert, I expected the Chilean authorities to be particularly sensitive to issues related to the
scarcity of water. However, many of those I spoke to about
desertification complain, off the record, that *for politicians,
it's not sexy enough, it doesn't win votes and therefore they tend to
neglect it.* A reforested plot takes at least twenty years to

reach maturity, while a new highway, bridge or tunnel can be inaugurated during a term in office.

For Latin America, the debate on water management and desertification is just beginning, but with global warming and the Niño phenomenon increasingly altering rainfall in the region, time may be running out, like the water itself.

Farewell. She may have hummed it under her breath, secretly terrified and glad to be travelling away from disaster, moving toward disasters still unknown, and therefore sweetened by hope.

> *Today is the day I leave,*
> *But I won't be off today,*
> *I'll leave tomorrow.*

Playfully, as if she had a choice, as if this journey were of her planning and her designing and therefore would bring her to somewhere or some new person she longed to be.

> *You'll see me off, playing*
> *A flute of fly-bone,*
> *Carrying a spider web for a flag.*

She sang cheerfully, as if the symbols that lit their journey and gave it meaning were of her choosing, came from the prayers and song, from the huacas, the local gods whose doorways to other, adjacent worlds had always punctuated the landscape, had always given hope that a plea would be heard, that a bargain could be made.

An ant's egg for my drum,
And my cap? my cap
Will be the nest of a hummingbird.

I am home to stay, stuck for some time at least, while this book, this world I've lived in/travelled through begins to make its own long journey northward, past the Atacama, away. I've been poring over a booklet I picked up on the Enchanted Valley, one last time. Here, yet again, the by now eternal story of an indigenous princess in love with a Spanish conquistador. This one is supposed to have thrown herself off one of the high rocks perched precariously above Rocky Creek. At four in the morning I grope around, searching the piles of books and papers around my office for more information. Instead I find the rough printout of a photograph from my friend Rosa Zañartu, at CODELCO. *A couple of mummies in 1912*, she's written on it. In the picture, an American who looks like a mining executive's idea of a cowboy squats beside the skeletal but well-preserved remains of a man. The mummy leans his head on his hand, apparently staring intently at the American. Time travellers the both of them now, they appear to be deep in conversation.

Call it karma, call it what-goes-around-comes-around, there's always a moment when conflicting realities finally clash and, if we're not quick to respond, quick to right injustice in clear and decisive ways, societies reach a point where no more negotiations are possible. For the Chileans, one such moment occurred when the English arrested General Pinochet in London on 16 October 1998. For his supporters at least, the General's government has always been a political issue and the reign of brutal terror that held it in place was not the point. If you were for him you were right (in both senses). If you were against him, you were left and wrong. And, as the country's national slogan proclaims: *Por la razón o la fuerza* (where reason fails: by force), a Chilean version of might makes right.

But for the rest of the world, what he did was not a matter of political opinion. It was legally and morally wrong. *Thou shalt not kill.* Pinochet thought he was safe in Thatcher's London, even when the French refused him a visa. But when the moment came, there was no one in power at the end of a telephone willing to let him go. The sabre-rattling, the military's veiled and not-so-veiled threats to elected government fell on deaf ears. No one trembled and held out the key for General Pinochet's release. His supporters were astounded to find their hero clutched in the jaws of a justice system different from Chile's, where virtually everything can be boiled down to the politics of expediency: in the end whoever has the power to pay, or apply the necessary dose of violence, will prevail.

Two world views, complete unto themselves, until they meet. It's true. Both romance and suicides occur.

Likewise, we may avoid coming to terms with our own past. We may ignore, rewrite, forget it. Or, in the Americas, we may pretend our past is only Europe. This means we gaze at our own present through half-closed eyes. We accept half-truths, half willing ourselves not to see.

But we can visit the Atacama, can gaze for a long time, in silence, at the desert Huillac Ñusta and thousands of years of indigenous travellers shaped with their feet, the calligraphy of menace and delight they carved across its open walls, its seemingly endless space. We can stand at the edge of the salar, surrounded by the absence of life that reaffirms its mystery. There, the pages of all the books never written lie open before us. She is telling us that it is inevitable, that our societies too will some day meet the Pizarros or Diego de Almagro and his men, marching out of the Atacama into our lives, the legions of severed heads and headless bodies, invading aliens bearing with them a new vision they will force us to kneel before. Perhaps they will come from other planets, as Hollywood never tires of predicting. But perhaps they will come from within—the forces of our own frustrated species, allying themselves with a planet so crushed and twisted out of shape that they bring with them the horrors of destruction, and all the terrifying fury and power and beauty of birth. The armed resistance of Chiapas, the guerrillas of Colombia and Ecuador, Peru's Shining Path, the Aymaras, the Atacamenians, the Mapuche of Chile who have spent over a year now rebelling, at first in peace. . . There is fear, and the brutality of injustice, but this is also a story of love.

And there is still time (there's always time, until there's none), to listen to her last song.

Look for me

If you seek me out, you'll find me
In the centre of a carnation
Or a rose.

If you don't find me there,
You'll say she's gone because I made her cry,
Because I made her suffer, she's gone, you'll say.

Say goodbye, wave goodbye to me
From the hilltop above your town
From the door to your house.

She's waiting there now. If I stop typing and walk down to the front door of my house, look outside, let the breath of the hill and the acacias blow through me, hand a pile of old papers to the recyclers who make their living by going through the garbage every night, I may see her. The whistles of the pan flutes, the mourning wails of the antara, the shadows of leaping dancers: they're all there, reminding me to look through the past to see the future, to seek the answers as much in what was as in what may never be. Her hand, dry as dust in the Iquique museum, or still frozen and swollen on some peak as though alive, the young girl leaning into her lap, a shared smile, perhaps, playing across both their lips.

Their twin hands reach back out through the glass case, through sheets of ice, through the rain that falls but never meets the earth, toward a cyclist pedalling her way across the desert, trying to find that single place that we all come from, the single dancing language that will allow us to really talk.

Still she stands there, on the hilltop above our town, visible from the threshold of our houses.

She's offering us goodbye, fare well and welcome, all in the same quick flick of her wrist.

ACKNOWLEDGMENTS

➤

I AM GRATEFUL to all the authors whose work helped to nourish my understanding of the Norte Grande and the events there over the centuries. Because so much of their work is available only in Spanish, I have on occasion quoted at greater length than I have in the case of the English-language writers (John Hemming, Harold Blakemore, Brian Loveman, Isaiah Bowman). To some I feel a special debt, for the vividness of their prose, the quality of their vision and their passion for their subject.

I celebrate especially the books by Juan van Kessel, the Jesuit anthropologist whose work, published, sadly, in footnote-sized lettering, explores with great depth and sensibility the reality of the desert's peoples today. I found his books not in Chilean bookstores but on a visit to Bolivia. Several key volumes were available only in the Pre-Columbian Museum's library.

And Andrés Sabella, the northern poet whose book I discovered well into the process of writing. We speak from different generations, different cultures and different genders, all of which exercise a powerful influence on how we see. But I would like to think that with all their differences, contradictions, common passions, notes of argument, our books carry on a conversation that began with the Conquest and will grow in richness in the coming years.

Special thanks too to:

Anne-Mette Herr, the editor whose assignment took me to the Norte Grande for the first time. Jorge Vergara, for the magnificent books he so generously loaned me, his comments, suggestions, the long arguments both patient and passionate. Rosa Zañartu, tireless researcher and impassioned thinker about Chile's mining history. Enrique Silva, studies head at Codelco, the Copper Corporation of Chile. María Elena Rozas, for the loan of two crucial books. Sonia Montecinos, for her thoughts on La Tirana herself within the context of the nature of mestizaje and machismo in Latin America. Rolf Foerster, for hours of wide-ranging conversation on themes that found their way into this book. Laura López, public relations officer for the United Nations Economic Commission for Latin America and the Caribbean and a great help in my search for information about water. Similarly, Claudio Mercado and José Pérez de Arce of the Museo Precolombino in Santiago, Micaela Navarrete of the National Library of Chile, and Max Salinas for his unorthodox religious opinions (bless him!). Thanks also, to Liz and Tony Tillett, for the many good reads and good information, which helped work on this book go a little easier, and to Joan Simalchik, historian and friend, and Robin Breon, an expert in many things

ACKNOWLEDGMENTS 351

surprising and also a great friend, for the loan of their home, the sharing of ideas, and access to the Robarts Library. Especially, and always, my patient parents, Lois and Don Batten, for the generous loan of a room and a place to get away and work, Denise Bukowski, my agent, who finally made this possible, and Diane Martin, my editor at Knopf Canada.

Above all this book was a search for the stories of the ghosts whose presence still haunts the desert.

ANNOTATED
BIBLIOGRAPHY

➤

In general, phrases in italic are quotations. Quechua poetry quoted is from the Spanish version collected in *Literatura Quechua*, unless otherwise noted. The translation to English is mine.

Advis, Luis. *Cantata popular Santa María de Iquique* (CD-ROM). Santiago: Alerce, 1997.

Agulhon, Maurice, et al. *Formas de sociabilidad en Chile 1840–1940*. Santiago: Fundación Mario Góngora, 1992.

Aldunate del Solar and Victoria Castro. *Las Chullpas de Toconce y su relación con el poblamiento altiplánico en el Loa Superior*. Santiago: Ediciones Kultrun, 1981.

Aldunate, Carlos. *Cronología y asentamiento en la región del Loa Superior*. Santiago: Dibam, 1986.

Ampuero Brito, Gonzalo and others. *Diaguitas: pueblos del norte verde*. Santiago: Museo Chileno de Arte Precolombino, 1986.

Ampuero, Gonzalo. *Arte rupestre en el Valle de El Encanto*. Ovalle: Ilustre Municipalidad y Otros, c. 1994.

————. *Cultura Diaguita*. Santiago: Ministerio de Educación, 1994.

————. *En busca de la identidad perdida*. La Serena: Dibam, 1998.

Anonymous. *Copper through the Ages*. Herts (England): Copper Development Association, 1955.

Aranda, Alfredo, ed. *Antología Atacameña: Poesía y cuento*. Santiago: Nascimento, 1978.

Aylwin, Mariana, Carlos Bascuñán and others. *Chile en el siglo XX*. Santiago: Emisión, 1986.

Barros Arana, *Historia general de Chile*. 20-volume history of Chile, Santiago. The quote from Cieza León in chapter 4 and much of the description of Diego de Almagro's journey over the mountains into the Atacama Desert came from this version of Chilean history, along with information in *The Conquest of the Inca* and much contemporary or near-contemporary testimony from Hidalgo, *Culturas proto-históricas del Norte de Chile, El testimonio de los cronistas* (including comments by Mariño de Lovera, Gerónimo de Bibar, Cristobal Molina). I also relied heavily on the vivid descriptions included in Barros Arana (Almagro bitterly concludes) for some of Almagro's thoughts on his defeat by the Atacama in chapter 6.

Baudin, Louis. *El imperio socialista de los Incas*. Santiago: Zig-zag. 4th Edition, 1955.

Bendezú, Edmundo. *Literatura Quechua*. Caracas: Biblioteca Ayacucho, 1980. This amazing book, organized chronologically from Pre-Conquest up to almost the present, offers prayers, songs, poems and stories carefully translated from Quechua to Spanish by distinguished Peruvian writers. I found it an endless source of insight and inspiration. The final prayer in chapter 1 is my translation of the version in Spanish by Jesus Lara, 1945. This prayer predates the Conquest. The poem/prayer "Padre Condor" is from the Spanish translation by Edmundo Bendezú (p. 18). The epigraph at the start of chapter 10 is from *¿Quién Soy?*, translated by José María Arguedas in 1963 (p. 237), and *Dios Santo* was translated to Spanish by José María Arguedas in 1963. "You will be my sweet deception," *Canción*, was translated from Quechua to Spanish by Jesús Lara, 1945. "An ant's egg" is from *Despedida*, translated from Quechua to Spanish by José Miguel Arguedas. "Look for me" was translated to Spanish by Sergio Quijada Jara.

Berenguer, José, et al. *El arte rupestre en Chile*. Santiago: Museo Chileno de Arte Precolombino.

———. *Los primeros Americanos y sus Descendientes*. Santiago: Museo Chileno de Arte Precolombino & Editorial Antártica, 1988. This book is virtually an encyclopaedia about the original peoples of the Americas. Carefully illustrated and prepared, it provided an excellent introduction to the Incas, Tiwanaku and the original peoples of Chile. The illustrations are particularly useful, blending photographs of some of the more extraordinary artefacts and drawings of people from different ethnic groups involved in daily activities. The work of the archaeologists William Isbell and Anita Cook was particularly useful to the chapter on Tiwanaku.

Berenguer, José. *Aspectos diferenciales de la influencia de Tiwanaku en Chile*. Thesis. Santiago: Library, Department of Anthropology, University of Chile, 1975.

Bermudez, Oscar. *El Oasis de Pica y sus nexos regionales*. Santiago: Ediciones Universidad de Tarapacá, 1987. For the history of the Pica/Matilla area (where not quoted from Bowman) and events in and around the town of La Tirana, I am indebted to the work of Oscar Bermudez. Most of the historical information about events in Pica/Matilla-La Tirana included in chapter 9 is based on accounts collected by Oscar Bermudez and he is quoted in this chapter ("Pica was still in ruins").

Bird, Junius. "The Copper Man." Included in *Pre-Columbian Metallurgy of South America*, a conference at Dumbarton Oaks, 18 and 19 October 1975, Elizabeth Benson, ed. Dumbarton Oaks Research Library, Harvard University.

All of the information about the Copper Man, included in chapter 8, is from this source, as are the quotes from the letter by Edward Jackson.

Blakemore, Harold. *British Nitrates and Chilean Politics, 1886–1896: Balmaceda and North*. London: Athlone Press, 1974. This excellent study of a crucial phase in Chilean history and international economics provided much of the background for chapter 5, in particular.

———. *Gobierno Chileno y salitre inglés. 1886–1896*. Santiago: Andres Bello, 1976.

Boletín del Museo Chileno de Arte Precolombino, no. 4. Santiago: Museo Chileno de Arte Precolombino, 1990.

———, no. 7. Santiago: Museo Chileno de Arte Precolombino, 1998.

Bollinger, Armin. *Así se alimentaban los Inkas*. La Paz: Los Amigos del Libro, 1993.

Botero, Luis Fernando. *Compadres y priostes*. Quito: Ediciones Abya-Yala, 1991.

Bowman, Isaiah. *Desert Trails of the Atacama*. New York: American Geographical Society, 1924. Undoubtedly this is one of the great classics of the Atacama Desert, written by a tireless and detailed observer. It took me a long time to find a copy, but eventually I managed to locate one in both Spanish (Pre-Columbian Museum in Santiago) and English (Robarts Library, University of Toronto). Bowman's comments were particularly useful to developing my own vision in chapters 3 and 5.

———. *Los Senderos del Desierto del Atacama*. Santiago: Sociedad Chilena de Historia y Geografía, 1942.

Bravo Elizondo, Pedro. "Matanza de la Santa María Las Versiones," published in a special edition of the magazine *Camanchaca*, Tarapaca, Mar.–April 1994. Several versions of the massacre that I did not find elsewhere were published here.

————. *Cultura y teatro obreros en Chile, 1900–1930.* Madrid: Ediciones Mechay, 1986. This book provides a nicely summarized history of the nitrate era as well as details about workers' culture and theatre as it developed in the north during the early twentieth century. It was particularly useful for reconstructing events and the atmosphere around theatres like the one in Humberstone (although Humberstone itself dates form a slightly later period and I have telescoped somewhat).

Bruce St. John, Ronald. *Boundaries, Trade, and Seaports: Power Politics in the Atacama Desert.* Amherst: University of Massachusetts Occasional Paper Series, no. 28, 1991.

Cajías, Fernando. *Provincia de Atacama.* La Paz: Instituto Boliviano de Cultura, 1975.

Castro, Victoria and Varinia Varela, eds. *Ceremonias de tierra y agua: Ritos milenarios Andinos.* Santiago: Fondart & others, 1994.

Castro, Victoria. "La dinámica de las identidades en la Provincia de El Loa, II Región." Resumen de Ponencia. Santiago: Department of Anthropology, University of Chile.

Catálogo. *Chile Antes de Chile.* Santiago: Museo Chileno de Arte Precolombino, 1997.

CEPAL/ECLAC (Environment and Development Division). *Progress in the privatization of water-related public services: A country-by-country review for South America.* Santiago: ECLAC, 1998.

————. *Recomendaciones de las reuniones internacionales sobre el agua: De Mar del Plata a París.* Santiago: ECLAC, 1998.

Cervellino, Miguel. "La Imagen del Sacrificador en el Arte Rupestre de la Región de Atacama Chile." Copiapó: Boletín del Museo Regional de Atacama, no. 4, 1992, pp. 161–174. (Copy courtesy of Claudio Mercado of the Museo Chileno de Arte Precolombino.) One of the few detailed descriptions of the differing accounts of the sacrificer, this paper was invaluable to forming an image of the elusive but omnipotent character.

Chaunu, Pierre. *Historia de América Latina*. Buenos Aires: Editorial Universitaria, 1972.

Chihualaf, Elicura. *Recado Confidencial a los chilenos*. Santiago: LOM, 1999. The quote about Mapuche beliefs ("We die three times") in chapter 9 is from p. 38.

Clissold, Stephen. *Chilean Scrap-Book*. London: Cresset Press, 1952.

Cornejo, Luis, and others. *Nasca: Vida y muerte en el desierto*. Santiago: Museo Chileno de Arte Precolombino, 1996.

Cotarelo y Mori, Emilio. *María del Rosario Fernández La Tirana*. Madrid: Impresores de la Real Casa, 1897.

Craig, Alan and Robert C. West, eds. "Copper Smelting in the Atacama: Ancient Metallurgy at the Ramaditas Site, Northern Chile," by Gray Graffam, Mario Rivera, Alvaro Carevic. "Black Legends and Silver Mountains: Spanish Mining in Colonial Spanish America Reconsidered," by Otis Young, Jr., was especially useful to chapter 8, for its invaluable descriptions of Spanish colonial mining mostly in Mexico and to a lesser degree in South America. *In Quest of Mineral Wealth, Aboriginal and Colonial Mining and Metallurgy in Spanish America*. Baton Rouge: Louisiana State University, 1994.

De Rokha, Pablo. *Interpretación dialéctica de América Los Cinco Estilos del Pacífico*. Buenos Aires: Ediciones Libertad, 1947.

Deves, Eduardo. *Los que van a morir te saludan*. Santiago: LOM, 1997. Deves's reflections on why these events should be studied and remembered, along with his detailed study of events leading up to, during and immediately following the massacre at the Santa María School in Iquique provided much of the chronological information in chapter 5.

Disselhoff, H. D. *Las grandes civilizaciones de la América antigua*. Translation: Agustina Fort. Barcelona: Ayma SA Editora, 1967.

Dourojeanni, Axel, and Andrei Jouravlev. *El código de aguas de Chile: Entre la ideología y la realidad*. Santiago: ECLAC, 1999.

Dourojeanni, Axel. *Politicas públicas para el desarrollo sustentable: La gestión integrada de cuencas*. Santiago: Cepal, 1994.

Fazio, Hugo. *Mapa actual de la extrema riqueza*. Santiago: LOM Ediciones, 1997.

Ffrench-Davis, Ricardo and Ernesto Tironi. *El cobre en el desarrollo nacional*. Santiago: Universidad Católica, 1974.

Finn, Janet. *Tracing the Veins*. Berkeley: University of California Press, 1998. This well-researched, well-written book provided an interesting dual view of one U.S.-based copper corporation's activities in both Chile and the U.S. The personal testimonies that she collected during interviews with the women of Chuquicamata were particularly useful for chapter 8.

Flores Galindo, Alberto. *Buscando un Inca: Identidad y Utopía en Los Andes*. Lima: Editorial Horizonte, 4ª edición, 1994.

Fuentes, Carlos. *El espejo enterrado*. Mexico: Fondo de Cultura Económica, 1994.

Gallardo, Francisco, et al. *Identidad y prestigio en Los Andes*. Santiago: Museo Precolombino, 1993/1994.

Gandarillas, Humberto and others. *Dios da el agua: ¿Qué hacen los proyectos?* La Paz: Hisbol/PRIV. 2d edition, 1994.

García de la Huerta, Marcos. *Chile 1891: La gran crisis y su historiografía*. Santiago: Centro de Estudios Humanísticos Universidad de Chile, 1979.

González Miranda, Sergio, ed. *A 90 años de los sucesos de la Escuela Santa María de Iquique*. Santiago: Ediciones DIBAM/LOM, 1998.

González Miranda, Sergio. *Hombres y mujeres de la pampa: Tarapacá en el ciclo del salitre*. Iquique: Taller de Estudios Regionales, 1991. This book, which includes the personal memories of many of those who worked in the nitrate offices, was very useful, particularly in the preparation of chapter 5.

González, Sergio, María Angélica Illanes, Luis Moulian, eds. *Poemario popular de Tarapacá (1899–1910)*. Santiago: Ediciones DIBAM/LOM, 1998. I found the workers' poetry in this collection very useful, particularly in chapter 5, when it came to trying to understand their perception of the events composing the boom and bust cycles of the nitrate era.

Grau, Dr. Juan. *Voces indígenas de uso común en Chile*. Santiago: Ediciones OIKOS Ltda, 1998.

Guamán Poma de Ayala, Felipe. *Nueva corónica y buen gobierno*. Biblioteca Ayacucho: Caracas. Franklin Pease edition, 1980. One of the few Incan accounts of the Conquest, this three-volume history, with its amazing pictures, was very revealing and invaluable to my understanding of the Incan empire.

———. *Nueva corónica y buen gobierno*. Editor: Franklin Pease. Volumes I–III. México etc.: Fondo de Cultura Económica, 1993.

Guerrero, Bernardo, ed. *Vida, pasión y muerte Pisagua*. Iquique: Centro de Investigación de la Realidad del Norte CREAR, 1990. This wonderful book, which I discovered in the University of Toronto's Robarts Library toward the end of my work on *Bone and Dream*, provided exactly the well-ordered chronology of events in Pisagua that I had sought in vain in Chile. It was particularly important for chapter 7, especially the opening chapter by Lautaro Núñez and Nelson Muñoz Morales' section.

Gutiérrez, Eulogio. *Chuquicamata Tierras rojas*. Santiago: Nascimiento, 1926. This book provided some unofficial insights into the past of Chuquicamata, from the perspective of someone who appears to have been something of a heretic in his day.

Halperin Donghi, Tulio. *Historia contemporánea de América Latina*. Madrid: Alianza Editorial, 1990.

Hemming, John. *The Conquest of the Incas*. London: Sphere Books, 1972. This wonderful book gave me my first glimpse of the world I would gradually come to know as I did the research for Ñusta's story. Particularly useful and vivid was his account of the meeting between Valverde and Atahualpa and the conflicts between the Pizarros and Diego de Almagro that culminated in the latter's death, which formed the basis for my own narration in chapter 2 and contributed to my version of Almagro's journey, primarily in chapter 4. His work was also the main source for many of the de Molina quotes in chapter 4.

Hidalgo, Jorge. *Culturas protohistóricas del Norte de Chile. El Testimonio de los cronistas.* Santiago: University of Chile, 1972. This collection of contemporary accounts of the Spanish chroniclers was extremely useful, particularly for the information about Tiwanaku in chapter 2. Most of the comments from Gerónimo de Bibar came from this source as well.

――――. *Indian Society in Arica, Tarapacá and Atacama 1750–1793 and Its Response to the Rebellion of Tupac Amaru.* London: University of London, 1986. Ph.D. thesis.

Hidalgo, Jorge, Virgilio Schiappaccasse, Hans Niemeyer, Carlos Aldunate del Solar and Iván Solimano, eds. *Culturas de Chile: Prehistoria.* Santiago: Andrés Bello, 1997.

Hiriart, Luis. *Braden.* Santiago: Editorial Andes, 1964.

Hutton, Ronald. *The Stations of the Sun.* Oxford: Oxford University Press, 1996.

Ibarra, Dick Edgar. *América en la prehistoria mundial.* Buenos Aires: Tipográfica Editora, 1982.

Jacobs, Birgit. *Costumbres mortuarias de la cultura San Pedro de Atacama, Tomo I y II.* Santiago: Manuscript library, Pre-Columbian Museum, 1986. Information on the Atacamenians' approach to death is based on work by Birgit Jacobs in her thesis, found in the library of Santiago's Museo Precolombino, as well as books by Lautaro Núñez, Claudio Mercado, Grete Mostny. Undoubtedly, this account is as fragile as the reconstruction of an ancient clay water jar, carefully fitted together, but still full of cracks and gaps. I also used an essay by Miguel Cervellino, "La Imagen del Sacrificador en el Arte Rupestre de la Región de Atacama, Chile" (from the Boletín del Museo Regional de Atacama, no. 4, 1992, (p. 163), Hidalgo's *Culturas Protohistóricas*, Mostny's

Ciudades Atacameñas and Cristóbal de Molina, quoted in Hemming's *The Conquest of the Incas* (p. 181).

Jarpa Yáñez, Patricio. *Los hombres del cobre 1955–1971*. Santiago, c. 1972.

Jocelyn-Holt, Alfredo. *El Chile perplejo*. Santiago: Planeta/Ariel, 1998.

———. *El peso de la noche*. Santiago: Ariel, 1997.

Kolata, Alan. *Valley of the Spirits: A Journey into the Lost Realm of the Aymara*. New York: John Wiley & Sons, 1996. This well-written book explores the ancient city of Tiwanaku within the context of the modern-day Aymara communities of the high plateaux of the Andes, as well as telling the fascinating tale of American and Bolivian anthropologists' and archaeologists' work in and around the site by Lake Titicaca.

Le Paige, Gustavo, S.J. *Continuidad o discontinuidad de la cultura Atacameña*. Antofagasta: Apartado de los Anales de la Universidad del Norte. no. 2, 1963.

Lee, Terence and Andre Jouravlev. *Prices, Property and Markets in Water Allocation*. Santiago: ECLAC, 1998.

León León, Marco Antonio. *Sepultura sagrada, tumba profana. Los espacios de la muerte en Santiago de Chile, 1883–1932*. Santiago: LOM Ediciones, 1997.

Martínez, José Luis. *Pueblos del chañar y el algarrobo*. Santiago: DIBAM, 1998.

Maturana, Andrea. *El daño*. Santiago: Alfaguara, 1997.

Mazuda, Shozo, et al., eds. *Andean Ecology and Civilization*. Tokyo: University of Tokyo Press, 1985.

Melgar Bao, Ricardo, et al. *Perú contemporáneo: El espejo de las identidades*. México: Universidad Nacional Autónoma de México, 1993.

Méndez Beltrán, Luz María. *Instituciones y problemas de la minería en Chile 1787–1826*. Santiago: Ediciones Universidad de Chile, 1979.

Mercado, Claudio, Luis Galdames. *De todo el universo entero*. Santiago: Fondo Matta, Museo Chileno de Arte Precolombino, 1997.

Mercado, Claudio, Patricia Rodríguez, and Mauricio Uribe. *Tiempo del verde, tiempo de lluvia, Carnaval en Aiquina*. Santiago: LOM Ediciones, 1996.

Mercado, Claudio, Patricia Rodríguez, Pablo Miranda. *Pa' que coman las almas*. Santiago: LOM Ediciones, 1997.

Molina, Juan Ignacio. *Historia natural y civil de Chile*. Santiago: Editorial Universitaria, 1976.

Montandón, Roberto. *Apuntes sobre el Pukara de Lasana*. Santiago: Consejo de Monumentos Nacionales, 1988. For the history of Lasana and the native people of that area of the Atacama, Montandon's historical essay was rich in both ideas and sensations that went into chapter 8, as was Grete Mostny's section on Turi, from *Ciudades Atacameñas*.

Mostny, Grete, Fidel Jeldes, Raúl González, F. Oberhauser. *Peine un pueblo Atacameño*. Santiago: Instituto de Geografía Facultad de Filosofía, 1954. For details of an Incan sacrifice (in chapter 9) I relied on Grete Mostny's comments in *La momia del cerro el plomo*.

Muñoz, Bernardo. *Procesos de cambios sociales en el área de San Pedro de Atacama: Pérdida y recuperación de la identidad étnica*. Bonn: Die Deutsche Bibliothek CIP Einheitsaufnahme Mundus Reihe Ethnologie, 1993.

Navarrete, Micaela. *Balmaceda en la poesía popular 1886–1896*. Santiago: DIBAM, 1993.

Niemeyer, Hans, Miguel Cervellino, Gastón Castillo. *Culturas prehistóricas de Copiapó*. Copiapó: Museo Regional de Atacama, 1998.

Núñez Atencio, Lautaro. *Cultura y conflicto en los oasis de San Pedro de Atacama*. Santiago: Editorial Universitaria, 1991. Most of the basic historical and anthropological information about the Atacamenian people comes from this fundamental study of their lives in and around San Pedro de Atacama.

This is a long, detailed scholarly text that brings together all the available information.

————. *La Tirana del Tamarugal*. Antofagasta: Universidad del Norte, 1989. This book was fundamental to my understanding of the historical and literary events that compose the story of La Tirana, Huillac Ñusta. It provides an excellent study of the original story by Cuneo Vidal (which it quotes at length, as I do) and tests it against verifiable historical information for this region. Cuneo Vidal is generally considered a historian, but as Núñez points out, because Cuneo Vidal seldom included the sources for his material, it is difficult to tell where history ended and literature, or the making of myths, began. Núñez is among those quoted (in a surrealistic way) in chapter 9.

Olivares Toledo, Juan Carlos. *El Roto: Escritos en antropología poética*. Santiago: Fondo Matta, Museo Chileo de Arte Precolombino, 1995.

Orellana, Mario. *Prehistoria y etnología de Chile*. Santiago: Bravo y Allende Editores, 1994.

Peña, Humberto, et al. *Resúmenes: VI jornadas del Comité Chileno para el Programa Hidrológico Internacional (PHI)* (and full papers included on CD-ROM). Santiago: UNESCO, 1999.

Pérez de Arce, José, et al. *Música en la piedra*. Santiago: Museo Precolombino, 1995. Information on the antara is based on the paper and graphics by José Pérez de Arce, "Polifonía en fiestas rituales de Chile Central," in the Revista Musical Chilena, Año L, Jan.–June, 1996, no. 185, at the Pre-Columbian Museum in Santiago, pp. 38–41, as well as Claudio Mercado's descriptions of how he feels when he plays the antara in the present-day ceremonies of the *Chinos* (servants, presumably of the Christian God) in central Chile and another essay by José Pérez de Arce, "El sonido rajado, una historia milenaria," published in Valles, Revista de Estudios Regionales, no. 3, 1997, listed below.

Plath, Oreste. *Geografía del mito y la leyenda*. Santiago: Grijalbo.

————. *L'animita*. Santiago: Grijalbo, 1995. For the information on animitas in chapter 5, Oreste Plath's work has no equal. He dedicated his life and extraordinary talent to rescuing oral beliefs and stories, giving them the kind of treatment usually reserved for written literature.

Ponce Sanginés, Carlos, et al. *Tiwanaku: Un estado precolombino*. La Paz: Centro de Investigaciones Antropológicas Tiwanaku, 1995. This collection of essays by Ponce himself and colleagues was extremely useful for background information on both the Incas and the culture of Tiwanaku itself. I relied on this work particularly for chapter 2. Restrepo's essay "Instituciones sociales, políticas y económicas de Tawintinsuyu" (p. 117) provides an excellent study of the Incan empire and how it fit within the cultural and social framework of Andean society in general. This essay (along with Núñez's) also offered innumerable examples of the surprising similarities between Christian and Incan religious culture.

Ponce Sanginés, Carlos. *Descripción del templete subterráneo de Tiwanaku*. 6th edition. La Paz: Juventud, 1990.

————. *Tiwanaku: 200 años de investigaciones arqueológicas*. La Paz: Producciones CIMA, 1995.

PRATEC. *Afirmación cultural Andina*. Lima: Proyecto Andino de Tecnologías Campesinas, 1993.

Prescott, Guillermo. *Historia de la Conquista del Perú*. Buenos Aires: Editorial Schapire, 1967.

Reyes, Enrique. *El desarrollo de la conciencia proletaria en Chile (el Ciclo Salitrero)*. Santiago: Editorial Orbe/Universidad del Norte, c. 1984.

Reyes, Salvador. *Andanzas por el desierto de Atacama*. Zigzag: Santiago, 1969. 10(854–25)

Rojas, Manuel. *A pie por Chile*. Santiago: LOM Ediciones, 1997.

Rudolph, William. *Vanishing Trails of the Atacama*. New York: American Geographical Society, 1963.

Sabella, Andrés. *Norte Grande*. Santiago: LOM Ediciones, 1997.

Sabella's enthusiasm for the endless possibilities of the barren desert where he was born and bred and his rich use of language were a source of delight and discovery, particularly useful in chapter 5 and in understanding the glories and dramatic contrasts of the nitrate era.

Salinas, Cecilia. *Las Chilenas de la Colonia, Virtud sumisa, Amor rebelde*. Santiago: LOM Ediciones, 1994.

Salinas, Maximiliano. *Canto a lo divino y religión del oprimido en Chile*. Santiago: Rehue Ediciones.

Sierra, Malú. *Donde todo es altar*. Santiago: Editorial Persona, 1991.

Silva, Víctor Domingo. *La trágica*. Santiago: Empresa Editorial Selecta de Masgrau y Cia, 1921.

Silverblatt, Irene. *Luna, sol y brujas: Género y clases en los Andes prehispánicos y coloniales*. Cuzco: Centro de Estudios Regionales Andinos, "Bartolomé de las Casas," 1990. This book provided most of the background on specific Incan ceremonies described in chapter 6, especially the contemporary Spanish voices describing the Incan ceremonies, Estete ("There were to be found in the city"), Hernández Silva ("Four young girls, enough feasts / And when the feasting was over"), Garcilaso ("Foreign tyranny bangs").

Solanes, Miguel, and David Getches. *Prácticas recomendables para la elaboración de leyes y regulaciones relacionadas con el recurso hídrico*. Washington: Interamerican Development Bank, 1998.

Stehberg, Rubén. *Instalaciones Incaicas en el norte y centro semiárido de Chile*. Santiago: DIBAM (Dirección de Bibliotecas, Archivos y Museos), 1995. This very scholarly book provided rare and useful information on the Incas' efforts in Chile, particularly the role their highways played in breaking up the kingdoms of existing native groups/organizations mentioned in chapter 4.

Steward, Julian, ed. *Handbook of South American Indians*. Washington: Smithsonian Institution, 1946. Volume 2.

Sutulov, Alexander. *El cobre Chileno*. Santiago: Corporación del Cobre, 1975.

————. *Minería Chilena 1545–1975*. Santiago: Centro de Investigación Minera y Metalúrgica, 1976.

Teitelboim, Volodia. *Hijo del Salitre*. Santiago: LOM, 1996.

Uribe-Echevarría, Juan. *Fiesta de La Tirana de Tarapacá*. Valparaiso: Ediciones Universitarias, c. 1976.

Van Kessel, Juan. *Cuando arde el tiempo sagrado*. La Paz: Hisbol, 1992.

————. *Holocausto al progreso: Los Aymarás de Tarapacá*. La Paz: Hisbol, 1992.

————. *Lucero del desierto*. Photocopied version of this book from the collection of the Pre-Columbian Museum library in Santiago. Both this book and *Holocausto al progreso* were crucial to chapter 9 and Van Kessel is quoted here ("Christian camouflage," "more isolated sanctuaries").

Vicuña Mackenna, Benjamín. *El libro del cobre y del carbón de Piedra de Chile*. Santiago: Imprenta Cervantes, 1883. This book provided both historical detail and some delicious side remarks, particularly useful to chapter 8.

————. *La edad de oro en Chile*. Buenos Aires: Editorial Francisco de Aguirre, 1968.

Vicuña Urrutia, Manuel. *La Imagen del Desierto de Atacama (XVI–XIX)*. Santiago: Editorial Universidad de Santiago, 1995.

Villalobos, Sergio. *La economía de un desierto*. Santiago: Ediciones Nueva Universidad, 1979.

Vivar, Jerónimo de (also spelled Gerónimo de Bibar). Angel Barral Gómez, ed. *Crónica de los reinos de Chile*. Madrid: Historia 16, 1988.

Wright, Ronald. *Stolen Continents*. Toronto: Penguin, 1992. A wonderful book for freeing eyes, heart, mind; teaching the soul to perceive differently, I found this one useful for both facts and inspiration.

Zauschquevich, Andrés and Alexander Sutulov. *El cobre Chileno*. Santiago: Codelco, 1975. Much of the background information on copper mining in Chile comes from Sutulov's work.

Zepeda, Ernesta and Senen Durán. *Oficina salitreras "Santiago Humberstone,"* booklet sold on site at the Humberstone national monument (the old nitrate office). This, along with Bowman, Blakemore and Sutulov, provided most of the background on the Humberstone office in particular, and the nitrate era in general.

INDEX OF PEOPLE AND PLACES